Final Report of the Thirty-fifth Antarctic Treaty Consultative Meeting

ANTARCTIC TREATY
CONSULTATIVE MEETING

Final Report of the Thirty-fifth Antarctic Treaty Consultative Meeting

Hobart, Australia
11–20 June 2012

Volume I

Secretariat of the Antarctic Treaty
Buenos Aires
2012

Antarctic Treaty Consultative Meeting (35th : 2012 : Hobart)
  Final Report of the Thirty-fifth Antarctic Treaty Consultative Meeting.
    Hobart, Australia, 11–20 June 2012.
  Buenos Aires : Secretariat of the Antarctic Treaty, 2012.
    v.

ISBN 978-987-1515-42-4 (v.I)

1. International law – Environmental issues. 2. Antarctic Treaty system.
3. Environmental law – Antarctica. 4. Environmental protection – Antarctica.

DDC 341.762 5

ISBN 978-987-1515-42-4 (v.I)

This book is also available from: *www.ats.aq* (digital version)
and online-purchased copies.

Contents

VOLUME I

VOLUME II

PART II. MEASURES, DECISIONS AND RESOLUTIONS (Cont.)

4. Management Plans
ASPA No 109 Moe Island
ASPA No 110 Lynch Island
ASPA No 111 Southern Powell Island and adjacent islands
ASPA No 112 Coppermine Peninsula
ASPA No 115 Lagotellerie Island
ASPA No 129 Rothera Point
ASPA No 133 Harmony Point
ASPA No 140 Parts of Deception Island
ASPA No 172 Lower Taylor Glacier and Blood Falls
ASMA No 4 Deception Island

PART III. OPENING AND CLOSING ADDRESSES AND REPORTS

1. Reports by Depositaries and Observers
Report of SCAR
Report of COMNAP
Report of the UK as Depositary Government of CCAS
Report of Australia as Depositary Government of CCAMLR
Report of Australia as Depositary Government of ACAP
Report of the USA as Depositary Government of the Antarctic Treaty and its Protocol
Report by the CCAMLR Observer

2. Reports by Experts
Report of IAATO
Report of IHO
Report of ASOC

PART IV. ADDITIONAL DOCUMENTS FROM ATCM XXXV

1. Additional Documents
Abstract of SCAR Lecture

2. List of documents

Working Papers
Information Papers
Secretariat Papers
Background Papers

3. List of Participants

Consultative Parties
Non-Consultative Parties
Observers, Experts and Guests
Host Country Secretariat
Antarctic Treaty Secretariat

Acronyms and Abbreviations

ACAP	Agreement on the Conservation of Albatrosses and Petrels
ASOC	Antarctic and Southern Ocean Coalition
ASMA	Antarctic Specially Managed Area
ASPA	Antarctic Specially Protected Area
ATS	Antarctic Treaty System or Antarctic Treaty Secretariat
ATCM	Antarctic Treaty Consultative Meeting
ATCP	Antarctic Treaty Consultative Party
CAML	Census of Antarctic Marine Life
CCAMLR	Convention on the Conservation of Antarctic Marine Living Resources and/or Commission for the Conservation of Antarctic Marine Living Resourcess
CCAS	Convention for the Conservation of Antarctic Seals
CEE	Comprehensive Environmental Evaluation
CEP	Committee for Environmental Protection
COMNAP	Council of Managers of National Antarctic Programmes
EIA	Environmental Impact Assessment
HCA	Hydrographic Committee on Antarctica
HSM	Historic Site and Monument
IAATO	International Association of Antarctica Tour Operators
ICG	Intersessional Contact Group
ICSU	International Council for Science
IEE	Initial Environmental Evaluation
IHO	International Hydrographic Organization
IMO	International Maritime Organization
IOC	Intergovernmental Oceanographic Commission
IP	Information Paper
IPCC	Intergovernmental Panel on Climate Change
IPY	International Polar Year
IPY-IPO	IPY Programme Office
IUCN	International Union for Conservation of Nature and Natural Resources
RFMO	Regional Fishery Management Organization
SATCM	Special Antarctic Treaty Consultative Meeting
SCAR	Scientific Committee on Antarctic Research

SCALOP	Standing Committee for Antarctic Logistics and Operations
SC-CAMLR	Scientific Committee of CCAMLR
SP	Secretariat Paper
SPA	Specially Protected Area
UNEP	United Nations Environment Programme
UNFCCC	United Nations Framework Convention on Climate Change
WG	Working Group
WMO	World Meteorological Organization
WP	Working Paper
WTO	World Tourism Organization

PART I
Final Report

1. Final Report

Final Report of the Thirty-fifth Antarctic Treaty Consultative Meeting

Hobart, 11–20 June 2012

(1) Pursuant to Article IX of the Antarctic Treaty, Representatives of the Consultative Parties (Argentina, Australia, Belgium, Brazil, Bulgaria, Chile, China, Ecuador, Finland, France, Germany, India, Italy, Japan, the Republic of Korea, the Netherlands, New Zealand, Norway, Peru, Poland, the Russian Federation, South Africa, Spain, Sweden, Ukraine, the United Kingdom of Great Britain and Northern Ireland, the United States of America, and Uruguay) met in Hobart from 11 to 20 June 2012, for the purpose of exchanging information, holding consultations and considering and recommending to their Governments measures in furtherance of the principles and objectives of the Treaty.

(2) The Meeting was also attended by delegations from the following Contracting Parties to the Antarctic Treaty which are not Consultative Parties: Canada, Colombia, Czech Republic, Malaysia, Monaco, and Slovak Republic.

(3) In accordance with Rules 2 and 31 of the Rules of Procedure, Observers from the Commission for the Conservation of Antarctic Marine Living Resources (CCAMLR), the Scientific Committee on Antarctic Research (SCAR) and the Council of Managers of National Antarctic Programmes (COMNAP) attended the Meeting.

(4) In accordance with Rule 39 of the Rules of Procedure, Experts from the following international organisations and non-governmental organisations attended the Meeting: the Agreement on the Conservation of Albatrosses and Petrels (ACAP), the Antarctic and Southern Ocean Coalition (ASOC), the International Association of Antarctica Tour Operators (IAATO), the International Hydrographic Organization (IHO), the United Nations Environment Programme (UNEP) and the World Meteorological Organization (WMO).

(5)   The Host Country Australia fulfilled its information requirements towards the Contracting Parties, Observers and Experts through Secretariat Notes, letters and a website with public and members-only sections.

Item 1: Opening of the Meeting

(6)   The Meeting was officially opened on 11 June 2012. On behalf of the Host Government, in accordance with Rules 5 and 6 of the Rules of Procedure, the Executive Secretary of the Host Government Secretariat Mr Andrew Jackson called the Meeting to order. He formally acknowledged the Mouheneener people, the traditional custodians of the land on which the Meeting was held. He noted the steps taken by Australia to reduce the environmental impacts of the meeting (BP 19). He proposed the candidacy of the distinguished diplomat and Senior Legal Adviser to the Australian Department of Foreign Affairs and Trade, Mr Richard Rowe, as Chair of ATCM XXXV. The proposal was accepted.

(7)   The Chair warmly welcomed all Parties, Observers and Experts to Hobart. Delegates observed a minute of silence in honour of the tragic loss of Lieutenant Roberto Lopes dos Santos and Lieutenant Carlos Alberto Vieira Figueiredo during the February 2012 fire at Brazil's Comandante Ferraz Station, and the sudden passing away in September 2011 of Mr Alexandre de Lichtervelde, Belgium's late CEP representative. He also warmly welcomed the recent accession of Malaysia and Pakistan to the Antarctic Treaty, and Pakistan to the Protocol on Environmental Protection to the Antarctic Treaty.

(8)   The Hon. David O'Byrne MP, Tasmanian Minister for Economic Development and Minister for Science, Innovation and Technology, welcomed delegates to Tasmania. The Minister said that Tasmania had opened its doors and hearts for the past one hundred years to expeditioners leaving for Antarctica, noted that Antarctic scientific research and logistics contributed A$180 million annually to Tasmania's economy, and he looked forward to continued growth in this area.

(9)   The Hon. Tony Burke MP, Australian Minister for Sustainability, Environment, Water, Population and Communities, encouraged delegates to reflect on the remarkable success of the Antarctic Treaty, noting that they were participating in the thirty-fifth such gathering, building on science and exploration from the past 100 years, and using scientific evidence from the ice that goes back more than one million years. He drew attention to the uniqueness of the Treaty in designating Antarctica as a zone of peaceful cooperation and international

scientific collaboration, and highlighted the significant role played by the Antarctic in our understanding of global processes. He saluted all Parties for their achievements in protecting the Antarctic environment and paid particular tribute to the contributions of the Hon. Michel Rocard, former Prime Minister of France and the Hon. Bob Hawke, former Prime Minister of Australia, to the Antarctic environmental protection regime.

(10)   The Chair thanked the Ministers for their inspiring words, and acknowledged the presence of the former statesmen.

Item 2: Election of Officers and Creation of Working Groups

(11)   Mr Jean-Arthur Regibeau, Representative of Belgium (Host Country of ATCM XXXVI) was elected Vice-chair. In accordance with Rule 7 of the Rules of Procedure, Dr Manfred Reinke, Executive Secretary of the Antarctic Treaty Secretariat, acted as Secretary to the Meeting. Mr Andrew Jackson, head of the Host Country Secretariat, acted as Deputy Secretary. Dr Yves Frenot of France continued as Chair of the Committee for Environmental Protection at CEP XV.

(12)   Three Working Groups were established:

- Working Group on Legal and Institutional Affairs;
- Working Group on Tourism and Non-governmental Activities; and
- Working Group on Operational Matters.

(13)   The following Chairs of the Working Groups were elected:

- Legal and Institutional Affairs: Professor René Lefeber of the Netherlands;
- Tourism and Non-governmental Activities: Ambassador Donald Mackay of New Zealand;
- Operational Matters: Dr José Retamales of Chile.

Item 3: Adoption of the Agenda and Allocation of Items

(14)   The following Agenda was adopted:

1. Opening of the Meeting
2. Election of Officers and Creation of Working Groups
3. Adoption of the Agenda and Allocation of Items

4. Operation of the Antarctic Treaty System: Reports by Parties, Observers and Experts

5. Operation of the Antarctic Treaty System: General Matters

6. Operation of the Antarctic Treaty System: Review of the Secretariat's Situation

7. Development of a Multi-year Strategic Work Plan

8. Report of the Committee for Environmental Protection

9. Liability: Implementation of Decision 4 (2010)

10. Safety and Operations in Antarctica

11. Tourism and Non-Governmental Activities in the Antarctic Treaty Area

12. Inspections under the Antarctic Treaty and the Environment Protocol

13. Science Issues, Scientific Cooperation and Facilitation, including the Legacy of the International Polar Year 2007-2008

14. Implications of Climate Change for Management of the Antarctic Treaty Area

15. Operational Issues

16. Education Issues

17. Exchange of Information

18. Biological Prospecting in Antarctica

19. Preparation of the 36th Meeting

20. Any Other Business

21. Adoption of the Final Report

(15)   The Meeting adopted the following allocation of agenda items:
- Plenary: Items 1, 2, 3, 4, 8, 19, 20, 21
- Legal and Institutional Working Group: Items 5, 6, 7, 9, 18
- Tourism and Non-governmental Activities Working Group: Item 11
- Operational Matters Working Group: Items 10, 12, 13, 14, 15, 16, 17.

The Meeting agreed that some documents submitted under Item 10 would be discussed in a joint meeting of the Tourism Working Group and the Operational Matters Working Group.

(16)   The Meeting decided to allocate draft instruments arising out of the work of the Committee for Environmental Protection and the Working Groups to the Legal and Institutional Working Group for consideration of their legal and institutional aspects.

Item 4: Operation of the Antarctic Treaty System: Reports by Parties, Observers and Experts

(17) Pursuant to Recommendation XIII-2, the Meeting received reports from depositary governments and secretariats.

(18) The United States, in its capacity as Depositary Government of the Antarctic Treaty and the Protocol on Environmental Protection reported on their status (IP 19). In the past year, there were two accessions to the Antarctic Treaty: Malaysia on 31 October 2011, and Pakistan on 1 March 2012. There was one accession to the Protocol: Pakistan acceded on 1 March 2012, and the Protocol entered into force for Pakistan on 31 March 2012. There are now 50 Parties to the Treaty and 35 Parties to the Protocol. Japan had ratified a number of outstanding Recommendations and Measures, and the United States encouraged other Parties to do the same.

(19) Malaysia thanked Parties for welcoming it into the Antarctic Treaty System. Malaysia noted that its investment in Antarctic research since 1999 made Malaysia one of very few tropical countries to have made a mark on polar research. Over the past ten years, the Malaysian Antarctic Research Programme (MARP) had organised 62 expeditions involving 24 research projects in biological and physical sciences, producing more than five doctorates in polar research and more than 20 higher degrees at the M.Sc. level. Malaysia was grateful for the support provided by several Parties in developing its Antarctic expertise. Malaysia had been a member of SCAR since 2008, and planned to accede to the Madrid Protocol as soon as possible. Antarctic legislation would be tabled in Parliament by the end of the year. Malaysia drew attention to the recent Antarctic visit of the 13th King of Malaysia, with the kind assistance of the governments of New Zealand and the United States, and its issuance of postal stamps with a polar theme.

(20) Australia, in its capacity as Depositary for the Convention on the Conservation of Antarctic Marine Living Resources (CCAMLR), reported one new accession to the Convention since ATCM XXXIV: Pakistan acceded to the Convention on 24 January 2012, and the Convention entered into force for Pakistan on 22 February 2012 (IP 9 rev1). There are currently 35 Parties to the Convention.

(21) The United Kingdom, as Depositary for the Convention on the Conservation of Antarctic Seals (CCAS), reported that there had been no accessions to the Convention since ATCM XXXIV. However, Pakistan wished to accede, and in line with the provisions of CCAS Article 12, the United Kingdom would

seek the consent of the Contracting Parties to invite Pakistan to accede. Spain also indicated its intention to accede to the Convention. Five seals were killed accidentally during scientific programmes between March 2010 and February 2011 (IP 5). The United Kingdom expressed its appreciation to Parties to the Convention for meeting the 30 June annual deadline for reporting the information referenced in paragraph 6 of the Annex to the Convention to SCAR and the Contracting Parties.

(22) Australia, in its capacity as Depositary for the Agreement on the Conservation of Albatrosses and Petrels (ACAP), reported that there had been no new accessions to the Agreement since ATCM XXXIV and that there were currently 13 Parties to the Agreement (IP 10).

(23) The Representative of ACAP noted that the Agreement was making solid progress in identifying and adopting appropriate measures for seabird conservation, and encouraged countries that are not yet Parties to join, in order to increase the Agreement's effectiveness.

(24) The CCAMLR observer reported on the outcomes of CCAMLR XXX which was held in Hobart, Australia in October-November 2011 (IP 27). He reported that vessels fishing in fisheries managed under CCAMLR conservation measures in 2010/11 had reported, by 24 September 2011, a total catch of 179,131 tonnes of krill, 11,254 tonnes of toothfish, and 11 tonnes of icefish. He also mentioned that a number of other species were taken as by-catch and that in addition, a reported 9,190 tonnes of toothfish were taken outside the Convention Area in 2010/11, compared with 12,441 tonnes in 2009/10. Seven members submitted krill fishing notifications in 2011/12, covering 15 vessels, with a notified total predicted catch of 401,000 tonnes. He further noted that fishing for krill inside ASMA 1 in 2010 may have been inconsistent with the management objectives of the ASMA. In relation to marine protected areas (MPAs), he referred to the work of a 2011 workshop in Brest, France, concerning the development of planning domains for representative systems of MPAs, and the work of New Zealand and the United States concerning the Ross Sea region, as well as the work of Australia and France in relation to the East Antarctic planning domain. He advised that CCAMLR had written to Singapore following the revocation of its Non-Contracting Party status, as well as to the Antarctic Treaty Secretariat in relation to CCAMLR's efforts in engaging with Malaysia to combat illegal, unreported and unregulated fishing. He highlighted other aspects of the report, including the EU/Netherlands-sponsored workshop on 'Antarctic Krill and Climate Change'; new bottom fishing initiatives;

low levels of incidental seabird mortality; and good levels of compliance with conservation measures.

(25) The ACAP Observer noted that ACAP's work was an integral component of the conservation of the Antarctic environment. He congratulated CCAMLR's efforts to address seabird by catch, and noted that because much remains to be done, ACAP needed more Parties to implement its work, and to support similarly rigorous by catch mitigation in regional fishery management organisations.

(26) The President of the Scientific Committee on Antarctic Research (SCAR) presented the SCAR annual report (IP 1), and advised that the July 2012 SCAR meetings would take important decisions, including determining the next generation of SCAR research programmes. He referred to SCAR's initial work towards a long-term strategy on managing future Antarctic conservation, which began with a meeting kindly hosted by South Africa. Other recent work of note included SCAR's role in the Southern Ocean Observing System and the Ice Sheet Mass Balance and Sea Level group. In addition, Prof. Diana H Wall of the United States would receive the 2012 SCAR President's Medal, Dr John Priscu, also of the United States, would receive the SCAR Medal for Scientific Excellence and Dr Ian Allison of Australia the SCAR Medal for International Cooperation..

(27) The Executive Secretary of the Council of Managers of National Antarctic Programmes (COMNAP) presented the COMNAP annual report (IP 3). She highlighted the launch of a new website with greater public access to information, as well as new products and tools. She also mentioned that Dr José Retamales of Chile had completed his term as COMNAP Chair and that Prof. Dr Heinrich Miller of Germany was elected as Chair for a three-year term of office.

(28) In relation to Article III-2 of the Antarctic Treaty, the Meeting received reports from other international organisations.

(29) The International Hydrographic Organization (IHO) Observer presented the IHO's report on Antarctic surveying and charting (IP 70), noting that there remained scope for improvement in coordination in this respect. The XVIII International Hydrographic Conference of April 2012 approved the tasks of conducting a risk assessment for the Antarctic region and improving Antarctic charting. He noted that the Hydrographic Committee on Antarctica (HCA) had been proactive in complying with ATCM Resolution 2 (2010) and had participated in several ATCM contact groups. He invited the ATCM

to consider how the IMO Polar Code, when introduced, would impact on hydrographic activities in Antarctica.

(30) Uruguay warmly invited all relevant member states to the October 2012 HCA Conference in Uruguay.

(31) The representative of the Antarctic and Southern Ocean Coalition (ASOC) presented the ASOC report (IP 85). She noted that ASOC had submitted a range of papers on key topics this year addressing issues including the review of tourism policies, the mandatory Polar Code, vessel incident reporting, and ATCM and CCAMLR cooperation regarding krill fishing. ASOC was also concerned about other issues, including climate change impacts, search and rescue information, a multi-year strategic plan, information sharing frameworks for bioprospecting and impacts on sub-glacial lakes from scientific sampling.

(32) The representative of the International Association of Antarctica Tour Operators (IAATO) presented its annual report (IP 36), which noted that there was a 22 per cent reduction in overall numbers of tourists during the 2011/12 season, and attributed the drop in cruise-only activity to the implementation of the ban on the use and carriage of heavy fuel oil. The report also highlighted progress on a number of initiatives on safety and communications and noted their policy of transparency over accidents and incidents in order to learn the lessons of experience.

(33) The World Meteorological Organization (WMO) had submitted an outline (IP 8) of the opportunities to mitigate risks to people and property in the Antarctic through improved environmental intelligence comprising meteorological and related observations and data, research, and services (including products such as weather forecasts). WMO Congress XVI (May-June 2011) had recognised the importance of the WMO's relationship with the ATCM, including through the new WMO Executive Council on Polar Observations, Research and Services, which had participated in ACTM intersessional processes, and the integration of all Antarctic networks and operational stations into an Antarctic Observing Network for climate data.

(34) During the discussion, Brazil expressed its thanks for the messages and statements of condolence regarding the Comandante Ferraz Station tragedy. Brazil had been commemorating its 30th anniversary of Antarctic programmes, and wished to state its determination to rebuild the station.

Item 5: Operation of the Antarctic Treaty System: General Matters

(35) The Chair reminded the Meeting of Resolution 1 (2011) on increasing the number of Parties to the Protocol on Environmental Protection to the Antarctic Treaty, and invited the leaders of the initiative to share their findings.

(36) The Hon. Michel Rocard AC, former Prime Minister of France, advised the Meeting that five states – Malaysia, Portugal, Colombia, Denmark and Hungary – had decided to ratify the Protocol, whilst five other states had indicated an interest in acceding. He acknowledged the assistance of many other Parties which had formally approached states that had not yet acceded to the Protocol. While congratulating Treaty Parties on the progress to date, France noted that the mission to achieve full ratification of the Protocol was still to be completed.

(37) The Hon. Bob Hawke AC, former Prime Minister of Australia, supported France's remarks, reiterated the unique value of the Antarctic Treaty and its Protocol, commended the cooperation embodied by the ATCM, and urged all Parties to ratify the Protocol.

(38) Spain also supported the Madrid Protocol Initiative, and noted that two factors sometimes cited as preventing Parties from ratifying the Protocol, namely costs and a low level of priority, were unacceptable in light of the importance of ratifications to the Antarctic Treaty system and the Antarctic environment. Spain encouraged all Parties that had signed the Protocol to ratify it as soon as possible.

(39) Colombia confirmed that it had initiated the internal procedures to accede to the Madrid Protocol.

(40) France introduced WP 31, *Strengthening Support for the Protocol on Environmental Protection to the Antarctic Treaty*, jointly prepared with Australia and Spain. The overall response of Treaty Parties not yet Party to the Protocol to the demarches was positive and reflected widespread support for the principles and objectives of the Protocol. Some States had already commenced procedures for accession or ratification, but not all of them were able to commit to accession at this time.

(41) The Meeting commended Parties that had participated in demarches for their work on this matter and confirmed that the issue was of importance to all Parties. Noting that some specific questions had been raised, particularly in relation to the financial and administrative implications of acceding to the

Protocol, the Meeting agreed that the intersessional work should continue and welcomed the offer by Australia, France and Spain to continue to coordinate this intersessional work and to report to ATCM XXXVI on the outcomes of follow-up representations in the 2012/13 intersessional period.

(42) The Meeting adopted Resolution 1 (2012), Strengthening Support for the Protocol on Environmental Protection to the Antarctic Treaty.

(43) Australia introduced WP 1, *Antarctic Treaty Consultative Meeting Communiqué*, which proposed that Parties issue at the conclusion of each ATCM a short, factual report, or communiqué, comprising a summary of matters discussed and decisions taken. Australia suggested that a communiqué could improve awareness among the general public and relevant international bodies of the unique features of Antarctica and the Antarctic Treaty System, and of the important work undertaken during the annual meetings of Parties.

(44) The Meeting agreed to develop an ATCM communiqué that would provide a factual reflection of the Meeting and be developed under the supervision of the ATCM Chair. In addition to posting on the Secretariat website, the communiqué should be disseminated actively to the international press and national media by the Antarctic Treaty Secretariat, Host Country Secretariat and Parties.

(45) France introduced WP 28, *Jurisdiction in Antarctica*, outlining the complexity of the exercise of jurisdiction in the Antarctic Treaty area and proposing an intersessional contact group to discuss questions related thereto. France referred to an incident in which French nationals damaged the historic site and monument Wordie House and in respect of which several questions on the exercise of jurisdiction in the Antarctic Treaty area had arisen, including the types of offences that could happen; the bases of the exercise of jurisdiction; the reporting of incidents; and the collection of evidence.

(46) The Meeting noted the need to improve cooperation among Parties by instituting discussion on issues of jurisdiction in the Antarctic Treaty area, and adopted Resolution 2, Cooperation on questions related to the exercise of jurisdiction in the Antarctic Treaty area.

(47) The Meeting agreed to establish an intersessional contact group (ICG), dedicated to cooperation on questions related to the exercise of jurisdiction in the Antarctic Treaty area.

(48) There was support for the view that the ICG should focus on an exchange on concrete situations.

(49)   It was further agreed that:

- Observers and Experts participating in ATCM XXXV would be invited to provide input to the ICG;
- The Executive Secretary would open the ATCM forum for the ICG and provide assistance to the ICG; and
- France would act as convener, and would report to ATCM XXXVI on the progress made in the ICG.

(50)   Chile introduced WP 64, *Establishing a Working Group on Antarctic Cooperation,* recalling the importance of scientific cooperation in the Antarctic Treaty and the Protocol on Environmental Protection.

(51)   The Parties, while recognising with appreciation the contribution of SCAR and COMNAP to scientific and logistical cooperation among the Treaty Parties, decided to establish an intersessional contact group (ICG), convened by Chile.

(52)   The ICG would work on identifying means of further improving cooperation in Antarctica, which might include issues such as: education and promotion of public knowledge about Antarctic issues; exchange of experiences on bilateral cooperation; implementation of the Antarctic Treaty System rules in domestic law and procedures; and identifying competent national authorities regulating tourism and non-scientific activities in Antarctica.

(53)   The ICG would prepare a report for ATCM XXXVI. The ICG would be established with the assistance of the Secretariat of the Antarctic Treaty within existing resources.

(54)   The Meeting adopted Resolution 3 (2012) Improving Cooperation in Antarctica.

(55)   The Executive Secretary presented SP 9, *Report of the Intersessional Contact Group on the Review of ATCM Recommendations on Operational Matters,* which continued the analysis of operational recommendations as agreed by ATCM XXXIV, coordinated by the Secretariat and contributed to by Parties and expert bodies. The ICG had reviewed twenty-eight recommendations in four categories.

(56)   The ICG identified eleven recommendations that are current; seven recommendations that are no longer current; and twelve recommendations containing current general principles but outdated operational paragraphs requiring updating; and eight technical recommendations relating to meteorology, on which advice was required from relevant expert bodies, including WMO,

COMNAP and SCAR. The Meeting adopted Decision 1 (2012) Measures on Operational Matters designated as no longer current.

(57) COMNAP noted that it had actively participated in the ICG on the status of recommendations (summarised in SP 9), and had provided detailed comments on the practical and technical aspects of the Recommendations. COMNAP offered to provide draft language for those Recommendations identified by the ICG as requiring updating, and also to suggest draft report language for next year's ATCM final report, in those cases where the general principles of the Recommendations might still be valid, but the technical and practical aspects may be outdated and therefore no longer current.

(58) Given the subject matter contained in the Recommendations that require updating, COMNAP would invite other organisations with expertise on particular technical topics, such as the WMO, IAATO and the IHO in particular, to contribute to the drafting work. Bearing in mind the discussions from the ICG and SP 9, the draft language would be presented by COMNAP as a working paper for consideration by ATCM XXXVI.

(59) The Meeting accepted the offer by COMNAP.

(60) ASOC noted the significance of the Polar Code negotiations, and highlighted the importance of leadership from Parties on this matter in order to achieve progress and a coherent outcome at the IMO. Some Parties endorsed this statement.

(61) The Meeting also welcomed the offer of the IHO to provide ATCM XXXVI with consolidated text for consideration in relation to past recommendations concerning hydrography.

(62) The Meeting discussed the use of an indicative template for terms of reference of intersessional contact groups and agreed to develop this at ATCM XXXVI.

Item 6: Operation of the Antarctic Treaty System: Review of the Secretariat's Situation

(63) The Meeting reviewed SP 2, *Secretariat Report 2011/12*; SP 3, *Secretariat Programme 2012/13*; SP 4, *Contributions Received by the Antarctic Treaty Secretariat 2009-2012*; and SP 5, *Five Years Forward Budget 2012–2017*.

(64) The Executive Secretary thanked Parties for their advice, and expressed appreciation to the Government of Argentina for its excellent support for the

activities of the Secretariat, including the provision of the new Secretariat office and costs associated with relocation.

(65) Reporting on the activities of the Secretariat, the Executive Secretary noted its support to the ATCM and CEP Meetings and thirteen intersessional contact groups, the update of the online CEP Handbook, the revision and improvement of the Electronic Information Exchange System (EIES), and the publication of the Non-Native Species Manual pursuant to Resolution 6 (2011). He also outlined several personnel matters.

(66) The Executive Secretary presented the audited financial report for 2010/11 and the provisional financial report for 2011/12. The conclusion of the auditor was that the financial reports presented fairly, in all material respects, the financial position of the Secretariat to 31 March 2011, as well as confirming that its financial performance for this period was in accordance with International Accounting Standards and the rules agreed by the ATCM.

(67) In outlining the anticipated activities of the Secretariat in 2012/13, the Executive Secretary highlighted the support that would be provided to Belgium as the Host Country for ATCM XXXVI and CEP XVI. Additionally, the Secretariat would continue to develop the EIES, and expand a number of information databases, including for protected areas. The Secretariat also intended to continue cooperation with the Scott Polar Research Institute in identifying all missing ATCM documentation and integrating it into the ATS database.

(68) The Executive Secretary noted that the forward budget profile reflected specific financial challenges that have resulted from global and local economic developments, and that the most notable factors that have contributed to increased forecast expenditure were inflation in Argentina and increased costs associated with translation and interpretation.

(69) Parties thanked the Secretariat for its work, including in compiling documents, and presenting comprehensive reports. In response to a query from Chile, the Executive Secretary indicated that to the best of his knowledge all papers that Parties had provided to the ATS to date for archiving had been included in the ATS database.

(70) Several Parties raised specific questions regarding the 2012/13 draft budget and 2013/14 forecast budget, and noted that many were facing strict budget constraints, which they needed to take into account when analyzing and approving the budget.

(71) Responding to Parties' questions, the Executive Secretary provided further information on, for example, translation and interpretation arrangements; the operation of the funds for staff replacement and staff termination; purchasing power in Argentina and the difference between paying salaries in US Dollars or Argentine Pesos.

(72) Following further discussions on the budget, the Executive Secretary produced revised figures (SP2 (rev.1) and SP3 (rev.1)). These were agreed by the Meeting which then adopted Decision 2 (2012), Secretariat Report, Programme and Budget.

(73) During these discussions, the Meeting decided to support the Executive Secretary through the establishment of an open-ended Intersessional Contact Group (ICG). The ICG, referred to in Decision 2(2012), will also consider ways to ensure a sustainable budget for future years, including consideration of:

1. possible avenues of developing income streams, other than from Consultative Parties' contributions;
2. options for reducing the costs of translation and interpretation;
3. possible amendments of ATCM rules and regulations, including Financial Regulations and Staff Regulations;
4. use of appropriate formulae to calculate the increase in costs, and the principles underlying such formulae;
5. salary scales for executive and general staff;
6. use of an appropriate multi-year forecast budget profile.

(74) Japan expressed its appreciation for the efforts made by the Secretariat in achieving a zero nominal growth budget. Japan also pointed out that the salary scale attached to the Staff Regulations (Decision 3 (2003)) was outdated and should be designated as no longer current.

(75) Australia introduced WP 24, *A Guide for Secretariat Systems and Information Sources*, proposing that the Meeting request the Secretariat to develop, and update as required, a concise and factual reference document or 'guide', in electronic format, on how to access and use its systems and information sources. The guide would provide information and instructions on the use of the systems and information resources administered by the Secretariat, and explain the practical aspects of participating in meetings and interacting with the Secretariat and other Parties.

(76) Following confirmation by the Executive Secretary that this could be accomplished within existing resources, the Meeting requested the Secretariat to develop an

electronic guide to its systems and information sources, to be integrated within the Secretariat website and referred to in the delegates' manual.

Item 7: Development of a Multi-Year Strategic Work Plan

(77) Australia introduced WP 30, *The Development of a Multi-Year Strategic Work Plan for the Antarctic Treaty Consultative Meeting*, jointly prepared with Belgium, Germany, the Netherlands, New Zealand, Norway, South Africa, Sweden, the United Kingdom and the United States. It noted that there were two supporting information papers, IP 11, *Topic Summary: The Development of a Multi-Year Strategic Work Plan for the Antarctic Treaty Consultative* Meeting and IP 12, *Examples to illustrate the proposed application of a Multi-Year Strategic Work Plan.* The proposal was for the Meeting to adopt a strategic approach to the conduct of its work, by developing a five-year rolling plan to be attached to its final report and made available on the website of the Secretariat.

(78) A delegate of the CEP provided a briefing on the CEP's experience of developing a rolling 5 year work-plan. It was noted in particular that the adoption of the plan had significantly helped the CEP to operate more efficiently and effectively in its work.

(79) While many Parties and ASOC supported the idea of a work plan and its potential to increase the efficiency of the work of the ATCM, a number of Parties expressed concerns, including how complex and time-consuming the setting of priorities could be, the need for the work plan to remain subordinate to the ATCM agenda and not to interfere with its regular development, and the potential cost implications of producing a work plan.

(80) New Zealand introduced WP 47, *Prioritisation of Issues in an ATCM Multi-Year Strategic Work Plan*, which proposed that the Meeting consider prioritising issues in three thematic groupings: (i) effective protection of the changing Antarctic environment; (ii) effective management of human activities in Antarctica; and (iii) effective operation of the Antarctic Treaty System; and suggested a prioritisation methodology based on the 'likelihood' and 'consequences' of events for Antarctica and the Antarctic Treaty System. It also referred to the supporting IP 16, *Prioritisation of ATCM Issues: Illustrative Table.*

(81) In response to the proposed risk-based methodology for identifying priorities, the Netherlands highlighted that the methodology did not take into account the policy dimension of prioritisation. In this sense, the United States

suggested that while the proposed model may be useful at a national level, there are other factors that Parties may wish to take into consideration when determining national priorities.

(82) Taking these concerns and considerations into account in the further discussion, the Meeting adopted Decision 3 (2012), The Development of a Multi-Year Strategic Work Plan for the Antarctic Treaty Consultative Meeting. The Meeting noted that proposals had been put forward with respect to a possible format for the plan. The Meeting requested that the Executive Secretary establish a Special Fund to receive voluntary contributions for interpretation services at the workshop established by Decision 3 (2012).

(83) The Meeting agreed to establish the Intersessional Contact Group (ICG), referred to in Decision 3 (2012), with the following terms of reference:

    a. To coordinate, electronically, input from Consultative Parties and other ATCM participants, on possible priority issues to be identified in the plan; and

    b. To compile a document reflecting input to be circulated to Consultative Parties and other ATCM participants no less than 3 months prior to ATCM XXXVI.

(84) It was further agreed that:

- Observers and Experts participating in ATCM XXXV would be invited to provide input to the ICG; and
- The Executive Secretary would open the ATCM forum for the ICG and provide assistance to the ICG.

(85) Australia and Belgium recognised that consensus for a format for the multi-year strategic work plan was not reached at this Meeting. Acknowledging this, Australia and Belgium would like the draft format presented in IP12, *Examples to illustrate the proposed application of a Multi-Year Strategic Work Plan*, to continue to be considered as a possible basis for the format of the plan, including at the workshop to discuss developing a draft work plan for consideration at ATCM XXXVI.

Item 8: Report of the Committee for Environmental Protection

(86) Dr Yves Frenot, Chair of the Committee for Environmental Protection (CEP), introduced the report of CEP XV. The CEP considered 44 Working Papers, 46 Information Papers, 5 Secretariat Papers and 13 Background Papers.

Strategic Discussions on the Future of the CEP (CEP Agenda Item 3)

(87)   The Committee revised and updated its Five-Year Work Plan, which was important for managing its work and priorities. The Committee decided to elevate to priority 2 the topics of 'Overview of protected areas system' and 'Site specific guidelines', and to identify as priority 3 (previously priority 2) the topics of 'Historic Sites and Monuments' and 'Exchange of information', which remain standing items.

(88)   The Committee also supported the concept of an on-line Antarctic Environments Portal, which would serve as the primary source of information on Antarctic environments, a link between science and policy, a way to facilitate and enhance the advisory roles of both SCAR and the CEP to the ATCM, and to assist in communicating information on Antarctic environments to the public. The Committee looked forward to intersessional work on a demonstration model towards further discussions in 2013.

(89)   The ATCM noted that the CEP continued to work strategically to prioritise issues though its 5 year work plan, which allows for the most important topics to be the focus of work while encouraging individual members to pursue areas of their expertise. The ATCM thanked the CEP for its responsiveness to requests for advice. The importance of full use of the EIES was reiterated.

Operation of the CEP (CEP Agenda Item 4)

(90)   The Committee discussed ongoing efforts to improve the exchange of information, and accepted the Secretariat's offer to facilitate further improvements to the environmental reporting components of the Electronic Information Exchange System (EIES).

Climate Change Implications for the Environment: Strategic approach (CEP Agenda Item 5)

(91)   The Committee discussed actions taken to address the recommendations of the 2010 Antarctic Treaty Meeting of Experts (ATME) on Climate Change. It considered a COMNAP report on best practices in energy management, and an outline from SCAR of its work to communicate the science of climate change. It also noted the proposal of ASOC, Australia and the United Kingdom to hold a coordinated switch-off of all non-essential lights at Antarctic research stations to mark Earth Hour on 30 March 2013, to demonstrate support for action to tackle the threat of climate change.

(92) The Committee endorsed the proposal of Norway and the United Kingdom to trial in the Antarctic the methodology of the Rapid Assessment of Circum-Arctic Ecosystem Resilience (RACER), a tool to assess ecosystem resilience and areas of conservation importance, while taking into account the need to adapt the methodology to the Antarctic context.

(93) The ATCM thanked the CEP for its work in advancing several recommendations from the meeting of experts on climate change and recalled that there were still a number of outstanding recommendations and encouraged further work in this area.

(94) Australia noted that the CEP was making progress on the environmental recommendations from the ATME, through its five-year work plan. It noted that a multi-year strategic work plan could similarly assist the ATCM to schedule its consideration of recommendations addressing other matters, as suggested in IP 12.

Environmental Impact Assessment (CEP Agenda Item 6)

Draft Comprehensive Environmental Evaluations

(95) No draft Comprehensive Environmental Evaluations (CEEs) were submitted to CEP XV.

Other EIA matters

(96) The Committee endorsed the study led by New Zealand on the environmental aspects and impacts of tourism and non-governmental activities in Antarctica, and forwarded the study and its 8 recommendations to the ATCM to support its consideration of tourism management. The study responded to a request by ATCM XXXII, and was a significant step towards identifying the known and unknown impacts of tourism and non-governmental activities. The Committee recognised that the study was a dynamic document that would require ongoing consideration by the CEP.

(97) The Meeting welcomed the timely advice from the CEP on the environmental aspects and impacts of tourism and noted that the CEP is ready to develop further work as needed.

(98) The Committee welcomed Brazil's efforts to minimise environmental impacts in the course of decommissioning and reconstructing facilities at Comandante Ferraz Station. It also received further information from the

Russian Federation on the penetration of subglacial Lake Vostok, including an explanation of why it had not transferred to the thermal drill technology as originally planned, and its intentions for future work to take samples from the water column of the lake.

(99) The Committee was informed of the preparation of 2 final CEEs:

- Final Comprehensive Environmental Evaluation (CEE) of the Construction and Operation of the Jang Bogo Antarctic Research Station, Terra Nova Bay, Antarctica (Republic of Korea)
- Final Comprehensive Environmental Evaluation (CEE) of the Proposed Exploration of Subglacial Lake Ellsworth, Antarctica (United Kingdom).

(100) The ATCM was grateful for these two final CEEs and commended Korea for the high quality CEE produced for the construction of the new Jang Bogo station and noted the thorough response to issues raised by the CEP in its review of the draft CEE.

(101) India presented a paper on the establishment and operation of its new research station Bharati at Larsemann Hills and thanked a number of Parties for their useful feedback during the CEE process.

Area Protection and Management (CEP Agenda Item 7)

Management Plans for Protected and Managed Areas

(102) The Committee had before it revised management plans for 14 Antarctic Specially Protected Areas (ASPAs) and 1 Antarctic Specially Managed Area (ASMA), and 3 proposals to designate new ASPAs. One of these had been subject to review by the Subsidiary Group on Management Plans (SGMP) and the others had been submitted directly to CEP XV.

(103) Accepting the CEP's advice, the Meeting adopted the following Measures on Protected and Managed Areas:

- Measure 1 (2012): Antarctic Specially Protected Area No 109 (Moe Island, South Orkney Islands): Revised Management Plan.
- Measure 2 (2012): Antarctic Specially Protected Area No 110 (Lynch Island, South Orkney Islands): Revised Management Plan.
- Measure 3 (2012): Antarctic Specially Protected Area No 111 (Southern Powell Island and adjacent islands, South Orkney Islands): Revised Management Plan.

- Measure 4 (2012): Antarctic Specially Protected Area No 112 (Coppermine Peninsula, Robert Island, South Shetland Islands): Revised Management Plan.
- Measure 5 (2012): Antarctic Specially Protected Area No 115 (Lagotellerie Island, Marguerite Bay, Graham Land): Revised Management Plan.
- Measure 6 (2012): Antarctic Specially Protected Area No 129 (Rothera Point, Adelaide Island): Revised Management Plan.
- Measure 7 (2012): Antarctic Specially Protected Area No 133 (Harmony Point): Revised Management Plan.
- Measure 8(2012): Antarctic Specially Protected Area No 140 (Parts of Deception Island): Revised Management Plan.
- Measure 9 (2012): New Antarctic Specially Protected Area (Blood Falls, Taylor Valley, McMurdo Dry Valleys, Victoria Land).
- Measure 10 (2012): Antarctic Specially Managed Area No 4 (Deception Island): Revised Management Plan.

(104) The Committee referred the following draft management plans and proposals for new ASPAs to the SGMP for intersessional review:

- ASPA 128 (Western Shore of Admiralty Bay, King George Island, South Shetland Islands).
- ASPA 132 (Potter Peninsula).
- ASPA 144 ('Chile Bay' (Discovery Bay), Greenwich Island, South Shetland Islands).
- ASPA 145 (Port Foster, Deception Island, South Shetland Islands).
- ASPA 146 (South Bay, Doumer Island, Palmer Archipelago).
- ASPA 151 (Lions Rump, King George Island, South Shetland Islands).
- New ASPA(High altitude geothermal areas of the Ross Sea region).
- New ASPA (Cape Washington and Silverfish Bay, Terra Nova Bay, Ross Sea).

CEP Subsidiary Group on Management Plans

(105) The Committee adopted the work plan for the SGMP's activities during the 2012/13 intersessional period, appointed Ms Birgit Njåstad from Norway as the new convener and thanked Mr Ewan McIvor from Australia for his convenership.

(106) The Meeting noted the large work load ahead of the SGMP in considering new and revised management plans and encouraged participation in that work, noting the effectiveness of the group. New Zealand suggested that the Committee might consider the utility of establishing additional subsidiary groups to facilitate its work. It was also noted that several of the management plans to be discussed will also be considered by CCAMLR in the coming intersessional period. The Meeting encouraged effective dialogue between SC_CCAMLR and the CEP on the matters of interest to the two committees.

Historic Sites and Monuments

(107) The Committee considered the report of intersessional discussions convened by Argentina on Historic Sites and Monuments and noted the proposed list of additional information that could be added to the description of HSMs, including information on the type of HSM, physical feature and local / cultural landscape, historical / cultural feature, description of the historical context, link to site guidelines for visitors if applicable, photos and maps, and ASPA designation if applicable. The Committee agreed that Parties should engage with heritage specialists and/or national representatives to external expert bodies when considering management mechanisms for HSMs.

(108) The Committee had before it 7 proposals to revise the descriptions of HSMs.

(109) Accepting the CEP's advice, the Meeting adopted Measure 11 on Historic Sites and Monuments:

- No 4 Pole of Inaccessibility
- No 7 Ivan Khmara's Stone
- No 8 Anatoly Scheglov's Monument
- No 9 Buromsky Island Cemetery
- No 10 Soviet Oasis Station Observatory
- No 11 Vostok Station Tractor
- No 37 O'Higgins Historic Site.

Site Guidelines

(110) The Committee discussed proposals for revised site guidelines for one site and new guidelines for three new sites. The Committee endorsed the new site guidelines for D'Hainaut Island, Mikkelsen Harbour, Trinity Island;

Port Charcot, Booth Island; and Pendulum Cove, Deception Island, South Shetland Islands.

(111) The Meeting considered and approved 3 new Site Guidelines by means of Resolution 4 (2012).

(112) The Committee discussed a proposal to revise the site guidelines for Aitcho Island/Barrientos Island, to modify the anchorage points and to change the designated walking route through a closed area. The Committee agreed that it would be appropriate to place a moratorium on access to the closed central area other than for reasons of scientific research and monitoring. It also agreed that it would be appropriate to: amend the site guidelines to take account of the moratorium; to encourage those national programmes active in the area to cooperate in collecting further data and information on the damage that had occurred to moss beds as well as on developing a monitoring programme to assess recovery of the site, and to reassess the issue, including the site guidelines, at CEP XVI.

(113) The Meeting considered and approved 1 revised Site Guidelines by means of Resolution 5 (2012).

(114) The Meeting welcomed the adoption of new and revised Visitor Site Guidelines, which are proving to be useful, and in the case of Barrientos/Aitcho Island, a proactive tool for managing impacts at tourist landing sites.

Human Footprint and Wilderness Values

(115) The Committee discussed the concept of footprint and wilderness values related to the protection of the Antarctic environment. The Committee welcomed an offer by New Zealand and the Netherlands to work with SCAR and other interested Parties in advance of CEP XVI, to develop guidance material to assist Parties to take account of wilderness values, and to explore possibilities for considering inviolate areas in conservation planning, and potential synergies with the protection of wilderness values.

(116) New Zealand highlighted the ongoing work on footprint and wilderness and the Committee's acknowledgment that there had been a gradual decline in some aspects of Antarctic wilderness; and noted that this work is pertinent to some of the longer term strategic questions being considered by the Tourism Working Group around the expansion and diversification of tourism activities.

Marine Spatial Protection and Management

(117) The Committee noted that the matter of krill fishing in ASMA 1 during 2009/10 raised by ASOC would be considered by the Management Group for ASMA 1 when reviewing and revising the Area management plan in the coming year. The SC-CCAMLR Observer also undertook to ensure that concerns regarding this issue were brought to CCAMLR's attention.

Other Annex V Matters

(118) The Committee considered a proposal from the United States and New Zealand on the protection of geothermal areas in ice caves on Mount Erebus, Ross Island. It agreed to encourage: interested Parties and their scientists to collaborate in generating an inventory of Mount Erebus ice caves; interested Parties and their scientists to collaborate in developing a Code of Conduct to prevent contamination; and scientists, interested Parties, and SCAR to work together to develop appropriate guidance material for other geothermal areas in Antarctica. The Committee also noted other recommendations to encourage Parties to adopt a temporary moratorium on informal visits or visits for any purpose other than scientific research; and on entry for any purpose into Mount Erebus ice caves that are believed to be pristine until a Code of Conduct can be agreed; and to encourage scientists to sterilise their gear and clothing.

(119) The Committee also considered an analysis presented by Australia, New Zealand and SCAR, which identified 15 biologically distinct ice-free regions (Antarctic Conservation Biogeographic Regions) encompassing the Antarctic continent and offshore islands within the Antarctic Treaty area. The Committee agreed that the Antarctic Conservation Biogeographic Regions should be used consistently and in conjunction with other tools agreed within the Antarctic Treaty system as a dynamic model for the identification of areas that could be designated as Antarctic Specially Protected Areas within the systematic environmental-geographic framework referred to in Article 3(2) of Annex V of the Protocol. The Committee also made requests of the Secretariat and Parties to contribute to the collection and accessibility of spatial data, and agreed to incorporate the map of the 15 Antarctic Conservation Biogeographic Regions into the CEP Non-Native Species Manual.

(120) The Meeting adopted Resolution 6 (2012) on Antarctic Conservation Biogeographic Regions.

(121) The Meeting welcomed the endorsement of the recently developed Antarctic Conservation Biogeographic Regions as a new tool to support the identification of areas for consideration of special protection or management, within a systematic environmental framework.

(122) The Committee discussed a proposal from the Russian Federation to require any Party reviewing a management plan for an Area primarily designated to protect living Antarctic values, to submit to the CEP the results of a scientific monitoring programme on the state of those values. While the Committee agreed with the need for long-term monitoring of protected areas, some Members expressed concerns about the potential consequences of a compulsory system, which they were concerned could include compelling access to protected areas, and discouraging management plan revision.

Conservation of Antarctic Fauna and Flora (CEP Agenda Item 8)

Quarantine and non-native species

(123) Following the SCAR lecture on the outputs of the SCAR-IPY 'Aliens in Antarctica' project, the Committee agreed:

- To include the spatially explicit, activity-differentiated risk assessments in further development of strategies to mitigate the risks posed by terrestrial non-native species.
- In collaboration with SCAR, COMNAP, IAATO, the IUCN and Parties, to develop a surveillance strategy for areas at high risk of non-native species establishment as identified by the Aliens in Antarctica project.
- To give additional attention, in collaboration with its partners, to the risks posed by intra-Antarctic transfer of propagules, given that such assessments only formed a small part of the Aliens in Antarctica project.

(124) The Committee also considered SCAR's paper on reducing the risk of inadvertent introductions of non-native species associated with fresh food and vegetable importation to the Antarctic, and agreed to: encourage Parties to implement the COMNAP/SCAR checklists for supply chain managers; and investigate further methods to reduce the risk of non-native species introductions to Antarctica associated with fresh food. It also agreed to include the guidelines proposed by Australia and France to minimise the

risks of non-native species and disease associated with Antarctic hydroponics facilities in the Non-Native Species Manual.

Other Annex II matters

(125) The Committee noted with interest the information from Germany and SCAR on anthropogenic sound in the Southern Ocean, and requested regular updates on further research in this area.

Environmental Monitoring and Reporting (CEP Agenda Item 9)

(126) The Committee continued its discussion started at CEP XIV on the potential use of remote sensing techniques for improved monitoring of environment and climate change in Antarctica. In response to a paper by the United Kingdom on remote sensing techniques to monitor vegetation change in ASPAs and the wider Antarctic environment, the Committee:

- acknowledged the significant value offered by the combination of satellite and aerial monitoring as a new technique for gathering detailed evidence of vegetation change, linked to localised climate change;
- encouraged Parties with work programmes related to vegetation change to consider collaboration with the UK in further developing and applying these monitoring techniques; in particular to identify particular geographic areas or scientific programmes suitable for these techniques; and
- invited Parties to comment on the methodology and to share their experiences of applying similar techniques.

(127) The Committee also agreed that Germany would coordinate and lead an informal intersessional contact group on the topic of remote sensing as an additional tool for monitoring Antarctic penguin populations, which would liaise with CCAMLR and report to CEP XVI.

(128) In response to a submission by New Zealand on simple and fast techniques using GIS analysis for monitoring vegetation changes at fine scales, the Committee:

- acknowledged the potential use of GIS techniques as a method for monitoring changes in species distribution and abundance at fine scales, which could be coupled with remote sensing technologies for monitoring changes at macro scales for both species and the environment;

- agreed to establish a network of sites for monitoring species distribution and abundance, with priority afforded to ASPAs designated for their flora and/or fauna diversity and abundance, where monitoring can occur during the management plan review process; and

- recognised the value of applying consistent methodologies at ASPAs so that changes in species diversity and abundance can be compared continent-wide to obtain a more comprehensive understanding of climate change effects in Antarctica.

(129) In response to a submission from Chile relating to the presence of human-associated microorganisms from sewage treatment plant discharges in the Antarctic, the Committee agreed that Members should strengthen their precautionary monitoring of microbial activity in areas near sewage treatment plant discharges, and noted that COMNAP would consider at its July 2012 Annual General Meeting the possibility of reviewing relevant information and guidelines concerning waste water management.

Inspection Reports (CEP Agenda Item 10)

(130) The Committee considered one Inspection Report: from the Russian Federation and the United States, on their joint inspection of Scott Base (New Zealand), Concordia Station (France and Italy), and Mario Zucchelli Station (Italy). France, Italy and New Zealand provided preliminary responses to the findings, and Dr H. Miller, as Chairman of the EPICA Project, gave complementary information on the historical and technical features of the deep ice core project at Dome C.

(131) In response to a review of inspections under Article 14 of the Madrid Protocol submitted by ASOC and UNEP, the Committee noted that the inspection mechanism was vital in underpinning the practical application of the Madrid Protocol, and several Members recommended that inspected Parties report back on measures they had taken in response to recommendations in inspection reports. In this respect, the Russian Federation informed the CEP of progress made in response to inspections of Molodezhnaya Station, Druzhnaya IV Station, Soyuz Station, Leningradskaya Station and Vostok Station carried out by Australia in 2010 and 2011.

Cooperation with Other Organisations (CEP Agenda Item 11)

(132) The Committee received the annual reports from COMNAP, SCAR, and CCAMLR. In light of the relevance of reports from other organisations to a

range of items on its agenda, the Committee decided to examine this agenda item earlier in future meetings.

Repair and Remediation of Environment Damage (CEP Agenda Item 12)

(133) The Committee reiterated that repair and remediation was of utmost importance, and decided to continue informal discussions during the intersessional period to further develop the draft Antarctic Clean-Up Manual proposed by Australia and the United Kingdom. The Manual will contain guidance to assist Parties to address their obligations under Annex III to the Environmental Protocol to clean up past waste disposal sites on land and abandoned work sites of past activities, and could be regularly updated.

(134) The Committee considered Australia's outline of key issues to respond to the request from ATCM XXXIII, in Decision 4 (2010), for advice on environmental issues related to the practicality of repair and remediation of environmental damage. The Committee established an ICG to be convened by Dr Neil Gilbert, New Zealand, under the following Terms of Reference:

- drawing on ATCM XXXV/WP 26 *Environmental issues related to the practicality of repair and remediation of environmental damage* (Australia) and, as appropriate, other papers submitted to CEP XV on the subject of repair and remediation of environmental damage:
- prepare a draft response to Decision 4 (2010), in which the ATCM requested the CEP to 'consider environmental issues related to the practicality of repair and remediation of environmental damage in the circumstances in Antarctica';
- where appropriate, seek to identify and present examples to help illustrate matters raised in the draft advice; and
- report to CEP XVI on the outcomes of this work.

(135) The ATCM welcomed the response of the CEP to the request of the ATCM put forward in Decision 4 (2010) and looks forward to the results of the proposed programme of CEP work on the issue of repair and remediation which are important to address the environmental legacy of sites of past activity.

General Matters (CEP Agenda Item 13)

(136) After considering COMNAP's report on its survey of oil spill contingency planning, the Committee urged Parties to continue improving their

contingency plans within the framework of their National Antarctic Programmes.

Election of Officers (CEP Agenda Item 14)

(137) The Committee re-elected Dr Yves Frenot from France as CEP Chair for a second two-year term.

(138) Ms Birgit Njåstad from Norway was elected as a Vice-Chair of the CEP.

(139) The Committee warmly thanked Ewan McIvor from Australia for serving as Vice-Chair for two terms, and for convening the SGMP.

Preparation for CEP XVI (CEP Agenda Item 14)

(140) The Committee adopted the provisional agenda for CEP XVI contained in Appendix [1] to the CEP's report.

(141) The Meeting thanked Dr Frenot for his excellent chairmanship, thanked the outgoing vice chair Ewan McIvor for having served the Committee in an outstanding manner during his two terms in office, and congratulated the Committee on its ability to constantly and in such a dedicated manner provide the ATCM with sound management advice based on solid background work.

Item 9: Liability: Implementation of Decision 4 (2010)

(142) Parties provided updated information on the status of their ratification of Annex VI of the Protocol. As of June 2012, six Consultative Parties had ratified Annex VI, and approximately six further Consultative Parties were expected to ratify before ATCM XXXVI. The Meeting welcomed the ongoing work of Consultative Parties and any other Parties, while noting that the Annex was unlikely to enter into force prior to ATCM XXXVI. Consultative Parties confirmed that they were committed to ratifying Annex VI, and attributed any delays in ratification to resource constraints and/or certain implementation challenges.

(143) The Russian Federation presented IP 71, *On preparation for ratification of Annex VI of the Protocol on Environmental Protection to the Antarctic Treaty*, outlining the relevant changes to its domestic legislation during the previous year. In 2012, the Russian Parliament considered a draft law on regulation of the activities of Russian citizens and legal entities in Antarctica

required by Measure 4 (2004) and Measure 1 (2005). In the course of the Meeting, the Russian Federation advised that the legislation in question had been already adopted by the Russian Parliament and entered into force on June 5, 2012.

(144) The Russian Federation noted the difficulty it had experienced in accurately calculating the cost of response measures, which required an understanding of the scope and nature of each measure, and a methodology for the calculation of the costs of these measures. It suggested there was a need to develop a unified framework for this, in order to avoid discrepancies between Parties.

Item 10: Safety and Operations in Antarctica

(145) COMNAP introduced WP 13, *Understanding Risk to National Antarctic Programme Operations and Personnel in Coastal Antarctica from Tsunami Events*, prepared jointly with SCAR, which reported that a preliminary analysis showed that risks of a moderate to concerning level to National Antarctic Programme operations and personnel in coastal Antarctica from tsunami may arise on occasion.

(146) The United Kingdom and Spain noted that they had undertaken some tsunami response procedures in some Antarctic stations after the 2010 Chilean earthquake and, in the case of Spain, the 2011 Japanese earthquake. The United States noted its significant investment and experience with tsunami warning systems. Argentina recalled the information it provided to ATCM XXXIV on this matter. IHO and WMO indicated that they would be willing to assist if needed.

(147) The Meeting supported COMNAP's recommendation that organisations with expertise in tsunami detection, modelling, research and warning system management should work together with COMNAP and SCAR on the next phase of this project, namely, to develop a simple, cost-effective, practical tsunami warning communications plan and tsunami awareness education materials.

(148) New Zealand introduced WP 49, *ATCM Response to CCAMLR Fishing Vessel Incidents*, which reported on two search and rescue responses in the Ross Sea during the 2011/12 season involving the Russian-flagged *FV SPARTA* and the Korean-flagged *FV JEONG WOO 2*. New Zealand proposed that Parties support the Torremolinos Protocol of 1993 and the IMO Polar Code, enhance the safety standards of vessels, urge CCAMLR to strengthen its Resolution 20/XXII, remind operators to provide contact details to the

responsible Marine Rescue Coordination Centre in advance of entering the Antarctic Treaty area, and agree to report efforts undertaken to limit the environmental impacts of stricken vessels to the CEP.

(149) While Parties agreed that vessel safety was an important issue and an appropriate area for ATCM consideration, a number of Parties expressed concern that the ATCM should not prejudge ongoing IMO negotiations, and noted the need for consistency with existing relevant CCAMLR resolutions.

(150) Australia welcomed the encouragement to vessels to make their contact details available to an MRCC when entering the Treaty area. In Australia's view, as a nation with responsibilities for the coordination of search and rescue in the Southern Ocean, it was also important that, once inside the Treaty area, vessels report to relevant MRCCs when entering a new area for which a different MRCC had responsibility. Australia believed that it was within the remit of the ATCM to promote vessel safety in the Antarctic, and that this issue should be further considered in the future.

(151) Following further discussions, the Meeting adopted Resolution 7 (2012) Vessel Safety in the Antarctic Treaty area.

(152) The USA presented WP 51, *Coordination of Maritime and Aeronautical Search and Rescue (SAR) – Proposal for Considering Means to Improve Antarctic SAR Coordination*. It noted that SAR was a key concern of all Treaty Parties, including their National Antarctic Programmes and those agencies that manage and implement SAR in Antarctica. In light of the growing number of maritime incidents in Antarctica in recent years, the United States believed that it was time to consider exploring various means to improve SAR coordination through, for example, the establishment of best practices or other arrangements. Discussions among Treaty Parties may improve the coordination regarding the circumstances under which the five States that operate Maritime Rescue Coordination Centres with SAR coordination responsibilities in the Antarctic Treaty area should seek assistance from National Antarctic Programmes and others engaged in scientific or other missions in specified areas of operation. As a result, it proposed that there be a focused discussion of SAR at ATCM XXXVI in a special working group that would meet for one day, with participation of Parties' SAR experts, who would be included on national delegations for these discussions.

(153) Parties welcomed this proposal and raised issues that could be considered by such a working group, include the prevention of accidents. Chile noted

that on any day during the season at least 20 vessels would be in their area of SAR responsibility of which half would be IAATO vessels. This indicated the need to share information on reporting schemes with other MRCCs. Germany requested the specific inclusion of DROMLAN experts in the special working group. Russia noted that a new ice vessel would be available for SAR in the Antarctic in 2012/13 if necessary. Sweden indicated its intention to involve experts with experience from cooperation under the new Arctic SAR agreement. IAATO stressed the importance of including aeronautical SAR, specifically position tracking and air traffic management policies. India noted that regional SAR groupings might be necessary, as many coastal stations are beyond the reach of MRCCs and ARCCs. Argentina, a State with SAR responsibility in Antarctica, stated that it was fully committed to its obligations and felt that whilst wishing to consider ways to improve coordination among the MRCCs, it was important that their specific responsibilities should not be eroded.

(154) COMNAP confirmed that it would make available the reports from its two previous SAR Workshops to support the special working group's consideration of this issue, and noted that this special working group would benefit from interpretation services. The United States would consult with interested Parties and ATCM participants intersessionally to prepare the agenda for the special working group discussion.

(155) The Meeting adopted Resolution 8 (2012) Improved Coordination of Maritime, Aeronautical and Land-Based Search and Rescue.

(156) The IHO presented IP70, *Report by the International Hydrographic Organization (IHO) on "Cooperation in Hydrographic Surveying and Charting of Antarctic Waters"*, which reported on the status of hydrographic surveys and nautical chart production in Antarctica. The IHO called on Parties to recognise the importance of this work, noting that increased exchange of hydrographic information by Parties was crucial to its aim to improve hydrography and nautical charting for the safety of navigation and protection of the marine environment in Antarctica. The IHO noted that the 11th Meeting of the IHO Hydrographic Commission of Antarctica in October 2011 had agreed that improving coordination at a national level should be an ongoing practice amongst Parties. The IHO drew attention to its 2013-2017 work programme, which included a risk assessment for the Antarctic region and the development of a work programme to improve Antarctic charting (2013/14).

(157) Parties welcomed the report and thanked the IHO for its work. The Meeting noted the importance of hydrographic charting to avoid loss of life and serious vessel incidents.

(158) New Zealand reported that it was actively seeking to collaborate with other National Antarctic Programmes to complete hydrographic survey coverage of shipping lanes in the Ross Sea, building on surveys conducted in the Ross Sea in 2001 and 2004, and supported the IHO's request to Parties to encourage voluntary participation in data activities.

(159) The United Kingdom noted that while it fully supported the work of the IHO, and its HCA in particular, it questioned whether, since the Polar Code was still in development, now was the time for the ATCM to communicate on the specific matter of voluntary participation in data collection.

(160) The United Kingdom introduced WP 4, *The Assessment of Land-Based Activities in Antarctica*, containing a list of questions for the consideration of competent authorities as part of the authorisation process for non-governmental land-based activities. The list (a reformulation of the checklist discussed at ATCM XXXIV) aims to enhance the consistency of assessments, and responds to comments received intersessionally via the forum on the ATS website.

(161) Many Parties expressed support for this work and thanked the United Kingdom. Norway noted that not all the questions would be relevant to all land-based activities. The Netherlands reiterated that it was the responsibility of competent national authorities to approve activities in line with domestic requirements, and that the list of questions should reflect this.

(162) The Meeting adopted Resolution 9 (2012) The Assessment of Land-Based Expeditionary Activities.

(163) COMNAP referred to IP 32, *COMNAP Survey of National Antarctic Programmes on Oil Spill Contingency Planning*, which had also been discussed by the CEP, and presented the results of a new COMNAP survey on oil spill contingency planning conducted in the 2011/12 intersessional period. Twenty-two of 28 COMNAP Member National Antarctic Programmes replied to the survey, which effectively updated the survey conducted by COMNAP in 1996.

(164) Welcoming this report, IAATO noted its participation in the survey and the benefits of collaboration with COMNAP.

Safety issues and tourism

(165) Germany, the United Kingdom and the United States introduced WP 17 rev.1, *Compiling Yacht Guidelines to Complement Safety Standards of Ship Traffic around Antarctica*, referring to the German-led ICG convened in 2011/12. The ICG reviewed and updated the check list of yacht-specific items presented in WP 37 at ATCM XXXIV, and provided guidelines for yachts travelling in open seas or polar regions.

(166) The Meeting adopted Resolution 10 (2012) Yachting Guidelines.

(167) New Zealand introduced WP 48, *Repeat Unauthorised Commercial Expedition: Nilaya/Berserk,* providing Parties with updated information on New Zealand's effort, with Argentina, Chile, Norway, the Russian Federation, and the United States, to cooperate in relation to this incident, and the repeated attempts made by the expedition organiser of the *Nilaya / Berserk* to undertake unauthorised expeditions to Antarctica. IP 75, *Relation of Activities Performed by Chile Regarding Nilaya/Berserk Yacht Situation* (Chile), and IP 81, *The Nilaya/Berserk Expedition* (Norway), provided further information concerning this incident. New Zealand also thanked IAATO for its cooperation in alerting its operators, and sought to encourage Parties to take practical steps toward limiting these activities, particularly further expeditions by the expedition organiser of the *Nilaya/Berserk.*

(168) Norway informed the Meeting that Norwegian authorities in April 2012 reported the responsible organiser of the *Nilaya* expedition to the prosecuting authorities for violations of the Norwegian Antarctic regulations. The report was based on lack of sufficient notification and IEE, and lack of search and rescue insurance. Currently the case is resting with the Norwegian prosecuting authorities, which have an independent role in the Norwegian legal system. No indications have been given as to when the investigation will be completed.

(169) Following the request of support made by New Zealand, Argentina required its immigration authorities, Port Control, MRCC, as well as Argentine Station Commanders in Antarctica, to report at the earliest any information on passengers travelling on board the vessel. Whilst waiting for the vessel to call at the Port of Ushuaia, there was frequent contact with New Zealand. On April 10th, at 5 pm, the vessel entered Ushuaia from Puerto Williams (Chile), flying the flag of Russia and under the name of "Berserk". The maritime authority reported this to the New Zealand consulate, which contacted its citizen on board the vessel, in order to progress immigration requirements.

(170) Chile thanked Argentina, New Zealand, the Russian Federation and IAATO for their cooperation on information sharing that made it possible to know the whereabouts of the *Nilaya/Berserk,* and reported that the vessel was currently in Puerto Williams and could be preparing for another expedition in the coming season. Unauthorised vessel expeditions to Antarctica (including the associated risks) were identified as a concern common to all Parties.

(171) Parties acknowledged that activities contrary to the Protocol and other relevant Treaty instruments in Antarctica, including those that are repeated and/or commercially funded, are a cause for serious concern. In this regard, Parties reaffirmed their commitment to taking appropriate preventative and enforcement action, in accordance with relevant domestic law, in response to activities contrary to the Protocol and other relevant Treaty instruments in Antarctica. Recalling Resolution 3 (2004), Parties also stressed the importance of continuing cooperation and information sharing regarding activities contrary to the Protocol and other relevant Treaty instruments.

(172) Referring to incidents involving unauthorised expeditions, Brazil introduced IP 64, *Brazilian Motor Yacht Accident.* Brazil stated that its navy would attempt to remove a yacht, which had been wrecked in Maxwell Bay, in the coming summer season.

(173) Echoing the concerns of Parties, IAATO presented IP 37, *Report on IAATO Operator use of Antarctic Peninsula Landing Sites and ATCM Visitor Site Guidelines, 2011-2012 Season*, reiterating its commitment to provide this information to the ATCM and the CEP annually.

(174) IAATO introduced IP 38, *Establishing IAATO Safety Advisories*, on IAATO's establishment of a formalised internal system that aims to enhance safety for operators in Antarctica, thereby ensuring that there was a readily accessible, searchable bank of 'local knowledge' on both general matters and site-specific advice, retained over time. IAATO presented the first dedicated Advisory, for Whalers Bay, Deception Island, and noted that previous recommendations to enhance safety will be converted into this format and redistributed via the IAATO Field Operations Manual.

(175) The United Kingdom said that this system was extremely useful and encouraged further liaison between IAATO and COMNAP on issues related to vessel safety.

(176) In response, COMNAP noted that it maintains an Accident, Incident and Near-Miss Reporting system that allowed National Antarctic Programmes

to share information on safety issues via instant email alert which can be supplemented with additional details.

(177) Reiterating, in this context, the importance of accurate data collection and reporting, the United Kingdom presented IP 42, *Data Collection and Reporting on Yachting Activity in Antarctica in 2011/12,* jointly prepared with IAATO. The report (an update of WP 20 presented at ATCM XXXIV) identified eight potentially unauthorised yachts operating in the Antarctic in the 2011/12 season. IAATO stated that while the number of unauthorised vessels had decreased over the last season, this issue would continue to require the close attention of Parties.

(178) In presenting IP 53, *Follow-up to Vessel Incidents in Antarctic Waters,* ASOC highlighted WP 49, *ATCM Response to CCAMLR Fishing Vessels Incidents* (New Zealand), WP 51, *Coordination of Maritime Search and Rescue (SAR) – Proposal for considering means to improve Antarctic SAR coordination* (United States) and WP 63, *Exchange of Real-time Information of the Maritime Traffic in Antarctica* (Chile), which demonstrated the potential dangers in Antarctic shipping, and underlined that further action was necessary to ensure maximum protection for human life and the environment. ASOC highlighted the lack of adequate reporting in most incidents, and called on Parties to take definitive action to address reporting, investigating, response, and follow-up of incidents.

(179) ASOC presented IP 56, *Progress on the Development of a Mandatory Polar Code,* and recalled Resolution 8 (2009), which expressed the desire of the Parties for the IMO to commence work as soon as practicable to develop mandatory requirements for ships operating in Antarctic waters. ASOC encouraged Parties to ensure that the Code would apply to new and existing vessels; require polar class standards for all vessels likely to encounter ice; apply to all vessels including fishing vessels and yachts; and include an environmental protection chapter. ASOC urged Parties to participate in the IMO correspondence group, the Design and Equipment subcommittee in February 2013, and the Marine Environment and Protection Committee in October 2012. ASOC reminded Parties that their strong leadership on this issue in the IMO would ensure the Code was effective.

(180) Parties noted the importance of continuing to engage in the development of the Code, because of its relevance to operations in Antarctica.

(181) The Russian Federation presented IP 73, *Russian Experience of Applying Automatic Aids to Approach of Heavy Transport Aircraft at the Antarctic*

Aerodromes using Satellite Navigation Systems, recalling that air safety was important in addressing the overall safety of Antarctic operations. Russian experiences in using satellite navigation systems specifically adapted to Antarctic conditions over the 2011/12 summer period showed that these systems could significantly improve air safety.

(182) COMNAP presented IP 4, *Management Implications of a Changing Antarctica – COMNAP Workshop Report,* noting that the paper was a summary of discussions amongst the managers and deputy managers of National Antarctic Programmes, who are the people that have the greatest first-hand knowledge of Antarctica. The Workshop provided an opportunity to discuss current change, and discuss practical and technical responses needed to support Antarctic science.

(183) COMNAP also referred to IP 31, *Best Practice for Energy Management – Guidance and Recommendations,* which had been discussed in the CEP. The paper showed that there are many examples of National Antarctic Programme energy saving initiatives.

Item 11: Tourism and Non-Governmental Activities

Overview of Antarctic Tourism in the 2011/12 season

(184) IAATO presented IP 39, *IAATO Overview of Antarctic Tourism: 2011-12 Season and Preliminary Estimates for 2012-13 Season*, which provided a report of tourist activity in Antarctica during the last season, as well as an overview of Antarctic tourism trends for the coming season. The total number of passengers and clients carried by IAATO operators during 2011/12 decreased to 26,519, which was a decline of approximately 22% from the previous season and marked the fourth consecutive year of decrease. IAATO clarified that the numbers represented in the paper referred only to its members' activities.

(185) IAATO stated that while worldwide economic factors were responsible for the declines across all forms of Antarctic tourism in 2008/09, 2009/10 and 2010/11, the sharp decrease during the 2011/12 season was due to changes to the International Maritime Organization's (IMO) MARPOL Annex I which came into effect on 1 August 2011. These changes banned the use and carriage of heavy fuel oil in the Antarctic Treaty area and had a significant impact on the number of overall tourists to Antarctica, as it reduced the number of voyages by IAATO cruise-only operators who use vessels carrying

more than 500 passengers. Estimates for the 2012/13 season forecasted an increase to 34,950 tourists, still below the 2007/08 season.

(186) In response to a query from Chile, IAATO advised that although cruise-only voyages had significantly decreased, other cruises, including those with landings, were increasing. IAATO also assured the Meeting that no vessel refuelling was taking place within the Treaty area.

(187) Argentina presented IP 86, *Areas of tourist interest in the Antarctic Peninsula and Islas Orcadas del Sur (South Orkney Islands) region. 2011/2012 austral summer season,* IP 87, *Antarctic tourism through Ushuaia. Comparison of the last four austral summer seasons,* and IP 88, *Report on Antarctic tourist flows and cruise ships operating in Ushuaia during the 2011/2012 austral summer season.* Argentina had been systematically recording the movement of passengers and vessels that visit Antarctica through the port of Ushuaia since the 2008/09 season, and providing the ATCM with that information. These papers gave details on all tourism voyages from Ushuaia including information on passengers, crew, expedition staff, tour operators, vessel owners and the registration of ships. While particularly focusing on those vessels that call at Ushuaia, the papers provide an alternative and/or complementary source of information to other currently available sources, in order to assist in the assessment of tourist activities in the Antarctic.

(188) Sweden expressed its gratitude to Argentina for the efficient assistance provided in a situation of a medical emergency occurred at Melchior Station, with assistance from Chile and IAATO.

Supervision and Management of Tourism

(189) Argentina introduced WP 43, *Final Report of the Intersessional Contact Group on Supervision of Antarctic Tourism,* which proposed a draft checklist aimed to support inspections of the on-ground conduct of visitors' activities, under Article VII of the Antarctic Treaty and Article 14 of the Madrid Protocol. Information obtained in this way would supplement (but not be a substitute for) information obtained from environmental assessment processes, information exchange, reports by Parties and Experts to the ATCM and CEP, and from documented industry practices and procedures (where applicable).

(190) While noting that a checklist would facilitate inspections, ASOC believed it was also important to increase the rate of inspections of tourist activities as underscored in XXXV ATCM IP 59 by UNEP and ASOC.

(191) Following further discussion and noting that the use of checklists was neither mandatory nor restrictive, the Meeting agreed upon a checklist to help facilitate inspections, by adopting Resolution 11 (2012) Checklist for visitors' in-field activities.

(192) The United States introduced WP 37, *Coastal Camping Considerations*, prepared jointly with Norway. Noting the increase in non-governmental requests for vessel-supported camping, the United States considered that it would be helpful to have guidance for competent authorities in conducting reviews of these applications. In the view of the United States and Norway, the guidance required related particularly to determining appropriate camp sites, appropriate human waste management practices, and ensuring adequate overnight supervision.

(193) The United States further observed that it would be helpful if new or revised Site Guidelines for Visitors include an explicit statement as to whether camping was advisable. It may be useful to develop camping guidelines that capture best practices, to aid in the review process and improve consistency between competent authorities.

(194) The Meeting discussed different approaches to visitor site guidelines, including whether site guidelines should advise on the suitability of camp sites, the acceptability of camping, the need for new or revised site guidelines, and the appropriateness of a single set of guidelines given the wide variation of activities that could be described as camping. Such camping guidelines could prove useful in capturing best practices which again would help in the review process and improve consistency between competent authorities.

(195) IAATO confirmed that there had been an increase in short overnight visits by its operators to Antarctica and that it would share its current guidelines on short overnight visits.

(196) New Zealand, the Netherlands and ASOC were concerned that consideration of camping and other nongovernmental activities should also include whether the activity was acceptable under the principles of the Antarctic Treaty System and the General Principles concerning tourism adopted under Resolution 7 (2009), and not be limited to a regulatory focus.

(197) Several Parties noted that this topic was of relevance to the CEP. Australia considered that guidelines for camping could assist Parties in implementing the environmental impact assessment provisions of the Protocol and noted that camping was not a new development. Argentina was of the view that

consideration camping expeditions should stem from National Antarctic Programmes' best practices.

(198) Some Parties agreed with the conclusions of WP 37, which encouraged Parties and Observers developing or revising Site Guidelines for Visitors to add an explicit statement as to whether camping was advisable to the "Landing Ashore" subsection of the "Visitors" section, and if advisable, give the maximum number of campers the site can accommodate, and show the preferred camp site(s) on the map. Those Parties also discussed encouraging IAATO to work with its operators that are experienced in coastal camping to generate a catalogue of sites potentially suited for camping, and developing camping guidelines to aid in the review process and to improve consistency between competent authorities in reviewing such activities. However, other Parties considered the question of the appropriateness of camping activities ashore should be considered on a case by case basis, taking into account the specifics of the proposed sites.

(199) The United States agreed with the observations made by a number of Parties that the issues highlighted in WP 37 would be of interest to the CEP. The United States offered to informally continue the discussion intersessionally.

(200) The Russian Federation presented IP 72, *Activity of the international air programme DROMLAN and its interaction with non-governmental activity in the Antarctic*, on the use of the programme carried out jointly by eleven National Antarctic Programmes, providing aviation support for expedition activities in Dronning Maud Land. The programme organises intercontinental flights to Antarctica to the ice air fields of Russia's Novolazarevskaya Station and Norway's Troll Station.

(201) Responding to Norway's inspection of the Russian Federation's facilities in Dronning Maud Land (which had been reported to ATCM XXXIII), the Russian Federation confirmed that DROMLAN programme participants had approved the use of DROMLAN infrastructure by tourist and non-government operators through an annex to its terms of reference, which came into force in 2011, and required the users of the DROMLAN infrastructure to comply with provisions of the Treaty and Protocol. Noting an increase in the cost of expeditions and budget pressures on National Antarctic Programmes, the Russian Federation said that in the 2011/12 season this measure had assisted in reducing the cost of air transport for Parties.

(202) Norway thanked Russia for its comprehensive and transparent report in response to the Norwegian inspection in 2010. ASOC thanked Russia for information regarding the DROMLAN air link and considered that the inclusion of tourism activities as part of the regular flights had to be assessed under Article 8 (3) of the Protocol.

(203) While the Netherlands welcomed the information presented by the Russian Federation, it reiterated its belief that the best guarantee to ensure sustainable management of tourist and non-government activities in Antarctica was to keep tourism ship-based.

(204) In response to a query raised by India, the United Kingdom confirmed that the non-governmental operator 'White Desert',which undertakes activities in the vicinity of the Russian and Indian station in Dronning Maud Land, was subject to its authorisation processes. As an IAATO operator, 'White Desert' also follows all IAATO operational guidelines.

(205) France introduced WP 29, *Improving the Functioning of the Electronic Information Exchange System (EIES) for Non-Governmental Activities in Antarctica*, and reiterated the importance of improving the functioning of the EIES in relation to non-governmental activities in Antarctica, in order to provide Parties with detailed information to manage these activities effectively. France noted that recent incidents in the Ross Sea illustrated the problems faced by competent authorities in dealing with infringements of regulations by non-governmental operators in Antarctica.

(206) Concepts to be considered included improving the usability of EIES data on non-governmental activities, the inclusion of more rigorous data for management purposes, and the possibility of a more structured role and a more user friendly mechanism for the forum of competent authorities initiated by Germany and the Netherlands at CEP VIII (2005) and CEP IX (2006).The Secretariat advised that it would be possible to accommodate information about prior authorisations and refusals and the cancellation of activities by operators in the Secretariat's EIES with only minor modifications.

(207) Parties confirmed the value of further development of the EIES, while noting that EIES reporting requirements should not overburden Parties and that the use of the EIES should remain voluntary.

(208) In welcoming France's proposal, ASOC noted that currently 25 per cent of Parties did not appear to be exchanging information through the database. ASOC expressed its desire to see Parties fully utilising the system in the next year.

(209) The Meeting adopted Decision 4 (2012) Electronic Information Exchange System, encouraging use of the system and modifying it in several respects; and Parties will continue to work with the Secretariat to refine and improve the EIES.

Review of Tourism Policies

(210) The Netherlands introduced WP 27 rev. 1, *Report of the Intersessional Contact Group 'Outstanding Questions' on Antarctic Tourism*, and referred to supporting information in IP 67, reporting on the work of the ICG. The five priority questions the ICG identified were on: improving information exchange and cooperation; measuring and managing cumulative impacts of visitation; the merits of regulatory instruments to prevent or regulate the further expansion of tourist activities; the increasing diversity of activities in Antarctica; and the potential development of regulations in respect of permanent facilities for tourism in Antarctica.

(211) In response to the suggestion that a multi-year work plan on tourism issues could be developed for inclusion in the broader ATCM multi-year work plan, several Parties stated they could agree on focusing the ATCMs discussion on tourism on the five priority questions identified by the ICG. New Zealand identified as a high priority for consideration the expansion of tourism to new areas lacking data or information regarding environmental sensitivity. Japan stressed the importance of using the existing frameworks such as ASMAs, ASPAs and site guidelines.

(212) ASOC presented IP 55, *Key Issues on a Strategic Approach to Review Tourism Policies,* and recommended three key activities: increased supervision of tourism activity via inspections carried out in compliance with the Antarctic Treaty and the Protocol; proactive management of tourism activities through legally binding regulation, especially with respect to tourism expansion, diversification and new site occupation; and the identification of environmental impacts of tourism separately from the impacts of other activities or environmental changes, in order to address expansion and cumulative impacts.

(213) Dr Neil Gilbert, for the CEP, introduced WP 22, *Environmental Aspects and Impacts of Tourism and Non-Governmental Activities in Antarctica,* and referred to the supporting information in IP 33, noting that the CEP had discussed the report appended to IP 33, endorsed it and forwarded it to ATCM XXXV to support the ATCM's consideration of tourism matters.

(214) In discussing priority question (d) in WP 27 rev. 1 on improving information exchange and cooperation, the Meeting referred to Recommendations 1 and 2 of the CEP Tourism Study –appended to IP 33. The United Kingdom and New Zealand registered their concern that the study had identified tourism data from the EIES as largely incomplete and inconsistent, and New Zealand suggested that the exchange of information be aligned in a way that was consistent with Resolution 6 (2005).

(215) Various points were raised in discussion of the priority question relating to monitoring and preventing cumulative impacts (question (g) in WP 27 rev.1). Several Parties emphasised the importance of the CEP's continuing role in addressing this issue. ASOC and Australia noted that Recommendation 7 of the CEP study could be a good first step to tackle this issue.

(216) Other options raised included: reviewing site guidelines, the possibility of making some guidelines mandatory, closing sites for a season or more, and setting precautionary limits on the number of visitors. New Zealand noted the substantive work undertaken by Oceanites Inc., which offered a comprehensive baseline of data. IAATO noted in their own reviews of visitor management practices they perceived value in focusing on three strands of monitoring: long-term monitoring programmes, research studies targeted towards answering specific questions and their own red flag system to highlight immediate problems.

(217) Various points were raised in discussion of the priority question relating to the potential adoption of regulatory instruments in relation to the expansion of tourist activities in Antarctica (question (h) in WP 27 rev.1).While Parties acknowledged that the Madrid Protocol applies to all activities, and was applied by each country in accordance with their national legislation, there was considerable discussion of how to address tourism and non-governmental activities in an appropriate manner. Some Parties also referred to the need to take into account the safety and self-sufficiency of an activity, in accordance with Measure 4 (2004), to ensure the proposed activity would have minimal or no impact on National Antarctic Programmes, without their prior agreement.

(218) Several Parties stated that the determinant of environmental impact assessments should be the impact of the activity and not its purpose, while others were of the view that the purpose of the activity was relevant to the application of the Protocol.

(219) The United Kingdom noted that in considering environmental impacts it was important that all human activities needed to be considered at sites of high

visitation. Therefore the recommendation for a redesign of and concerted use of the EIES should also include greater site specific information on all visitations including IAATO operators, non-IAATO operators and national programmes. The inclusion of information on non-Party activities, where available, would also be useful.

(220) In response to the comments of Germany and the Netherlands on potential to exclude certain types of tourist activities, the United Kingdom agreed that whilst, in principle, it was open to discussing which kinds of activities should be prohibited, it was difficult to foresee what kind of activities would be acceptable under the requirements of the Environmental Protocol and Measure 4 (2004), but that Parties might still consider unacceptable.

(221) ASOC noted that there was a lack of site specific information for particular tourist sites and highlighted that impact assessments do not normally reflect the cumulative impact of repeated visits to a site.

(222) There was a broad view that there were gaps in the current framework of regulation for land-based activities, in particular the expansion of tourism activities into the Antarctic interior. Parties recognised that this required consideration of how to regulate use of pristine areas, as interior areas are less likely to have been exposed to human impacts.

(223) IAATO welcomed the CEP's work on wilderness values and bioregionalisation, which offered potential for a strategic approach to area management. IAATO also noted the difficulties in isolating cumulative impacts from tourist activities alone, as highlighted in the CEP *Study on the Environmental Aspects and Impacts of Tourism and Non-Governmental Activities in Antarctica.*

(224) In relation to the closure of pristine areas, Argentina noted that Annex V of the Protocol provided Parties with guidance as to whether this was necessary. The United Kingdom noted in general it was not of the view that areas should be made off-limits, without environmental justification. Japan noted that scientific research and monitoring activities should not be prohibited in pristine areas and that the framework for identifying and designating ASPAs may be useful in the consideration of pristine areas. ASOC noted that Annex I and V could regulate some activity but not all, and argued for the need for inviolate and reference areas for science.

(225) In relation to permanent tourist facilities, Parties recalled the extensive discussions on this matter at previous Meetings, including the challenges of defining what constituted a permanent facility. Several Parties agreed that

tourism activities should not be approved if they would have more than a minor or transitory impact, and the United States suggested that Parties could seek to apply a threshold for such regulating activities, such as to exclude activities requiring a Comprehensive Environmental Evaluation (CEE).

(226) IAATO reiterated its commitment to ensuring that the activities of its Members have no more than a minor or transitory impact and that no IAATO member demonstrated interest in establishing permanent facilities in Antarctica. However, facilities classed as 'semi-permanent', and accompanied by site-remediation which can occur within a season, could be acceptable. There was substantial support for the view that tourism activities likely to have more than a minor or transitory impact should not be authorised.

(227) The Russian Federation noted that non-governmental property in Antarctica could be mortgaged, leased, sold, and inherited. The new owner may be a citizen of a country which is not a Member of the Antarctic Treaty and the Protocol. In this case permanent structures may be used not for their initially intended purpose even if an EIA was available.

(228) While recalling that tourist activities should be subject to regulation, Argentina states that it reserves the right to have an interpretation centre for tourist purposes with some lodging capacity at any time in any of its stations, and not detrimental of its scientific programmes, similar to already existing ones. In its view, these seem not to have had an adverse impact on the Antarctic environment.

(229) Japan noted that facilities should be restricted by their impact on the environment rather than by their purpose.

(230) In summary, there were two sets of concerns that required different approaches. The first concern was the possible cumulative impact of tourism on sites already visited, particularly but not limited to those where visits were increasing. Under this concern, the challenges of data limitations and data access were identified, as was the concern that the environmental impact assessment process addressed the impacts of a proposed activity on a visited site, but not the cumulative impact of many visits. The second concern was the possible diversification and expansion of activities, particularly in previously unvisited areas. This raised questions on how the Protocol was being applied, and it would be useful at a later stage to compare practices in this respect.

(231) The United States stated that it was open to new binding, enforceable regulatory mechanisms that would help Parties to regulate tourist and non-governmental activities. Such mechanisms should be based on sound science

and a precautionary approach in the sense that lack of full scientific certainty should not be used as a reason for postponing cost-effective measures to prevent environmental degradation in Antarctica. The United States recommended further work on area management, and the recommendations from the tourism study, in particular the potential for cumulative impacts. The United States noted that possible priorities for future work include a consideration of: permanent infrastructure, land-based adventure activities, marine safety and search and rescue, enforcement of existing regulations and protection of the marine environment. Priorities identified by the Meeting should be integrated with the multi-year strategic plan.

(232) New Zealand noted that its search and rescue coordination responsibilities for a vast part of the Southern Ocean necessitated a cautious approach to tourist and non-governmental activities in the region. New Zealand placed an emphasis on preventative safety measures. New Zealand noted that, in addition to the possible environmental impacts of tourism activities, the practical burdens that search and rescue could place on National Antarctic Programmes as well as legal issues relating to tourism which had been raised by Parties in discussions, together suggested a need for greater supervision of tourism by Parties. In this regard, New Zealand suggested that Parties should improve their supervision of such activities through enhanced information collection and exchange, systematic and targeted environmental monitoring, and greater use of the inspection tool.

(233) The Meeting agreed that the Netherlands would convene an informal contact group working until ATCM XXXVI to prepare for the ATCM's review of tourism policies with the following terms of reference. The group will:

- Identify examples of activities that contribute to a diversification of tourism in Antarctica;
- Exchange information on experiences and challenges with applying domestic law in respect of those activities;
- Exchange views on the question (j) identified by Parties in WP 27 rev.1, of whether further policy guidance from the ATCM on this issue is desirable, taking into account the Protocol and other existing instruments on tourism in Antarctica.

(234) The Meeting noted that question (j) related to formulation of policy guidance from the ATCM in view of the continuing increase of the diversity of tourism and other non-governmental activities in Antarctica, and question (h) related to the adoption of regulatory instruments to prevent or regulate the further

expansion of tourist activities in Antarctica. (IP 67, *Outstanding Questions' on Antarctic Tourism: An Inventory and Discussion.*)

(235) The Meeting discussed the CEP Study on Environmental Impacts and Aspects of Tourism. Several Parties supported the work that had been done by New Zealand. The United States noted there would need to be a prioritisation of these recommendations during the Parties' discussion of how future work would proceed.

(236) Australia, in supporting the recommendations, noted that some required further CEP attention whilst others required the attention of the ATCM.

(237) In discussing Recommendation 1 of the study presented by WP 22, on developing a centrally-managed database to provide the ATCM with a complete picture of tourism activities, ASOC noted that Parties should be mindful that cumulative impacts and the expansion and diversification of activities should not be discussed in isolation from each other, and that this may require new mechanisms relating to data collection for EIA. The United States cautioned that this additional work in relation to Recommendation 1 would require agreed additional funding and staffing of the Secretariat would be necessary. It may be possible that a Party could second a data expert to the Secretariat or provide a voluntary contribution for this work.

(238) IAATO suggested that the challenge before Parties was two-fold, involving first consideration of the implications on the wilderness nature of the region and limits of acceptable change, and second, the practical aspects to addressing visitor management. IAATO focused on educating their visitors to become ambassadors for the protection of the Antarctic and within that context the concept of wilderness was important. They confirmed their commitment to collaborating with Parties.

(239) In commending IAATO for its provision of useful information, and noting that data currently provided by Parties was incomplete and inconsistent, the United Kingdom stressed the need to ensure that site specific data collection reflected visitation from all visitors, including non-tourists, such as scientists and national programme personnel.

(240) Parties noted that potential sources of data in addition to that provided by IAATO could include post-season summaries from data collected by MRCCs (taking into account concerns to avoid the dissemination of commercial-in-confidence data), which includes information provided by IAATO, COMNAP, satellite data as well as sightings from stations. IAATO also suggested that their system of reporting sightings of yachts might be taken up by coastal stations.

(241) The Meeting agreed that there was a need for the development of a centrally managed database of tourism activities, noting that the EIES may provide a useful mechanism for such a database, pending further clarification of the type of data required, gaps in existing data sources, and guidance on how to collect and manage the data.

(242) In response to Recommendation 2, on developing a centrally-managed database of tourist sites, Parties raised various queries and suggestions. The United Kingdom reiterated its view that the ATCM should refer to sites of high visitation and sensitivity that require management, and did not agree to the term 'tourist sites'. Australia suggested that further advice should be requested from the CEP on the scope and type of information that should be collected; while Germany suggested that perhaps a single database could collect data on both activities and sites. The Netherlands suggested that a policy debate on cumulative impacts would be necessary in taking this recommendation forward. Argentina made reference to an earlier ATCM discussion during which it was agreed that the term 'environmental sensitivity' was difficult to define and measure and should be replaced by a more suitable term.

(243) Recalling Recommendations 1 and 2 of the CEP Study on the Environmental Aspects and Impacts of Tourism and Non-governmental Activities in Antarctica, the Meeting agreed to establish an Intersessional Contact Group, for the purposes of ensuring that the ATCM has readily available to it a more complete picture of tourism activities in Antarctica and to facilitate regular assessments of the potential and actual environmental impacts at visited sites, with the objective of identifying the items of information that are required for management purposes, with the following terms of reference:

  a. Clearly articulate the questions that need to be answered to address the objectives stated above, consider whether existing data and information sources address those questions, and identify what information or data need to be collected and shared to answer those questions. These questions will inform a more efficient and effective design of the EIES; and

  b. Report back to the ATCM on a summary of findings.

(244) It was further agreed that:

  • Observers and Experts participating in ATCM XXXV would be invited to provide input to the ICG;

  • The Executive Secretary would open the ATCM forum for the ICG and provide assistance to the ICG; and

- New Zealand would act as convener, and would report to ATCM XXXVI on the progress made in the ICG.

(245) On Recommendation 3, regarding the appropriate method of assessing site sensitivity, several Parties suggested that the CEP would be best placed to determine the most appropriate method. In addition, Norway offered to share its experiences on this matter from the Arctic. The United Kingdom stressed that activities should be assessed in the context of previous visits made to that site, regardless of whether those visits had been conducted by tourists or others. While the Netherlands supported scientifically-based assessment methods, it also emphasised the importance of applying a precautionary approach and not delaying management measures because of a lack of knowledge of a site. It also suggested that the concept of relative sensitivity might be useful. IAATO noted that it was important to distinguish between site sensitivity and visitation rates, stating that some sites with low visitation were sensitive to impact.

(246) In welcoming and agreeing in principle to Recommendation 3 of the CEP Study, the Meeting agreed to request the CEP, *as a matter of priority,* to:

- Develop an appropriate definition and method of assessing site sensitivity and undertake a relative sensitivity analysis for at least the most heavily visited sites in Antarctica, as appropriate, including, for example, consideration of the vulnerability of visited sites to non-native species establishment, for the purpose of more rigorously assessing appropriate management needs.
- In this respect, the Meeting also noted that site sensitivity considerations should also be included in the environmental assessment process for tourism and non-governmental activities as recommended in Recommendation 3.

(247) In welcoming and agreeing in principle to Recommendation 4 of the CEP Study, the Meeting agreed to request the CEP to:

- Consider the means by which site specific guidelines are reviewed and updated, including the appropriate frequency of review and the information required to support a review.

(248) In relation to Recommendation 5, on the regular review of trends in tourist activity at selected tourist sites, the United Kingdom noted that the CEP was already considering the extent to which management provisions, for example ASMAs, Site Guidelines or National Programme Guidelines, were in place for the most highly visited sites. In welcoming and agreeing in principle to this recommendation, the Meeting agreed to:

- Undertake a regular review of trends in tourist and other visitor activity at selected sites, particularly those with high levels of visitation or those considered to be particularly sensitive to impact.

(249) On Recommendation 6, regarding the development of an ATCM-approved on-site monitoring programme, the discussion noted that the CEP would need to consider the extent to which other schemes could contribute to such a programme, including the long-term *Oceanites* monitoring scheme, which helped to identify background trends; New Zealand's visitor site assessment scheme (VISTA); research asking specific questions about impacts, for example the impact of tourism on the breeding success of a particular species; and IAATO's 'red flag process' which triggered an immediate response. ASOC noted that an ATCM monitoring programme to address data deficiencies may require additional resources to be provided by Parties, the tourism industry, tourists or partnerships.

(250) In welcoming and agreeing in principle to Recommendation 6 of the CEP Study, the Meeting agreed to request the CEP, *as a matter of priority,* to:

- Consider how to target monitoring efforts (eg, appropriate frequency, level of effort, and location of monitoring) to inform environmental management; and
- Develop a pilot on-site monitoring study to assess potential impacts and the effectiveness of site guidelines at one or more visitor sites.

(251) In relation to Recommendation 7, on developing a series of 'best estimate' trigger levels to assist in guiding monitoring efforts, the United Kingdom cautioned that careful consideration would need to be given to any triggers to ensure that there were no perverse incentives that might lead to an 'Olympic' style race to visit sites before trigger levels were reached. The United States suggested that this could be done through policy responses, while scientific research could provide the necessary basis for any mechanism. Australia and IAATO said that triggers might inform the level of monitoring required for a particular site, rather than being necessarily linked to site closures. IAATO also noted the difficulty of obtaining real-time data on visitor numbers during the season, and stated that any triggers would need to be site-specific. ASOC noted that the CEP tourism study had already identified a need for monitoring the actual and potential environmental impacts of tourism and that it was important to take action to address this need.

(252) In welcoming and agreeing in principle to Recommendation 7 of the CEP Study, the Meeting agreed to request the CEP to:

- Consider developing a series of management parameters or environmental indicator triggers to assist in guiding monitoring efforts. This could include identifying certain parameters that would, if reached, trigger a need for a review of the effectiveness of current management at the site. Such an approach would be underpinned by the site sensitivity definition and analysis to be developed by the CEP.

(253) ASOC noted that Article 8 (3) of the Protocol stated that EIA procedures applied, *inter alia*, to any change in an activity whether the change arose from an increase or decrease in the intensity of an existing activity, or from the addition of an activity, and that therefore keeping track of parameters such as the number of landed tourists per season at a site was relevant to environmental impact assessment as it applied to tourism.

(254) Options that were discussed to address the suggestion in Recommendation 8 to identify a range of potential management options that might be applied to managing tourism activities included area closures, resting periods, and the clustering of sites as ASPAs or ASMAs where sites were identified as vulnerable. The Netherlands emphasised the need for a pro-active and precautionary policy focus, which IAATO suggested should not override careful consideration of management options, including their perceived benefits and their scientific basis. The United Kingdom and IAATO queried how options to cover vessels and vessel operations would intersect with other regulatory frameworks, such as the regulations of the IMO.

(255) With respect to Recommendation 8 of the CEP Study, the Meeting agreed:

    i. Bearing in mind Recommendation 8 of the CEP Study on Environmental Aspects and Impacts of Tourism and Non-governmental Activities in Antarctica, as well as question (g) identified by Parties in WP 27 rev.1, Parties are invited to identify potential management options that might be considered for possible application in the future;

    ii. Bearing in mind the questions (j) and (h) identified by Parties in the intersessional contact group reported in WP 27 rev.1 on the present and potential diversification and expansion of tourism activities into previously unvisited areas of Antarctica, the Meeting agreed on the importance of sharing experience and issues regarding their application of the Protocol, including on the Environmental Impact Assessment process to such activities.

(256) It was noted that, with respect to Recommendation 8ii, the term 'unvisited' may include areas that have been the subject of rare visits.

(257) The CEP Chair thanked the Chair of the Tourism Working Group for the comprehensive discussion on the CEP study on environmental aspects and impacts of tourism and NGO activities. The CEP Chair also noted that he will work with the CEP Members during the intersessional period in order to provide answers to the ATCM's requests in due time.

Item 12: Inspections under the Antarctic Treaty and the Environment Protocol

(258) One inspection was undertaken since the last Meeting. The Russian Federation and the United States presented IP 47, *United States – Russian Federation Report of Inspection*, reporting on the first joint inspection by both states – which was the first inspection conducted by the Russian Federation, and the thirteenth conducted by the United States. The two Parties inspected Scott Base (New Zealand), Concordia Base (France/Italy), and Mario Zucchelli Station (Italy), from 23 to 28 January 2012.

(259) Inspections took place in accordance with the relevant provisions of the Antarctic Treaty and the Madrid Protocol, and enjoyed the full cooperation of the Parties whose stations were inspected. The inspecting Parties reported that no infringements of environmental rules were observed, and that they were impressed by the scope and nature of the research activities taking place at the three stations. While Concordia Station was highlighted as a positive example of international cooperation, it was noted that this also presented certain issues relating to coordination between National Antarctic Programmes which have different administrative and legal regimes.

(260) In response Italy thanked the United States and the Russian Federation inspection team and highlighted that: since the start of Italian activities a great concern had been environmental issues, that prevention and adequate personnel selection and training were key features in obtaining compliance; that if needed, Italy could together with France implement a monitoring programme of the EPICA borehole, and stressed the fact that this issue was likely to concern all the other National Antarctic Programmes with drilling activities. New Zealand would certainly give consideration to the report in its aim to continue to improve its activities at Scott Base, and reported that its joint wind farm with the United States on Ross Island had

resulted in energy savings well beyond expectations, and referred to BP 41, *Antarctic Heritage Trust Conservation Update,* which reported on heritage conservation activities on Ross Island.

(261) Responding to a query from Spain regarding recommendations or procedures relating to drilling exercises, SCAR referred to its Code of Conduct for the Exploration and Research of Subglacial Environments, and its Expert Group on Advancing Technological and Environmental Stewardship for Subglacial Exploration in Antarctica (ATHENA).

(262) Japan was pleased to note that India had implemented recommendations as a result of its 2010 inspection of Maitri Station, as reflected in BP 22 submitted to the CEP.

(263) ASOC presented IP 59, *Review of the Implementation of the Madrid Protocol: Inspections by Parties (Article 14),* jointly prepared with UNEP, which reviewed the practice of inspections. It noted that inspections were a core element of the Treaty system and were valuable in identifying issues for further attention, and as a learning experience. Since the entry into force of the Protocol in 1998, 83 facilities and sites had been inspected, with a rising average frequency of inspections per year. Twelve of the 28 Consultative Parties had conducted inspections. Forty-five of the 101 facilities on the COMNAP list have never been inspected. One ASMA, 6 ASPAs, and 7 HSMs were inspected, while only 7 vessels were inspected during the period.

(264) Several Parties reinforced the importance of inspections to the Treaty System, and thanked ASOC and UNEP for this clear overview, which the United States indicated would assist in planning inspections, and the United Kingdom recommended that in future development of the ATS website, linking Antarctic facilities to previous inspection reports would be very helpful for future inspection programmes.

(265) Australia welcomed the report of the inspection conducted by the United States and the Russian Federation. Australia referred to WP 51, and IP 39, and IP 40 presented at ATCM XXXIV which reported on inspections conducted in 2009/10 and 2010/11. Australia recalled the Russian Federation's undertaking at that Meeting to provide further information to the Parties on some environmental concerns raised in those reports, and indicated that it looked forward to such information being provided to the ATCM in future.

Item 13: Science Issues, Scientific Cooperation and Facilitation, Including the Legacy of the International Polar Year 2007-2008

(266) SCAR presented IP 2, outlining the efforts of *The Southern Ocean Observing System (SOOS)* to develop an efficient and coherent observation system. The Science Plan for the System had been published, an international Steering Committee had convened its first meeting, and a new website was soon to be launched.

(267) In response to a query from Norway, SCAR confirmed that there were strong and developing links between SOOS and the Sustaining Arctic Observing Networks – the equivalent system that had been operating in the Arctic for several years.

(268) Chile presented IP 18 *Contribuciones chilenas al conocimiento científico de la Antártica: Expedición 2011/12*, presenting its activities during this expedition, with the aim of stimulating cooperation with other Parties. It reported that the Chile's National Antarctic Programme had 60 projects, 36 of which were land-based, involving 72 researchers, and supporting up to 95 researchers from foreign programmes.

(269) SCAR presented IP 40 rev.1, *SCAR Products available to support the deliberations of the ATCM*, noting it had several products available to support the work of the Antarctic scientific research community.

(270) Presenting IP 48, *Japan's Antarctic Research Highlights in 2011–2012*, Japan emphasised the importance of cooperation in all aspects of Antarctic research – particularly in logistics and in light of increasing financial constraints. Highlights of Japan's national Antarctic programme over the last year included its wind and plasma parameters observation programme called PANSY from the surface up to 500 km above, involving the construction of the largest atmospheric radar ever installed in Antarctica. Japan thanked Belgium for its support to the Japanese field party at Princess Elisabeth Station.

(271) Belgium noted the importance of collaboration to its Antarctic programme, which had operated since 1985 with the support of a number of other Parties.

(272) Other papers submitted under this Agenda item included:

- IP 21, *Anthropogenic Sound in the Southern Ocean: an Update* (SCAR)
- IP 35, *Antarctic Conservation for the 21st Century: Background, progress, and future directions* (SCAR, IUCN, New Zealand)

- IP 83, *Medical scientific cooperation between Romania and UK within the SCAR for the study of biometeorological human adaptation in a changing climate* (Romania)
- BP 4, *Report on Scientific Activity of Ukraine for 2011/2012 Season* (Ukraine)
- BP 6, *La base Belgrano II: un punto aventajado para observaciones científicas en el extremo austral del Mar de Weddell* (Argentina)
- BP 7, *Evaluación institucional del Instituto Antártico Argentino* (Argentina)
- BP 9, *Scientific & Science-related Collaborations with Other Parties During 2011-2012* (Republic of Korea)
- BP 21, *Icebreaker Oden and her Southern Ocean missions* (Sweden)
- BP 26, *XI Meeting of Iberoamerican Antarctic Historians Playa Hermosa, Piriapolis-Uruguay – November 24 - 25th 2011* (Uruguay)
- BP 27, *Actividades de investigación y proyectos científicos coordinados por el Instituto Antártico Uruguayo en la campaña 2011 – 2012* (Uruguay)
- BP 33, *Programa de cooperación binacional en asuntos antárticos "Ecuador-Venezuela"* (Ecuador)
- BP 35, *Biorremediación con microorganismos antárticos* (Ecuador)
- BP 37, *Scientific results of Russian studies in the Antarctic in 2011* (Russian Federation)
- BP 39, *Law-Racovita-Negoita Base. An example of cooperation in Antarctica* (Romania)
- BP 40, *ERICON Aurora Borealis Icebreaker. A new era in the polar research* (Romania).

Item 14: Implications of Climate Change for Management of the Antarctic Treaty Area

(273) Australia introduced WP 32, *ATCM Interests in International Climate Change Discussions – Options for Enhanced Engagement*, which offered several options for the Antarctic Treaty Parties to collectively pursue enhanced engagement in international discussions on climate change, as recommended by the 2010 ATME. Options included registering the Antarctic Treaty Secretariat as an observer organisation to United Nations Framework Convention on Climate Change (UNFCCC) negotiating sessions; issuing a joint statement on

Antarctic issues to the UNFCCC Conference of Parties (COP) or a subsidiary body; engaging in the Nairobi Work Programme on Impacts, Vulnerability and Adaptation to Climate Change of the UNFCCC's Subsidiary Body for Scientific and Technological Advice as a Partner organisation; and hosting a side event on Antarctic issues during the UNFCCC COP.

(274) Australia said that pursuing closer engagement with the UNFCCC would be consistent with the provisions of the Antarctic Treaty, and with the practice of establishing effective working relationships with other international organisations where necessary to advance the protection and management of the Antarctic region. The options were not intended to be prescriptive but sought to establish an effective working relationship with the UNFCCC rather than formal institutional linkages.

(275) ASOC also supported greater outreach to the international community about climate change research in Antarctica, and suggested that the Antarctic Treaty rather than the Secretariat might apply for Observer status to the UNFCCC. It noted that the communications plan supported by Norway, the United Kingdom and ASOC (as set out in IP 44, *Communicating the Science of Climate Change*, submitted by SCAR) was making good progress.

(276) The United Kingdom noted the importance of updating the ACCE report delivered by SCAR and sent to the Intergovernmental Panel on Climate Change (IPCC), and suggested using this to update the UNFCCC. Argentina suggested that the Meeting could develop a declaration to submit to the UNFCCC, which could highlight the implications of climate change for Antarctica, and the shared responsibilities and objectives of ATCPs. Several delegations suggested encouraging Parties to inform their national delegations to the UNFCCC and other relevant for a about polar issues, and the holding of Antarctic side events at such meetings.

(277) Parties welcomed the discussion of options to take forward ATME recommendations. While Parties believed that there was value in ensuring that the UNFCCC is made aware of relevant facts related to Antarctica and Antarctic science, and several recalled that a system of exchanging letters between the UNFCCC and the ATCM had previously been pursued, several Parties raised concerns about the merits and costs of registering the ATS as an observer at the UNFCCC, the merits of tasking the Secretariat with a policy liaison role, and the challenges of negotiating a statement by all Consultative Parties.

(278) SCAR advised that it was an observer to the UNFCCC and that through its parent organisation, the International Council of Science, interacted with the

IPCC. Due to a limited budget for these activities their interaction was mainly with the IPCC. Some delegations considered SCAR's status as an Observer to UNFCCC provided opportunities to outreach on Antarctic climate issues.

(279) In response to WP 39, *Invitation to the WMO* introduced by the United Kingdom and Norway, which proposed that the Meeting invite the WMO to the next ATCM to update Parties on the activities of its Panel of Experts on Polar Observations, Research and Services, the Meeting agreed to invite the WMO to ATCM XXXVI, and hoped it would continue to engage with the ATCM in the future.

(280) The Meeting welcomed WMO's attendance at ATCM XXXV and presentation of IP 8, *Contemporary opportunities for weather and related Polar Observations, Research and Services - leading to improved mitigation of risk*, which reported on the work of the Executive Council (Panel of Experts on) Polar Observations, Research and Services (EC-PORS). This body aims to bring together the work of the WMO in order to improve services and maximise opportunities in meteorological (and related) observations, research and services for both Arctic and Antarctic areas.

(281) The Meeting thanked the WMO for its work and welcomed closer cooperation between the ATCM and the WMO, particularly to update technical recommendations relating to meteorology as a result of the Review of ATCM Recommendations on Operational Matters (SP 9).

(282) COMNAP presented IP 4, *Management Implications of a Changing Antarctica – COMNAP Workshop*, which summarised the discussion held in the margins of the COMNAP XXIII Annual General Meeting, in Stockholm, Sweden, and referred to IP 31, *Best Practice for Energy Management – Guidance and Recommendations,* which had been discussed at CEP XV.

(283) Spain commented on IP 4, stressing that there were important challenges for Antarctic management both from climate change and from financial pressures. Therefore Parties needed to try and find ways to proactively cooperate on these issues in order to address them more efficiently.

(284) Bulgaria, due to the rapid global changes, strongly supported the Spanish statement.

(285) The Meeting welcomed SP 8, *Actions taken by the CEP and the ATCM on the ATME Recommendations on Climate Change*, and encouraged the Secretariat to continue providing these useful updates to the Meeting.

(286) SCAR presented IP 45, *Antarctic Climate Change and the Environment: an Update,* a third update report which included a comprehensive assessment of scientific information on the climate system and ecosystem responses to change in the Antarctic and the Southern Ocean.

(287) Other papers submitted under this agenda item included:

- BP 17, *Energy Efficiency and Carbon Reduction Initiatives* (New Zealand)
- BP 25, *Energy Efficiency project in Antarctic Research Station Artigas* (Uruguay).

Item 15: Operational Issues

(288) COMNAP presented IP 7, *Review of COMNAP Working Papers and Information Papers presented to the ATCM 1988 – 2011*, which sets out the work that COMNAP had authored and co-authored since 1988.

(289) Ecuador presented IP 69, *Proyecto para que la Estación Científica Ecuatoriana "Pedro Vicente Maldonado" tenga el carácter de permanente*, which detailed Ecuador's project of transforming its summer station *Pedro Vicente Maldonado* into a permanent station.

(290) Argentina presented BP 5, *Cambio de nombre a una base antártica de Argentina,* which referred to the change of name of an Argentinean Station from *Base Jubany* to *Base Carlini*, to honour one of Argentina's most renowned scientists.

(291) Other papers submitted under this agenda item included:

- IP 63 *Renovación del Parque de Tanques de combustible de la Base Científica Antártica Artigas* (Uruguay)
- IP 62, *The Dirck Gerritsz Laboratory at the UK's Rothera Research Station* (The Netherlands and the United Kingdom)
- BP 8, *The Second Antarctic Expedition of Araon (2011/2012)* (Republic of Korea)
- BP 28, *Renovación del Parque de Tanques de combustible de la Base Científica Antártica Artigas (BCAA)* (Uruguay)
- BP 29, *Maintenance of the Scientific Station T/N Ruperto Elichiribehety, Hope Bay, Antarctica Peninsula* (Uruguay)
- BP 38, *Retiro de chatarra desde la base Presidente Eduardo Frei Montalva, isla Rey Jorge* (Chile).

Item 16: Education Issues

(292) Papers submitted under this agenda item included:

- IP 44, *Communicating the Science of Climate Change* (SCAR)
- BP 2, *Estrategias para acercar la Antártica a los ciudadanos* (Chile)
- BP 20, *Australia's Antarctic Centenary celebrations* (Australia)
- BP 23, *A Hundred Years of the South Pole Conquest: events organised by Uruguay* (Uruguay)
- BP 24, *Educational, cultural and outreach activities of the Uruguayan Antarctic Institute in 2011-2012* (Uruguay)
- BP 30, *Re-Edición del "Acta Antártica Ecuatoriana", publicación científica oficial del Ecuador sobre investigación antártica* (Ecuador)
- BP 31, *II Concurso Intercolegial sobre Temas Antárticos, CITA 2011* (Ecuador)
- BP 32, *Seminario Taller "Ecuador en la Antártida: Historia, Perspectivas y Proyecciones"* (Ecuador).

Item 17: Exchange of Information

(293) France introduced WP 29, *Improved Functioning of the Electronic Information Exchange System (EIES) for Non-Governmental Activities in Antarctica*, proposing improvements to the EIES in order to provide Parties with faster and more complete information concerning non-governmental activities conducted in Antarctica. France proposed that the use of the EIES be mandatory in light of the lack of information exchange between Parties. France highlighted that it would be valuable for the EIES to allow Parties to record the history of prior authorisations and refusals of permits, in order to provide a 'memory' to inform future decisions. In addition, France proposed that different sections of the EIES be updated regularly throughout the year so that information could be made available in real-time by the other Parties.

(294) Chile introduced WP 63, *Exchange of Real Time Information of the Maritime Traffic in Antarctica*, proposing a coordinated real-time information exchange system for all maritime traffic in Antarctica. This was intended to provide a better understanding of all vessels operating in Antarctic waters, and would facilitate SAR activities. Chile recognised that while different systems existed under IAATO, COMNAP and CCAMLR in relation to the

exchange of vessel monitoring information, an integrated system providing more detailed information would be valuable. This could be managed by the ATS and MRCCs.

(295) The United States welcomed Parties' interest in maritime safety issues, and noted the value of further work on these matters at future ATCMs.

(296) Argentina supported in general terms the recommendations made by Chile in the document WP 63, while stressing the need to work on the development of a communications system through the MRCCs with SAR responsibility in Antarctica. Such a system should enable the exchange of information in real time with respect of vessels operating in Antarctica.

(297) In response to a query from Japan, Chile confirmed that this information would need to be handled confidentially, and that each organisation would be responsible for ensuring that information it received was managed accordingly.

(298) COMNAP drew attention to its existing ship reporting system. This system was designed to allow vessels of National Antarctic Programmes to provide comprehensive information, which could be added to and updated daily by Parties. This information is updated every 24 hours and automatically provided via email to all five MRCCs with SAR responsibility in Antarctic waters and to designated national contact points. The COMNAP website also provides a full list of vessels registered in the system, including their last positioning information.

(299) IAATO noted that its ship positioning system provides hourly tracking data for SOLAS passenger vessels, excluding yachts. MRCCs have access to this database and to the IAATO vessel database, with all information contained in it, provided on a commercial-in-confidence basis. IAATO noted that if it was proposed to use this information more broadly, it would require further clarification in order to seek approval from its members.

(300) The Secretariat presented SP 10, *Report on the Informal Contact Group on the Improvement of the EIES and other Information Exchange Matters*, outlining improvements made to the EIES and providing an overview of its current usage by Parties. Nine Parties took part in the ICG, which covered all aspects of information exchange and aimed to identify aspects of the EIES which were problematic for Parties, and to make improvements to the system.

(301) Several Parties and ASOC commended the Secretariat for its work and follow-up activities. ASOC stated that improvements in the rate of compliance with information exchange requirements over the last year were impressive.

(302) ASOC suggested that a compliance rate among Parties of 75 per cent on annual reports and 82 per cent on pre-season information was still inadequate. Bearing in mind the Treaty and Protocol obligations to exchange information they urged that further efforts were needed. ASOC indicated it would be useful to hear from those Parties not yet achieving compliance to indicate what other changes – technical or otherwise – might assist them.

Item 18: Biological Prospecting in Antarctica

(303) Belgium presented IP 22, *Report on the Bioprospecting Activities Carried out by Belgian Scientists since 1998,* informing the Meeting of Belgium's bioprospecting activities, and use of Antarctic genetic resources in line with Resolution 7 (2005) and Resolution 9 (2009).

(304) The Netherlands presented IP 63, *An Update on Biological Prospecting in Antarctica and Recent Policy Developments at the International Level,* prepared jointly with Belgium, Finland, Sweden, and UNEP, which provided an update on relevant bioprospecting activities since the last ATCM, and recent policy developments at the international level.

(305) In response to a suggestion to state in the report of this Meeting that the ATCM was prepared to address the collection and use of Antarctic biological material at some point in the future, some Parties indicated that it may not be necessary to address the issue and other Parties noted that other for a may address the issue if the ATCM does not. France insisted on the fact that biological prospecting should remain on the agenda of the ATCM and that the ATCM was the only competent forum to deal with biological prospecting in Antarctica. The Meeting agreed to monitor developments in other for a and to keep the Meeting updated on this issue.

(306) Parties recalled Resolution 9 (2009) which reaffirmed that the Antarctic Treaty System is the appropriate framework for managing the collection of biological material in the Antarctic Treaty area and for considering its use. Argentina also stated its view that Antarctica was not to be considered as an area beyond national jurisdiction.

(307) ASOC also reminded the Meeting of the importance of continuing to exchange and make freely available relevant information as agreed in Resolution 7 (2005), and in accordance with Article III of the Treaty.

Item 19:Preparation of the 36th Meeting

a. Date and place

(308) The Meeting welcomed the kind invitation of the Government of the Kingdom of Belgium to host ATCM XXXVI in Brussels from 20 to 29 May, 2013.

(309) For future planning, the Meeting took note that the following likely timetable of upcoming ATCMs:

- 2014 Brazil
- 2015 Bulgaria

(310) Belgium presented a preliminary agenda and a draft schedule for the 36th Antarctic Treaty Consultative Meeting, Belgium, 2013.

(311) The Meeting welcomed the proposed schedule for ATCM XXXVI.

b. Invitation of International and Non-Governmental Organisations

(312) In accordance with established practice, the Meeting agreed that the following organisations having scientific or technical interest in Antarctica should be invited to send experts to attend ATCM XXXVI: the ACAP Secretariat, ASOC, IAATO, IHO, IMO, IOC, the Intergovernmental Panel on Climate Change (IPCC), IUCN, UNEP, WMO and WTO.

c. Preparation of the Agenda for ATCM XXXVI

(313) The Meeting approved the Preliminary Agenda for ATCM XXXVI.

d. Organisation of ATCM XXXVI

(314) Pursuant to Rule 11, the Meeting decided as a preliminary matter to propose the same Working Groups at ATCM XXXVI as at this Meeting.

e. The SCAR Lecture

(315) Taking into account the valuable series of lectures given by SCAR at a number of ATCMs, the Meeting decided to invite SCAR to give another lecture on scientific issues relevant to ATCM XXXVI.

Item 20: Any Other Business

(316) Argentina recalled Article IV of the Antarctic Treaty with regard to all matters, included documents presented at ATCMs.

(317) With regard to incorrect references to the territorial status of the Malvinas Islands, South Georgias Islands and South Sandwich Islands made in documents, cartography and publications available and presentations made at this Antarctic Treaty Consultative Meeting, Argentina rejects any reference to these islands as being a separate entity from its national territory, thus giving them an international status that they do not have and affirm that the Malvinas, South Georgias and South Sandwich Islands and the surrounding maritime areas are an integral part of the Argentine national territory.

(318) Furthermore, it rejects the shipping register operated by the alleged British authorities thereof and any other unilateral act undertaken by such colonial authorities, which are not recognised and are rejected by Argentina. The Malvinas, South Georgias and South Sandwich Islands and the surrounding maritime areas are an integral part of the Argentine national territory, are under illegal British occupation and are the subject of a sovereignty dispute between the Argentine Republic and the United Kingdom of Great Britain and Northern Ireland, recognised by the United Nations.

(319) In response, the United Kingdom stated that it had no doubt about its sovereignty over the Falkland Islands, South Georgia and the South Sandwich Islands and their surrounding maritime areas, as is well known to all delegates. In that regard, the United Kingdom has no doubt about the right of the government of the Falkland Islands to operate a shipping register for UK & Falkland flagged vessels.

(320) Argentina rejects the United Kingdom's statement and reaffirms its well-known legal position.

Item 21: Adoption of the Final Report

(321) The Meeting adopted the Final Report of the 35th Antarctic Treaty Consultative Meeting.

(322) The Chair of the Meeting Mr Richard Rowe made closing remarks.

(323) The Meeting was closed on Wednesday, 20 June at 2.40 pm.

2. CEP XV Report

Report of the Committee for Environmental Protection (CEP XV)

Hobart, June 11–15, 2012

Item 1: Opening of the Meeting

(1)   The CEP Chair, Dr Yves Frenot (France), opened the meeting on Monday 11 June 2012 and thanked Australia for arranging and hosting the meeting in Hobart.

(2)   The Committee welcomed Pakistan as a new Member, following its accession to the Environmental Protocol.

(3)   The Committee expressed its sympathy and condolences to Brazil for the loss of Lieutenant Roberto Lopes dos Santos and Lieutenant Carlos Alberto Vieira Figueiredo during the February 2012 fire at Brazil's Comandante Ferraz Station, and to Belgium for the sudden passing away in September 2011 of Mr Alexandre de Lichtervelde, Belgium's late CEP representative.

(4)   The Chair summarised the work undertaken during the intersessional period. This included four informal contact groups, the SGMP work and other studies contributing to papers submitted to CEP XV. All the planned work decided at the end of CEP XIV was achieved.

(5)   It was emphasised that most of this work was conducted according to the tasks planned in the CEP 5 year work plan for the 2011-2012 intersessional period.

Item 2: Adoption of the Agenda

(6)   The Committee adopted the following agenda and confirmed the allocation of 44 working papers (WP), 46 information papers (IP), five secretariat papers (SP) and 13 background papers (BP) to the agenda items:

1. Opening of the Meeting

2. Adoption of the Agenda

3. Strategic Discussions on the Future Work of the CEP

4. Operation of the CEP

5. Climate Change Implications for the Environment: Strategic Approach

6. Environmental Impact Assessment (EIA)

   a. Draft Comprehensive Environmental Evaluations

   b. Other EIA Matters

7. Area Protection and Management Plans

   a. Management Plans

   b. Historic Sites and Monuments

   c. Site Guidelines

   d. Human Footprint and Wilderness Values

   e. Marine Spatial Protection and Management

   f. Other Annex V Matters

8. Conservation of Antarctic Flora and Fauna

   a. Quarantine and Non-Native Species

   b. Specially Protected Species

   c. Other Annex II Matters

9. Environmental Monitoring and Reporting

10. Inspection Reports

11. Cooperation with Other Organisations

12. Repair and Remediation of Environmental Damage

13. General Matters

14. Election of Officers

15. Preparation for Next Meeting

16. Adoption of the Report

17. Closing of the Meeting

Item 3: Strategic Discussions on the Future Work of the CEP

(7)   New Zealand introduced WP 57, *Antarctic Environments Portal*, jointly prepared with Australia and the Scientific Committee on Antarctic Research (SCAR), which reported on a concept of developing an online Antarctic Environments Portal. The portal would be an efficient means to strengthen the link between Antarctic science and policy, enhance the CEP's advisory role to the ATCM, facilitate SCAR's advisory role to the ATCM and CEP, and assist in communicating information on Antarctic environments to the public.

(8)   Members welcomed the proposal, noting the importance of having ready access to information to support the Committee's work, and expressed their interest in contributing to the development of the portal during the intersessional period. Norway volunteered to share its experience with the Barents Portal, developed under the Joint Norwegian-Russian Commission on Environmental Protection, and the websites of relevant Arctic Council working groups. Belgium noted that it was actively involved with the Biodiversity Portal ANTABIF and offered to collaborate. Key questions raised by some Members were: resource implications, potential duplication of information published by SCAR and the Secretariat, multi-language in the four languages of the Antarctic Treaty, long-term ownership and management of the portal and its contents, how publications would be endorsed by the CEP, and the principles to govern what kind of information would be included.

(9)   New Zealand advised that these matters would be considered in the development and planning of the portal.

(10)   The Committee supported the concept of an Antarctic Environments Portal and looked forward to hearing from New Zealand, SCAR, Australia and interested Members next year on progress in developing a demonstration model.

(11)   The Committee revised and updated the Five-Year Work Plan, noting its continued utility (Appendix 1).

(12)   The Committee highlighted the importance of the Five-Year Work Plan for managing its work and priorities and agreed in future to discuss the Plan at the end of each agenda item.

Item 4: Operation of the CEP

(13)　The Secretariat presented SP 10, *Report of the Informal Contact Group on the improvement of the EIES and other Information Exchange matters*, which reported information about the current usage of the Electronic Information Exchange System (EIES) and recent improvements, and posed a series of questions concerning information exchange. Nine Members had been active participants in the Informal Contact Group. The Secretariat offered to continue working to improve the EIES.

(14)　The Chair noted that the EIES was an essential tool for exchanging information on current activities being undertaken in Antarctica, and commended the Secretariat for the ongoing improvement which would support the work of the CEP.

(15)　Chile and the United States encouraged further enhancements to the EIES to enable the submission of data spanning multiple species, sites and years. The United Kingdom noted that Members would need to continue to contribute all available data to the EIES in order to achieve a critical mass.

(16)　The Committee expressed its gratitude to the Secretariat for its work on improving the EIES, as well as for the broad range of tasks the Secretariat had undertaken to support the CEP, ATCM and intersessional work, and encouraged Members to accept the Secretariat's offer to facilitate additional adjustments to the EIES.

(17)　France noted that in this respect WP 29, *Improving the Functioning of the Electronic Information Exchange System (EIES) for Non-Governmental Activities in Antarctica*, submitted under ATCM Agenda Item 17, was of relevance.

Item 5: Climate Change Implications for the Environment: Strategic Approach

(18)　The United Kingdom introduced WP 33, *RACER – 'Rapid Assessment of Circum-Arctic Ecosystem Resilience': a tool from the Arctic to assess ecosystem resilience and areas of conservation importance, and its possible application to Antarctica*, prepared jointly with Norway, which introduced a new conservation tool developed by the WWF for identifying and mapping places of conservation importance across the Arctic on the basis of ecosystem resilience. The paper was presented in response to Recommendation 29 of the Antarctic Treaty Meeting of Experts (ATME) on Climate Change (Svolvær, Norway, 2010), which stated that the CEP should *'remain alert to the development of climate change related conservation tools elsewhere in the world that may also have application in an Antarctic context'.*

(19)   Members and ASOC welcomed the initiative as a potential contribution to the suite of tools available to the CEP, and noted its potential complementarity with existing tools, such as the Environmental Domains Analysis and the Antarctic Conservation Biogeographic Regions, in developing large-scale representative ecoregions.

(20)   While SCAR noted that the RACER methodology could assist in defining areas of high resilience within Antarctic Conservation Biogeographic Regions, he also raised a concern about the establishment of non-native species in such areas which is not considered in the model at the moment. SCAR offered to work with the United Kingdom and Norway intersessionally.

(21)   Australia welcomed the paper, noting that progress on the outstanding ATME recommendations could only be made if Members brought forward proposals for the Committee's consideration. Australia indicated that it would be pleased to participate in discussions with the United Kingdom and Norway. As initial feedback, it noted the importance of considering the different management context and conservation objectives of the Arctic and Antarctic regions.

(22)   Several Members noted that significant differences in physical conditions and human activity between the Arctic and Antarctic would necessitate some adaptation of the methodology. Other points that were raised were: the need to reach agreed understandings of resilience and acceptable adaptation, the need to protect vulnerable areas, and the impact of other factors on resilience, such as ozone depletion. Spain also noted that an appropriate Spanish translation for the word 'resilience' would be required.

(23)   Brazil suggested that Admiralty Bay may be a useful test area, taking into account data available for both terrestrial and marine areas.

(24)   The Committee endorsed work to trial the RACER methodology in the Antarctic, while taking into account the need to adapt the methodology to the Antarctic context, and requested that the results of the trial be presented to CEP XVI to facilitate further discussion.

(25) The Secretariat presented SP 8, *Actions taken by the CEP and the ATCM on the ATME Recommendations on Climate Change*, informing the Committee of actions taken under each of the 30 ATME recommendations.

(26) New Zealand thanked the Secretariat for its work, noting that it was important not to lose sight of the recommendations of the ATME.

(27) COMNAP presented IP 31, *Best Practice for Energy Management – Guidance and Recommendations*, in response to ATME (2010) Recommendation 4 (2), which requested that COMNAP report on progress made to implement best practice in energy management and to update Parties on the details of best practices in energy efficiency and alternative energy deployment. This report indicated that while reducing the use of fuel on Antarctic stations remained important, the major use of fuel was on ships and aircraft, in which respect energy savings had been generated by improving operational planning.

(28) ASOC welcomed the initiatives from the United Kingdom and Norway in WP 33 and from COMNAP in IP 31 as useful contributions to the development of the CEP's strategic approach to climate change.

(29) In response to concerns raised by France and the United States about the low rate of response by national Antarctic programmes to COMNAP's energy management survey, COMNAP indicated that the survey was conducted during the austral summer season, when most of its members were in Antarctica. However, COMNAP would continue to seek further survey responses, and endeavor to provide this information to CEP XVI.

(30) SCAR presented IP 44, *Communicating the Science of Climate Change*, which responded to the Recommendation from the ATME on Climate Change and Impacts for Management and Governance for the Antarctic Region (2010),which identifies the need to develop an Antarctic climate change communication plan to bring the findings of the SCAR ACCE report to the attention of decision makers, the general public and the media. SCAR has showed how with funding from Norway, the United Kingdom and ASOC, it was actively implementing innovative ways to improve communication in this area. SCAR also to referred to IP 45, *Antarctic Climate Change and the Environment: an Update.* SCAR has been working on a major update to the Executive Summary of the ACCE report, making this a much more comprehensive update than previous ones. This update will be submitted to a peer reviewed journal.

(31)   The United Kingdom further recalled that it had jointly engaged in work to communicate the science of climate change with Norway and ASOC.

(32)   IAATO noted that it placed a high priority on educating its members' clients on climate change in Antarctica and, for example, was currently creating a generic climate change lecture for its members' use. As such IAATO offered to assist SCAR with their communication initiative.

(33)   ASOC presented IP 58 rev.1, *Earth Hour Antarctica (2013)*, jointly prepared with Australia and the United Kingdom, which proposed a coordinated continent–wide switch off of all non-essential lights at Antarctic research stations for Earth Hour on 30 March 2013, within all operational and safety constraints, to demonstrate support for real action to tackle the threat of climate change.

(34)   Members whose stations had participated in previous Earth Hour initiatives, including the United Kingdom (Halley and Rothera Stations), Australia (Casey and Mawson Stations) and New Zealand (Scott Base) encouraged other national programmes to participate, and indicated that they would be happy to answer any questions on practical requirements regarding operational constraints.

(35)   COMNAP suggested that the 2012 COMNAP annual general meeting of July 2012 could be an appropriate forum to determine the practical, technical or operational issues associated with the Earth Hour initiative.

Item 6: Environmental Impact Assessment

6a) Draft Comprehensive Environmental Evaluation

(36)   There were no papers submitted under this item.

6b) Other EIA matters

(37)   The Republic of Korea presented IP 23, *Final Comprehensive Environmental Evaluation (CEE) for the Proposed Construction and Operation of the Jang Bogo Station, Terra Nova Bay, Antarctica*, which sought to address a number of queries and recommendations from Parties regarding the draft CEE presented at CEP XIV (2011). These included cumulative impacts relating to the concentration of bases in Terra Nova Bay; water recycling;

replacement of a proposed incinerator with a food waste reducer; introduction of a management plan for visits to a nearby skua colony, and a monitoring programme relating to this colony; non-native species introduction; an energy management plan with solar and wind energy; and further information on station decommissioning aided by the modular system design. The construction would start in December 2012.

(38) Several Members acknowledged the high quality of the final CEE which provided responses to most of the concerns raised at CEP XIV on the basis of the draft CEE. While ASOC appreciated efforts to make Jang Bogo Station more environmentally friendly, it identified its continuing concerns regarding the cumulative impact of station construction and activity in Terra Nova Bay. ASOC further noted that the new station would place Korea at the forefront of science in the region, and hoped that Korea would take a leading role in the protection of the Ross Sea region. Germany noted that it would like information on modelling of the wind noise on the station structure, and data relating to the Skua colony, once the station is functioning.

(39) Italy noted that it had already initiated several joint scientific projects with Korean scientists.

(40) The Committee congratulated the Republic of Korea on the comprehensive nature of the final CEE. Members also expressed their best wishes to the Republic of Korea in operating Jang Bogo Station, and looked forward to further international cooperation and research activity in Terra Nova Bay.

(41) The United Kingdom introduced IP 30, *The Final Comprehensive Environmental Evaluation (CEE) for the* Proposed *Exploration of Subglacial Lake Ellsworth, Antarctica*, and once again thanked Members for comments that had been made to the Draft CEE, both directly to the United Kingdom and to the ICG led by Norway. The Russian Federation noted that the United Kingdom's work would enrich humanity's knowledge.

(42) The Committee congratulated the United Kingdom for the comprehensive nature of its final CEE.

(43) Several Members acknowledged the way in which the proponents of each of the CEEs had followed the process of addressing Parties' comments, in order to limit and avoid environmental impacts in line with the Environmental Protocol.

(44) New Zealand introduced WP 22, *Environmental Aspects and Impacts of Tourism and Non-governmental Activities in Antarctica*, and referred to IP 33 on the same subject. These papers outlined the results of a comprehensive study undertaken by New Zealand pursuant to a request by ATCM XXXII.

(45) New Zealand summarised the study's findings, which provide an overview of tourism trends over time, the current characteristics of Antarctic tourism, a consideration of the potential environmental impacts that could arise from Antarctic tourism, a review of the sites visited by tourists, a review of the published literature on the impact of tourism in Antarctica, a summary of regulatory measures adopted by the Treaty Parties, an assessment of regulatory controls in place, and eight recommendations for future work. New Zealand noted that independent, reliable and complete data on all forms of Antarctic tourism were difficult to obtain, and suggested that the lack of comprehensive data and information readily available to the ATCM made any assessment of the environmental impacts of Antarctic tourism challenging.

(46) The Committee thanked New Zealand for its dedication and hard work on this issue, and recognised the good level of participation from other Members and Observers. It noted that the study provided a significant step towards identifying the known and unknown impacts of tourism and non-governmental activities, and was an example of the CEP's ability to respond effectively to requests made by the ATCM.

(47) Members acknowledged that the available information was incomplete, however it was considered unlikely that further research and refinement would significantly alter the findings. While expressing support for the aims of the study and associated recommendations, some Members suggested that these recommendations should be viewed as a menu of options for consideration by the ATCM rather than a fixed package to be adopted all at once. They also highlighted the need for further work to address current data gaps, noting that the study was a dynamic document requiring ongoing consideration by the CEP. The Committee agreed to include some of the recommendations in its 5 year work plan, when appropriate.

(48) China appreciated the work done by New Zealand and looked forward to more discussions. It thanked IAATO for providing data, as IAATO had done a great deal of work on this topic.

(49) ASOC commended New Zealand for producing a thorough study based on the information that was available. ASOC noted that although the publications cited stated that there had not been any conclusive evidence that tourism had had any impacts on the Antarctic environment, it was not possible to conclude that tourism had not had any impacts, due to the lack of data. Long term site occupation was not mentioned in the report, while in fact it was a form of actual impact and suggested that the CEP should acknowledge that tourist access to previously untouched areas fundamentally altered their pristine state. ASOC supported the recommendations from the study, although considered that it left out the critical need to develop a "vision" for Antarctic tourism, which would enable Parties to shape tourism developments instead of reacting to them.

(50) IAATO thanked New Zealand for its work, noting that it was pleased to have provided data. IAATO would continue to engage in these discussions both in the CEP and ATCM.

(51) Following discussion, the Committee agreed to endorse the study and forward it to the ATCM for consideration, noting that it would not be necessary to take forward all recommendations simultaneously, and that the ATCM could refer matters back to the CEP for further consideration and advice. The study contained the following recommendations:

Recommendation 1: To ensure that the ATCM has readily available to it a complete picture of tourism activities and to facilitate regular assessments of the environmental impacts of Antarctic tourism by the ATCM, the ATCM should develop a centrally managed database of tourism activities, which might be achieved through a redesign and concerted use of the EIES. Consideration will need to be given as to the data required, though much of the information currently collected through the post-visit reporting process would be of relevance, supplemented with accurate reporting of all authorised tourist activities including yacht visits and land-based expeditions.

Recommendation 2: To improve site-specific management a centrally managed ATCM database of tourist sites, including information on their environmental sensitivities, should be established, alongside the visitation database referred to in Recommendation 1.

Recommendation 3: An appropriate method of assessing site sensitivity should be developed and a relative sensitivity analysis undertaken for at least the most heavily visited sites in Antarctica, including, for example, consideration of the vulnerability of tourist sites to non-native species establishment, for the purpose of more rigorously assessing appropriate management needs. Site sensitivity considerations should also be included in the Environmental Impact Assessment process for tourism activities.

Recommendation 4: Consideration should be given to the means by which site specific guidelines are reviewed and updated, including the appropriate frequency of review and the information required to support a review.

Recommendation 5: Consideration should be given to the regular review of trends in tourist activity at selected tourist sites, particularly those with high levels of visitation or those considered to be particularly sensitive to impact.

Recommendation 6: Consideration should be given to establishing an ATCM-approved on-site monitoring programme for the purposes of i) assessing the effectiveness of site-specific guidelines and ii) monitoring for impacts.

Recommendation 7: Consideration should be given to developing a series of 'best estimate' trigger levels to assist in guiding monitoring efforts. This could include identifying certain parameters (eg, the number of landed tourists per season at a site) that would, if reached, trigger a need for a review of the effectiveness of current management at the site. Such an approach would be underpinned by the site sensitivity analysis referred to in Recommendation 3 above.

Recommendation 8: Consideration should be given to identifying a range of potential management options that might be applied to managing tourism activities, including vessels and vessel operations while transporting tourists, as well as to the data and information needed to support the application of such measures

---

CEP Advice to the ATCM

(52) The Committee endorsed the study on *Environmental Aspects and Impacts of Tourism and Non-governmental Activities in Antarctica*, and agreed to forward the study to the ATCM to support its consideration of tourism management.

---

(53)   Brazil introduced WP 53, *Comandante Ferraz Station: Proposed Plan for the Demolition and Construction of Antarctic Emergency Modules.* The paper outlined a plan for the demolition and removal of the main building which was destroyed by the fire, and the construction and operation of Antarctic Emergency Modules (AEM) at the location of the Comandante Ferraz Station. Brazil indicated that the new station plan would be submitted to the ATCM as soon as the plan was prepared.

(54)   Brazil described the events surrounding the fire at its station and the tragic loss of life which resulted, and expressed gratitude to Chile, Argentina, Uruguay, the Russian Federation, Poland and the United Kingdom for their assistance during and after the fire, and to all those that conveyed their sympathy and solidarity. Brazil emphasised its efforts to uphold the Environmental Protocol and to mitigate the environmental impacts of the incident, both during the immediate aftermath of the fire, and through its plans for comprehensive ongoing clean-up activities, taking into consideration sampling conducted by Brazil and modelling based on meteorological and other data.

(55)   Members expressed their condolences to Brazil for the loss of Brazilian lives and the destruction of Comandante Ferraz station, which they noted had carried out invaluable scientific work. They welcomed Brazil's thorough and ongoing efforts to uphold its obligations under the Environmental Protocol, and to mitigate and avoid environmental impacts, despite the tragic and difficult circumstances. Members offered practical assistance to Brazil with its reconstruction efforts and to ensure Brazilian Antarctic science could continue.

(56)   Bulgaria thanked Brazil for saving the life of the Bulgarian Base Commander, who suffered a heart attack onboard the Brazilian ship *Almirante Maximiano.*

(57)   Some Members offered constructive suggestions on station design and how best to minimise the risk of similar tragedies occurring in the future. The Russian Federation, which had suffered three station fires and had lost lives as a result, and Spain, which was remodelling its station, favoured a modular design for stations, and offered to assist Brazil in this respect.

(58)   Thanking all Members who offered their condolences and support, Brazil expressed its determination to continue with its Antarctic research and to return to Antarctica during the 2012-13 austral summer. Brazil indicated that it was confident that it could work with others to rebuild its station, and reiterated its intention to do so while respecting and upholding the Environmental Protocol.

(59) The Russian Federation introduced WP 34, *Technology for investigating the water layer of subglacial Lake Vostok through the ice borehole 5G at the Russian Antarctic Vostok station*, which described the technological design that would enable direct observations and sampling of the lake as early as 2014–15. Russia also referred to IP 74, *Results of Russian activity for penetrating subglacial Lake Vostok in the season 2011-2012,* which reported that there had been a clean penetration from an ecological perspective, of 3679.60 metres of ice. The Russian Federation noted that the release of a significant amount of drilling fluid at the surface of the borehole, immediately pumped, confirmed that the liquid water of the lake rose up in the bottom of the borehole, preventing any contamination of the lake by the drilling fluid. A video about the activity was shown.

(60) A number of Parties congratulated the Russian Federation for its significant scientific and technological achievement, which would generate an important leap in scientific knowledge of sub-glacial lakes.

(61) While congratulating the Russian Federation, others raised questions about the process. Belgium asked why the thermal drill and organosilicon fluid that had originally been envisaged for the activity were not utilised, and whether there was any effect from the change in technology. Belgium also inquired whether it might have been possible to use the thermal drilling method and avoid potential pollution of the lake, if further progress had been delayed until the beginning of the following season. ASOC remained concerned about contamination, and in this respect asked for clarifications of the fate of leaked drill fluid, and contact of drill fluid with lake waters. ASOC noted the need to follow well-formulated research and operating protocols, even if this may result in a delay in obtaining scientific results, in order to safeguard Antarctica's environmental and scientific values.

(62) In response, the Russian Federation clarified that it had no time to transfer to the thermal drill technology with the organosilicon fluid, because the precise thickness of the ice sheet was unknown and there was no clear indication of how close the drill was to penetrating into water. Furthermore, the thermal drilling technology would not have allowed for a core sample to be taken from the site. The option of inserting organosilicon fluid into the bore hole, and to wait another year before assuming drilling, had been dismissed due to the unknowns involved. The Russian Federation stated that drill fluid would not contaminate the lake, because there was no way that a liquid with a lighter density could have penetrated into the lake water under the pressure of four

atmospheres. Rather, the kerosene and Freon was contained within the centre of the freshly frozen bore hole, as lake water travelled up the drill shaft. It noted that pure water samples were expected to be collected in 2012/13, and that new technologies would be applied in 2014/15 to research on the water column, including procedures that would maximise clean conditions.

(63) Italy presented IP 41, *Starting a feasibility study for the realization of a gravel runway near Mario Zucchelli Station*, which highlighted its intention to explore two sites for building a new gravel runway due to problems with the current ice runway. In the 2012/2013 season, a stratigraphical survey by drilling, helicopter radar surveys and the collection of meteorological data would be conducted for further analysis of the suitability of these sites for the proposed runway and in preparation for any necessary environmental impact assessment.

(64) The Republic of Korea noted that a new gravel runway would be very useful for scientists in the region, and offered its strong support for cooperation with Italy to make this project possible.

(65) ASOC noted that it looked forward to seeing the CEE before the project proceeded, and expressed its view that such a CEE should include an assessment of the cumulative impact of this and other facilities in the area.

(66) India presented IP 43, *Establishment and Operation of New Indian Research Station "Bharati" at Larsemann Hills*, and thanked a number of Parties for their useful feedback during the CEE process.

(67) The Committee congratulated India on the successful completion of Bharati Station in 2012, and looked forward to its contribution to collaborative scientific research in the area. China also thanked India for its kind assistance with cargo transportation in the Larsemann Hills during the construction of Bharati Station, after the loss of a Chinese helicopter.

(68) Other papers submitted under this item were:

- SP 6, *Annual list of Initial Environmental Evaluations (IEE) and Comprehensive Environmental Evaluations (CEE) prepared between April 1st 2011 and March 31st 2012* (Secretariat).

- BP 36, *Resumen de la Auditoría Ambiental de Cumplimiento de la Estación Científica Ecuatoriana Pedro Vicente Maldonado* (Ecuador).

Item 7: Area Protection and Management Plans

7a) Management Plans

i) *Draft Management Plans which have been reviewed by the Subsidiary Group on Management Plans*

(69) Australia introduced WP 14, *Subsidiary Group on Management Plans – Report on 2011/12 Intersessional Work,* on behalf of the Subsidiary Group on Management Plans (SGMP). The Group had in the intersessional period reviewed one revised management plan: for ASPA No. 140, Parts of Deception Island, prepared by the United Kingdom.

(70) The SGMP advised the Committee that the final revised management plan prepared by the United Kingdom was well written, of high quality, and adequately addressed the key points raised during its review. Accordingly, the SGMP recommended that the CEP approve the revised plan.

(71) The Committee endorsed the SGMP's recommendation and agreed to forward the revised management plan for ASPA 140 to the ATCM for adoption.

ii) *Draft revised Management Plans which had not been reviewed by the Subsidiary Group on Management Plans*

(72) The Committee considered revised management plans for 13 Antarctic Specially Protected Areas (ASPAs) and one Antarctic Specially Managed Area (ASMA) under this category:

- WP 2, *Revised Management Plan for Antarctic Specially Protected Area (ASPA) No. 151 Lions Rump, King George Island, South Shetland Islands* (Poland).

- WP 3, *Revised Management Plan for Antarctic Specially Protected Area (ASPA) No. 128 Western Shore of Admiralty Bay, King George Island, South Shetland Islands* (Poland).

- WP 8, *Revision of the Management Plan for Antarctic Specially Protected Area (ASPA) No. 129 Rothera Point, Adelaide Island* (United Kingdom).

- WP 9, *Revision of the Management Plan for Antarctic Specially Protected Area (ASPA) No. 109 Moe Island, South Orkney Islands* (United Kingdom).

- WP 10, *Revision of the Management Plan for Antarctic Specially Protected Area (ASPA) No. 111 Southern Powell Island and adjacent islands, South Orkney Islands* (United Kingdom).

- WP 11, *Revision of the Management Plan for Antarctic Specially Protected Area (ASPA) No. 115 Lagotellerie Island, Marguerite Bay, Graham Land* (United Kingdom).

- WP 12, *Revision of the Management Plan for Antarctic Specially Protected Area (ASPA) No. 110 Lynch Island, South Orkney Islands* (United Kingdom).

- WP 42, *Review of the Management Plan for ASMA No. 4: Deception Island* (Argentina, Chile, Norway, Spain, United Kingdom and United States).

- WP 44, *Revised Management Plan for Antarctic Specially Protected Area (ASPA) No. 132 Potter Peninsula* (Argentina).

- WP 52, *Review of the Management Plan of Antarctic Specially Protected Area (ASPA) No. 133 Harmony Point* (Argentina and Chile).

- WP 54, *Revised Management Plan for Antarctic Specially Protected Area (ASPA) No. 145 Port Foster, Deception Island, South Shetland Islands* (Chile).

- WP 58, *Management Plan for Antarctic Specially Protected Area (ASPA) No. 112 Coppermine Peninsula, Robert Island, South Shetland Islands* (Chile).

- WP 60, *Management Plan for Antarctic Specially Protected Area (ASPA) No. 146 South Bay, Doumer Island, Palmer Archipelago* (Chile).

- WP 61, *Management Plan for Antarctic Specially Protected Area (ASPA) No. 144 'Chile Bay' (Discovery Bay), Greenwich Island, South Shetland Islands* (Chile).

(73) In introducing WP 2, which presented a revised management plan for ASPA 151, and WP 3, which presented a revised management plan for ASPA 128, Poland noted that only minor amendments were proposed.

(74) Several Members sought clarification on a number of issues, particularly in relation to ASPA 128, including measures for the management of non-native flora species that had been identified in the Area, the consideration of ATCM Measures regarding control of overflights (which Chile raised), and the expanded boundaries (which IAATO requested should be clearly marked). Further, the United States noted that its field camp in ASPA 128 had been in place since before the area was declared an ASPA, and that it would raise other queries to improve the utility of the revised plan during the intersessional period.

(75) The Committee agreed to refer the revised management plans for ASPAs No.s 128 and 151 to the SGMP for intersessional review.

(76) With respect to WP 8 (ASPA 129), WP 9 (ASPA 109), WP 10 (ASPA 111), WP 11 (ASPA 115) and WP 12 (ASPA 110), the United Kingdom outlined minor changes, which included reformatting to comply with the *Guidelines for the Preparation of Management Plans for ASPAs*, information about access to the Areas, provision of coordinates for the boundaries of the Areas, and, where relevant, information about field camps.

(77) The United Kingdom explained that the revisions to the management plan for ASPA 129 (in WP 8), which was originally established as a control area against which the effects of human impact from the adjacent Rothera Research Station could be monitored in an Antarctic fellfield ecosystem, comprised formatting changes and the addition of an introduction, noting that whereas the Area itself had little intrinsic nature conservation value, it did have value as a biological research and monitoring site.

(78) Changes to the management plan for ASPA 109 (in WP 9), which was established to protect a representative sample of the maritime Antarctic ecosystem, environmental values (primarily terrestrial flora and fauna), and as a control site for comparison with areas subject to scientific activities, included a description of the Area's position in the Environmental Domains framework, and information on access and boundaries.

(79) Introducing WP 10, the United Kingdom explained that the proposed revisions to the management plan for ASPA 111, which protected predominantly breeding bird and seal populations, and to a lesser extent terrestrial vegetation, comprised the addition of an introduction, a reference to the Area's position in the Environmental Domains framework, information on access and boundaries, and the designated campsite.

(80) Changes to the management plan for ASPA 115, which protected environmental values, primarily terrestrial flora and fauna and avifauna, also addressed access, the Environmental Domains context, and information about structures within the Area.

(81) When discussing WP 12, which covered ASPA 110, the United Kingdom explained that management of this Area, which protected one of the largest areas of *Deschampsia antarctica* in the Treaty area, needed to be revised in light of an increase in the level of fur seal presence within the Area and the recognition of the increased biodiversity of the terrestrial communities.

(82) The Committee agreed to forward the revised management plans for ASPA No.s 109, 110, 111, 115 and 129 to the ATCM for adoption.

(83) With respect to WP 42, prepared jointly by Argentina, Chile, Norway, Spain, the United Kingdom and the United States, Norway explained that the Deception Island Management Group had conducted its first five-yearly review of the Management Plan for ASMA 4, which protects areas of unique and important natural, scientific, historic, educational and aesthetic value, and which were also subject to a wide range of competing demands. In this context, Norway also thanked ASOC and IAATO for their contributions to the five-yearly review.

(84) Norway remarked that the proposed changes to the Management Plan included: protection of areas not subjected to substantial human activity; guidance that Deception Island should not be used as an emergency harbour, if possible; updated census figures for chinstrap penguins in the ASMA, which indicated a marked and significant decline; an extensive package of visitor guidelines and changes to the visitor code of conduct; and inclusion of guidelines to reduce the risk of non-native species introduction to Deception Island.

(85) Spain highlighted that Deception Island is an active volcano and this posed additional risks to human activities, both for those entering the area and

anyone required to provide emergency assistance. Based on this, Spain emphasised that all activities needed to be considered carefully, and that restrictions and prohibitions may be warranted in some circumstances.

(86) The Russian Federation praised the scientific basis of the revised Management Plan and emphasised the importance of management decisions responding to scientific data.

(87) The Committee approved the revised Management Plan for ASMA 4 and agreed to forward it to the ATCM for adoption.

(88) With respect to WP 44, Argentina outlined the proposed changes to the management of ASPA 132, originally designated as a site of special scientific interest, as including editorial changes, revised maps, revised data and new information.

(89) The Committee agreed to forward the revised Management Plan for ASPA 132 to the SGMP for review.

(90) On behalf for Argentina and Chile, Argentina presented WP 52, which outlined minor changes to the management plan for ASPA 133. The Committee approved the revised Management Plan for ASPA 133 and agreed to forward it to the ATCM for adoption.

(91) With respect to WP 54 (ASPA 145), WP 60 (ASPA 146) and WP 61 (ASPA 144), Chile said the proposed revisions were for the management of ASPAs that included marine areas, and that it would therefore be appropriate to refer them to the Commission on the Conservation of Antarctic Marine Living Resources (CCAMLR) before further consideration by the Committee. Chile also advised Members that further revisions would be made to the map of ASPA 145 (WP 54) before forwarding to CCAMLR.

(92) Noting the proposed revisions and the need to consult CCAMLR, the Committee agreed to forward the management plans for ASPAs No.s 144, 145 and 146 to the SGMP.

(93) Concerning WP 58, submitted by Chile, the Committee approved the revised Management Plan for ASPA 112 and agreed to forward it to the ATCM for adoption.

iii) New draft management plans for protected/managed areas

(94)   The Committee considered three proposals to designate new Antarctic Specially Protected Areas (ASPAs) under this category:

- WP 19, *The proposed designation of an Antarctic Specially Protected Area for high altitude geothermal areas of the Ross Sea region* (New Zealand).

- WP 40, *Proposal for a new Antarctic Specially Protected Area at Cape Washington and Silverfish Bay, Terra Nova Bay, Ross Sea* (Italy & United States).

- WP 41, *Proposal for a new Antarctic Specially Protected Area at Taylor Glacier and Blood Falls, Taylor Valley, McMurdo Dry Valleys, Victoria Land* (United States).

(95)   In introducing WP 19, New Zealand noted that three sites in the Ross Sea area contain high altitude geothermal activity - Mount Erebus (ASPA No. 130: Tramway Ridge, Mount Erebus, Ross Island) Mount Melbourne (ASPA No. 118: Summit of Mount Melbourne, Victoria Land), and Mount Rittman in Victoria Land. All three sites contain unique biodiversity in warm geothermal soils. New Zealand proposed the designation of one ASPA for these three geothermal areas of the Ross Sea region and presented a draft management plan for a multi-site ASPA.

(96)   New Zealand suggested that this manner of ASPA designation represented a more strategic approach to protecting a rare environment type in Antarctica, and applied consistent measures to protect the highly sensitive and unique species assemblages to the same high standard in a single management plan.

(97)   The Committee welcomed New Zealand's proposal, and the United States, noting the mutual interest between New Zealand and the United States in high altitude geothermal areas, suggested that joint field work using shared logistical support might be possible during the 2012/13 field season to refine the proposed management plan.

(98)   The United Kingdom commended New Zealand on its proposal and suggested that intersessional discussion should consider whether the three areas considered under the proposal would be best protected as three separate ASPAs or as one larger ASPA.

(99) ASOC commented that New Zealand's proposal represented a creative and strategic initiative to protect unusual or rare habitats, and encouraged other Members to take a similar approach.

(100) In accordance with suggestions outlined in WP 19, the Committee agreed to refer the draft management plan for a proposed new ASPA for high altitude geothermal areas of the Ross Sea region to the SGMP for initial review and comment by October 2012, prior to the 2012/13 summer field season. New Zealand planned to address any identified issues during the 2012/13 season and to submit both a revised draft management plan and an outline of its responses to the SGMP's advice. Following further review by the SGMP, a final draft management plan would be submitted to CEP XVI.

(101) In introducing WP 40, the United States and Italy highlighted the scientific value of the area proposed for designation as an ASPA, noting that it includes one of the largest emperor penguin colonies in Antarctica and a rich Antarctic silverfish nursery. While the penguin colony had attracted interest for tourism, the boundaries proposed would reduce the area available for tourism. In view of the size of the marine component proposed in the ASPA, they also proposed forwarding the draft plan to CCAMLR for consideration in accordance with Decision 9 (2005).

(102) New Zealand noted the scientific importance of this part of the Ross Sea, and that it viewed the proposal as complementary to developing proposals for wider marine protection within CCAMLR and offered to contribute to the development of the proposed management plan. Similar offers were made by the Republic of Korea, which was in the process constructing a station in the vicinity of the proposed ASPA, and Germany, which had an existing research station in the area (Gondwana).

(103) While expressing support for the designation of a new ASPA in this area, the United Kingdom questioned whether it was necessary to exclude tourist visits to the area proposed for designation. IAATO expressed its appreciation that the intersessional consultations, to which it offered to contribute, would consider the tourism issues. Given the low levels of visitation at very defined periods of the year, IAATO hoped that they might find a way to allow controlled visitation to the area without compromising other values.

(104) The Committee agreed to forward the draft management plan for a proposed new ASPA for Cape Washington and Silverfish Bay to the SGMP. The SGMP would

provide advice to the United States and Italy on the draft management plan, to be considered first by CCAMLR and to then be discussed by CEP XVI.

(105) In introducing WP 41, the United States noted that the proposed management plan had been developed following extensive consultation with the scientific community, SCAR and interested CEP members. Increased activity on the Taylor Glacier and recent ice-core drilling projects highlighted the need to protect the Blood Falls as these activities have the potential to influence the unique microbial community and chemistry of the feature. They further noted that this would be the first sub-glacial ASPA and the first to be explicitly designed in three dimensions.

(106) The Committee commended this proposal as the first ASPA defined in three dimensions, approved the proposed designation of a new ASPA for Taylor Glacier and Blood Falls and agreed to forward it to the ATCM for adoption.

Advice to the ATCM

(107) In reviewing the advice of the SGMP, and following the Committee's assessment, the Committee agreed to forward the following management plans to the ATCM for adoption:

#	Name
ASPA 109	Moe Island, South Orkney Islands
ASPA 110	Lynch Island, South Orkney Islands
ASPA 111	Southern Powell Island and adjacent islands, South Orkney Islands
ASPA 112	Coppermine Peninsula
ASPA 115	Lagotellerie Island, Marguerite Bay, Graham Land
ASPA 129	Rothera Point, Adelaide Island
ASPA 133	Harmony Point
ASPA 140	Parts of Deception Island
New ASPA	Blood Falls
ASMA 4	Deception Island

iv) Other matters relating to management plans for protected/managed areas

(108) Australia introduced further elements of the intersessional work of the SGMP (in WP 14).

(109) The Committee thanked the SGMP for its work which it saw as important for the efficiency of its meetings.

(110) The Committee appointed Ms Birgit Njåstad from Norway as the new convenor of SGMP. The Committee thanked Mr Ewan McIvor from Australia for his convenership over the past 4 years.

(111) Mindful of the heavy workload of proposed management plans to be reviewed, the Committee agreed to defer the SGMP's consideration of actions arising from the ASMA workshop and revised the proposed 2012/13 work plan accordingly:

Terms of Reference	Suggested tasks
ToR 1 to 3	Review draft management plans referred by CEP for intersessional review and provide advice to proponents
ToR 4 and 5	Work with relevant Parties to ensure progress on review of management plans overdue for five-yearly review
	Review and update SGMP work plan
Working Papers	Prepare report for CEP XVI against SGMP ToR 1 to 3
	Prepare report for CEP XVI against SGMP ToR 4 and 5

(112) The Republic of Korea presented IP 24, *Management Report of Narębski Point (ASPA 171) and Ardley Island (ASPA 150) during the 2011/2012 period*, which provided a summary of flora and fauna surveys undertaken in these ASPAs.

(113) Chile congratulated the Republic of Korea for conducting the surveys, and Argentina and Germany for their assistance, and expressed a willingness to contribute to further data collection in the area in the future.

(114) IAATO presented IP 38, *Establishing IAATO Safety Advisories*, which described the establishment by its members of a formalised internal system that aims to enhance safety for operators in the Antarctic. When operators are involved in incidents, a process is followed to ensure review of the incident and, where appropriate, record the lessons learned and make the lessons available to the whole industry. Following the grounding of the MV *Sea Spirit* on December 9, 2011, IAATO prepared the first dedicated Advisory for Whalers Bay, Deception Island. IAATO further noted that previous

recommendations to enhance safety will be converted into this format and redistributed via the IAATO Field Operations Manual.

(115) India presented IP 61, *Report of the Larsemann Hills Antarctic Specially Managed Area (ASMA) Management Group,* prepared jointly with Australia, China, Romania and the Russian Federation. India noted that discussions within the management group on the first five-yearly review of the management plan had raised a number of issues which were being further discussed, and a revised management plan would be submitted to the CEP XVI.

(116) Belgium welcomed the management group's deliberations on the issue of designating the Stornes Peninsula as an ASPA to serve as a reference site and suggested that the protection could be extended to the Broknes Peninsula for its biological and paleolimnological value. Generally speaking, Belgium highlighted the value of the lakes on the Broknes and Grovnes Peninsula for biological and paleolimnological research.

(117) Brazil presented IP 66, *Working Plan Proposal for the Review of the Admiralty Bay Antarctic Specially Managed Area Management Plan (ASMA No. 1),* and reported that the management group planned to establish a discussion forum on the Secretariat website and to visit all stations and refuges during the next summer season, in preparation for submission of a revised management plan for consideration at CEP XVI.

(118) The United States presented IP 78, *Amundsen-Scott South Pole Station, South Pole Antarctica Specially Managed Area (ASMA No. 5) 2012 Management Report*, which summarised the continuing challenges in managing diverse activities in the ASMA. The United States expressed its satisfaction at the constructive relationship established with the tourist industry in expectation of high visitor numbers associated with celebrations of the centenaries of Roald Amundsen and Robert Falcon Scott reaching the South Pole, drawing particular attention to the success of the visitor centre. The United States also invited Members to provide advice to enhance the management of the ASMA, and material which might enhance the utility of the recently launched website *www.southpole.aq.*

(119) IAATO thanked the United States for its productive cooperation during the centenary year. In response to a query from ASOC, IAATO indicated that a decline in visitor numbers was expected in the short term, but numbers could not be accurately predicted beyond the next few years.

(120) Norway presented IP 82, *Deception Island Specially Managed Area (ASMA No 4) Management Group Report*, prepared jointly with Argentina, Chile, Spain, the United Kingdom and the United States, which summarised the activities undertaken within the Deception Island ASMA, and the work of the management group during the intersessional period.

(121) In response to a query from France concerning an incident involving the scattering of barley seeds at Telefon Bay, IAATO indicated that the seeds had been scattered unexpectedly as part of a religious ceremony by tourists. The operator had collected the seeds, reprimanded the group and threatened them with no longer being allowed ashore. While enquires within the science community indicated that any seeds inadvertently not collected were probably not viable, IAATO has instituted a 'barley watch' at the site to monitor for any possible introduction and will report back to the CEP.

(122) Other papers submitted under this Item included:

- SP 7, *Status of Antarctic Specially Protected Area and Antarctic Specially Managed Area Management Plans.*

7b) Historic Sites and Monuments

(123) The Russian Federation introduced WP 36, *Proposal on Revision of Historic Sites and Monuments under Management of the Russian Federation*, encompassing revisions to the descriptions of HSM No. 4 (Lenin's Bust), HSM No. 7 (Kharma's Stone), HSM No. 8 (Shcheglov's Monument), HSM No. 9 (Soviet Expedition Cemetery), HSM No. 10 (Oasis Station Observatory) and HSM No. 11 (Vostok Station Tractor). The changes made included updated descriptions (including titles) and corrections to the coordinates.

(124) Chile introduced WP 56 rev.1, *Proposal for modification of Historic Site No. 37*, which proposed modifications to the description of the HSM, to incorporate associated structures.

(125) The Committee approved the revised descriptions for HSM No.s 4, 7, 8, 9, 10, 11 and 37 and agreed to forward them to the ATCM for adoption.

Advice to the ATCM

(126) After considering the revisions of the descriptions of seven Historic Sites and Monuments the Committee agreed to forward the revised descriptions to the ATCM for adoption:

#	Name of site/monument
HSM 4	Pole of Inaccessibility Station Building
HSM 7	Ivan Khmara's Stone
HSM 8	Anatoly Shcheglov's Monument
HSM 9	Buromsky Island Cemetery
HSM 10	Soviet Oasis Station Observatory
HSM 11	Vostok Station Tractor
HSM 37	O'Higgins Historic Site

(127) Argentina introduced WP 46, *Final Report of the Informal Discussions on Historic Sites and Monuments*, held during the intersessional periods 2010-11 and 2011-12, under Argentina's leadership. The following Members and Observers actively contributed to these discussions: Argentina, Australia, Brazil, Germany, India, New Zealand, Norway, United Kingdom, Uruguay, IAATO and ASOC.

(128) Argentina reported that discussions in the second intersessional period had focused on the exploration of possible wider use of 'Site Guidelines for Visitors', the potential application of management plans, or equivalent, to HSMs, and the role of specialists and external experts, particularly given the material and situational diversity of Antarctic heritage.

(129) Members warmly thanked Argentina and the other participants for their productive work, noting in particular the efforts made to incorporate all views. Specific mention was made of the personal contribution of Lic. Rodolfo Andrés Sánchez.

(130) Members agreed that sharing of experiences in management of HSMs was very valuable given the no 'one size fits all' diverse nature of HSMs, and supported continuing discussion.

(131) The informal discussion group had prepared a list of additional information that could be added to the list of HSMs adopted under Resolution 5 (2011)

to improve transparency and accessibility to a wider audience, as follows. It was proposed that the Party or Parties responsible for the establishment of the particular HSM should play the primary role in establishing whether any additional information would be useful.

(132) Several Members supported this approach. The United States noted that additional information, including a specific name for each HSM, would be very useful to meet their domestic requirements.

INTRODUCTION
• HSM number and name*
• Original proposing Party*
• Party undertaking management*
• Type (historic site or monument/commemorative)
DESCRIPTION OF THE SITE
• Location*
• Physical Features & Local/Cultural Landscape
• Historical / Cultural Features
DESCRIPTION OF THE HISTORICAL CONTEXT
SITE GUIDELINES FOR VISITORS (link, if applicable)
PHOTOS AND MAPS
ASPA Designation (if applicable)
• Management Plan link
Those items as marked * are information to be provided by Parties according to Resolution 5 (2011). The CEP notes that, according to such a Resolution, 'if it is desired to keep any additional background information on the record, this material may be annexed to the report of the CEP for inclusion in the Final Report of the ATCM'.

(133) The Committee also agreed with the conclusion that any review and revision of an existing Site Guidelines for Visitors (SGVs) should ensure that the guidance addresses the need to protect any historical or cultural values of the site. In order to achieve this goal the following criteria on how to deal with SGVs -in relation to HSMs- should be taken into consideration: a) The presence of an HSM in a heavily visited area could be a strong motivation to consider the development and adaptation of SGV for the site; b) The presence of a particularly vulnerable HSM in an area less visited could also potentially be a motivation for developing and adopting an SGV for the site; and c) There could be merit in considering whether existing SGVs provide sufficient protection to the HSMs Parties are responsible for (and if not, initiate a review in cooperation with other relevant/interested Parties, as appropriate).

(134) Finally, the Committee agreed that Parties should engage with heritage specialists, and/or with national representatives to external expert bodies (eg, the ICOMOS International Polar Heritage Committee) when preparing management plans (or other applicable management mechanisms) specifically tailored to HSMs.

(135) China presented IP 14, *Brief Introduction of the Maintenance and Conservation Project of No.1 Building at Great Wall Station*. This building was designated as HSM No. 86 under Measure 12 (2011). Japan thanked China, and stated that it looked forward to China providing more data once the restoration work is completed.

(136) Other papers submitted under this item included:

- BP 41, *Antarctic Heritage Trust Conservation Update* (New Zealand)

7c) Site Guidelines

(137) The Committee discussed proposals for revised site guidelines for one site and new guidelines for three new sites.

(138) The United Kingdom introduced WP 15, *Site Guidelines for D'Hainaut Island, Mikkelsen Harbour, Trinity Island,* prepared jointly with Argentina and the United States, in conjunction with IAATO; and WP 16, *Site Guidelines for Port Charcot, Booth Island*, prepared jointly with Argentina, France, Ukraine, the United States, in conjunction with IAATO.

(139) On behalf of the Deception Island Management Group (Argentina, Chile, Norway, Spain, United Kingdom and the United States), in conjunction with IAATO, Norway introduced WP 45, *Site Guidelines for Visitors, Pendulum Cove, Deception Island, South Shetland Islands,* which aim to minimise the risk of visitor-related pressures at this site of outstanding natural and historic value, as well as to safeguard visitor safety. Norway noted an amendment under landing requirements of ships, deleting Landing Requirement "Maximum 2 ships per day (midnight to midnight)".

(140) The Committee approved the three sets of Guidelines and agreed to forward them to the ATCM for adoption.

Advice to the ATCM

(141) After considering the new site guidelines for three sites the Committee agreed to forward the following site guidelines to the ATCM for adoption:

- D'Hainaut Island, Mikkelsen Harbour, Trinity Island

- Port Charcot, Booth Island

- Pendulum Cove, Deception Island

(142) Ecuador introduced WP 59, *Review of the Site Visitor Guidelines for Aitcho Islands*, prepared jointly with Spain. Proposed changes to the existing guidelines included replacement of anchoring points and replacement of a designated route crossing the island to avoid further impacts on the moss beds.

(143) The Committee thanked Ecuador and Spain for their important paper and acknowledged the important work they had undertaken to assess the damage to the moss beds and to bring the information to the Committee.

(144) The Committee strongly expressed its significant concern over the tracks through the moss beds on Barrientos Island - Aitcho Island and the damage that had occurred.

(145) The Committee agreed on the importance of removing opportunities for further damage to the site and considered a number of options to achieve that aim. Several Members noted the importance of further monitoring and research at the site in order to assess recovery of the moss beds and to ensure adequate information is available to inform decisions on future activities at the site.

(146) The Committee recognised IAATO's intent to introduce a moratorium on walks through closed area B among its members at least for the 2012/13 season and recognised the importance of removing all visitation to at least the area of damage so as to allow opportunities for longer term management to be considered.

(147) The Committee agreed to place a moratorium on access to the central area of Barrientos Island - Aitcho Island other than for reasons of scientific research and monitoring; to amend the site guidelines to take account of the moratorium; to encourage those national programmes active in the area

to cooperate in collecting further data and information on the damage that has occurred as well as on developing a monitoring programme to assess recovery of the site; and to reassess the issue, including the site guidelines, at CEP XVI.

(148) On this basis the Committee prepared a draft Resolution and recommended its adoption by the ATCM.

Advice to the ATCM

The Committee agreed to forward to the ATCM for adoption the revised Site Guidelines for Aitcho/Barrientos Island and a related draft Resolution.

---

(149) IAATO introduced IP 37, *Report on IAATO operator use of Antarctic Peninsula Landing Sites and ATCM Visitor Site Guidelines, 2011-2012 Season.* The United Kingdom indicated its intention to carry out work to propose Site Guidelines for Orne Island in the coming season, working with other Parties and Observers.

7d) Human footprint and wilderness values

(150) New Zealand introduced WP 50, *Concepts for Wilderness protection in Antarctica using tools in the Protocol* and referred to further information in IP 60, *Further information about wilderness protection in Antarctica and use of tools in the Protocol,* both prepared jointly with the Netherlands. These papers sought to progress the discussion on how areas of wilderness significance could be better protected, and proposed the development of practical guidance material to support the protection of wilderness values when applying the environmental impact assessment and area protection tools of Annex I and Annex V of the Protocol.

(151) New Zealand noted that while wilderness could be conceived of as an area untouched by humans, and the Antarctic had long been considered as such an area, it was becoming progressively less untouched due to the cumulative impact of human activity. The paper sought to quantify the tangible aspects of wilderness, and acknowledged that intangible aspects, such as aesthetic value, were the subject of ongoing discussion. New Zealand and Netherlands thanked ASOC and others for their assistance in preparing the two papers.

(152) The Committee commended New Zealand and the Netherlands on their work, acknowledged that there had been gradual degradation of some aspects of Antarctic wilderness, and discussed the importance of inviolate areas in conservation planning.

(153) Acknowledging the inherent difficulties in defining, assessing and managing wilderness values, the United States noted that the CEP's slow and steady pace on addressing this topic had proven a useful approach. Norway informed the Committee that it would contribute working examples of its consideration of wilderness values in the high Arctic, to assist CEP discussions. IAATO noted the importance of Antarctic wilderness to tour operators and their clients, and stood ready to provide support to the CEP.

(154) The Committee welcomed the offer of New Zealand and the Netherlands to bring further work to CEP XVI resulting from intersessional work to:

(a) develop guidance material to assist Parties to take account of wilderness values when undertaking environmental impact assessment of proposed activities and/or developing proposals for protected areas on the basis of their wilderness values; and

(b) explore possibilities for consideration of inviolate areas in conservation planning, and potential synergies with protection of wilderness areas in the development of proposals for protected areas in conjunction with SCAR.

(155) The Committee also welcomed SCAR's offer to collaborate in this work.

(156) ASOC presented IP 49, *Annex V Inviolate and Reference Areas: Current Management Practices,* which suggested that the designation of inviolate areas in accordance with Annex V of the Protocol should be applied widely as a tool to help protect wilderness and scientific values. ASOC noted that only 30 square kilometres of the Antarctic Treaty area were designated as inviolate areas within the present 71 existing ASPAs.

(157) The Committee thanked ASOC for its paper, and some Members highlighted the value of designating inviolate areas for future potential scientific research. The United Kingdom encouraged Members to incorporate restricted areas into new and existing ASPAs, as had been done for ASPA No. 126 on Byers Peninsula.

(158) Belgium stressed that the designation of inviolate areas would be an invaluable tool for scientific research and considered that scientific progress could be hindered by the lack of reference areas preserved from human footprint.

(159) ASOC presented IP 52, *Data Sources for Mapping the Human Footprint in Antarctica*, which proposed the compilation of available data on research, logistics, tourism and fishing into a common format as a first step toward the construction of a model of the human footprint in Antarctica. ASOC suggested that the CEP could discuss with SCAR and COMNAP how best to integrate and analyse this information, and that it should be added to the five year work plan. During discussion, it was noted that the proposed Antarctic Environments Portal (WP 57) could serve as a tool for addressing ASOC's proposal.

7e) Marine spatial protection and management

(160) Ukraine presented IP 68, *Progress of Ukraine on Designation of Broad-scale Management System in the Vernadsky Station Area*, in response to increasing scientific, logistic and tourism activities in the area, and invited interested Parties to take part in further discussion on environmental protection and management for this area.

(161) Dr. Polly Penhale (United States), in her capacity as CEP Observer to CCAMLR, presented IP 80, *Report of the CEP Observer to the CCAMLR Workshop on Marine Protected Areas, Brest, France, 29 August to 2 September 2011*. She referred Members to the full report on the CCAMLR website *(http://www.ccamlr.org/pu/e/e_pubs/sr/11/a06.pdf)*. She noted that the Workshop considered regionalisation analyses for the circumpolar pelagic environment and for the Crozet Basin and northern Kerguelen Plateau region (Indian Ocean) and reviewed progress on draft proposals for circumpolar pelagic habitats, newly exposed benthic habitats created by ice-shelf collapse, East Antarctica, and the Ross Sea Region. She further noted that the Workshop recognised that SC-CCAMLR and CEP have common interests in marine protection which may result in having ASPAs and ASMAs designated by the ATCM within CCAMLR MPAs.

(162) ASOC presented IP 54, *Implications of Antarctic Krill Fishing in ASMA No. 1 – Admiralty Bay*, which highlighted the occurrence of krill fishing in ASMA 1 during 2009/10, an activity not explicitly identified in the ASMA's

Management Plan. ASOC reminded Members that the Area was established, in part, because Admiralty Bay had a high concentration of breeding seabirds and seals, and stated that penguin numbers in the Area had decreased, and that the scientific research of the past several decades into fish, krill, benthic communities and seabirds in the Area could be jeopardised by fishing. This was the first instance of reported fishing in an ASMA and set a precedent of concern.

(163) To address these concerns, ASOC recommended an immediate review of the Management Plan and an interim prohibition of all commercial fishing in the Area, and expressed its view that CCAMLR should implement a precautionary closure of fisheries in ASMAs with marine components, as well as complementary conservation measures and incident reporting to the ATCM.

(164) Poland pointed out that monitoring of penguins in Admiralty Bay by the USA is part of the CCAMLR system and has been conducted for 40 years. Since krill is a critical item of penguin diet it was surprising to see trawlers catching krill in Admiralty Bay, potentially damaging this long term data set. Poland considers that krill harvesting near biological monitoring sites has to be totally forbidden to avoid such cases in the future. The restricted zone should be determined by penguin feeding activity, which could be up to 50km from the rookery. This restriction could be introduced to management plans of ASMAs and ASPAs and it could also be the first step in MPA designation. Poland also pointed out that other monitoring activity by its scientists in King George Bay could be threatened by fishing activities.

(165) Japan expressed its view that prohibition on fishing should be introduced only when it is necessary to achieve the objectives of a management plan.

(166) The SC-CAMLR Observer to CEP advised the Committee that as there was no mention of harvesting in the management plan for ASMA 1, in contrast to the management plan for ASMA 7, it was unclear whether the fishing in ASMA 1 was compatible with the objectives of the ASMA and therefore it had brought this matter to the attention of the CEP in IP 28 *Report by the SC-CAMLR Observer to the Fifteenth Meeting of the Committee for Environmental Protection.*

(167) The Committee thanked ASOC for raising this issue. In the light of the concerns raised by several Members and ASOC that krill fishing may not

be compatible with the scientific values of the ASMA, Brazil agreed to send a revised version of IP66 to SC-CAMLR's Working Group on Ecosystem Monitoring and Management in order that the issue of krill fishing in ASMA 1 could be addressed during the intersessional period following the established procedure.

(168) The SC-CAMLR Observer to CEP thanked the CEP for its clear advice on this issue and undertook to ensure that the concerns raised by the Committee regarding krill fishing in ASMA 1 were included in the discussions held in CCAMLR in order to improve awareness of the interaction of spatial management measures in the region.

(169) ASOC presented IP 50, *Antarctic Ocean Legacy: A Marine Reserve for the Ross Sea* and the related information in IP 51, *Antarctic Ocean Legacy: A vision for circumpolar protection* which called for the creation of a network of marine protected areas and no-take marine reserves in the Southern Ocean.

(170) ASOC explained that these proposals were developed by the Antarctic Ocean Alliance and were based on rigorous scientific research. They identify three additional areas that could be included in a Ross Sea MPA / marine reserve and 19 marine areas around Antarctica worthy of protection.

(171) Other papers submitted under this Item were:

- IP 34, *Using ASMAs and ASPAs when necessary to complement CCAMLR MPAs* (IUCN)

7f) Other Annex V matters

(172) The United States introduced WP 38, *Developing Protection for a Geothermal Area; Volcanic Ice Caves at Mount Erebus, Ross Island,* jointly prepared with New Zealand, which encouraged Parties to develop strategies to protect the unique environments of geothermal areas in the vicinity of Mount Erebus.

(173) The United States observed that these areas attracted significant scientific research interest from a range of disciplines. The Mount Erebus ice caves are home to microbial communities that are isolated from surface dwelling microbes and have developed a unique lifestyle. In recent years, the ice caves at the summit have become popular shelters for those working in

the area. These sites are particularly vulnerable to contamination through introduced microbes or organic matter and such contamination decreases their value to science. Contamination has already been observed in some ice caves.

(174) The United States recommended that interested Parties and SCAR develop an inventory of ice cave features, a Code of Conduct to address current contamination and minimise further contamination, and a voluntary moratorium on entering any cave other than for scientific purposes until a Code of Conduct could be implemented.

(175) In thanking the United States and New Zealand for this initiative, the United Kingdom and Chile both strongly supported the development of appropriate guidance material for other geothermal areas in Antarctica, and drew this to the attention of the Deception Island Management Group.

(176) Following a query from France, the United States clarified that the Code of Conduct would be complementary to the protection within the framework of the proposed ASPA for high altitude geothermal areas of the Ross Sea region.

(177) SCAR noted its willingness to work alongside Parties to further develop this initiative.

(178) In response to the proposal, the Committee adopted the following recommendations:

- Encourage interested Parties and their scientists to collaborate in generating an inventory of Mount Erebus ice caves that identifies the location, size, history of human activity and current microbial community characteristics in each ice caves.

- Encourage interested Parties and their scientists to collaborate in developing a Code of Conduct that recognises the current level of microbiological contamination in the Mount Erebus ice caves and strives to prevent further contamination in ice caves of interest for microbiology studies.

- Encourage scientists, interested Parties, and SCAR to work together to develop appropriate guidance material for other geothermal areas in Antarctica.

(179) The Committee also noted the other recommendations in the proposal:

- Encourage Parties to adopt a temporary moratorium on informal visits or visits for any purpose other than scientific research inside all Mount Erebus ice caves until a Code of Conduct is agreed.

- Encourage Parties to adopt a temporary moratorium on entry for any purpose into Mount Erebus ice caves that are currently believed to be pristine until a Code of Conduct can be agreed.

- Encourage scientists working in Mount Erebus ice caves to sterilise their gear and clothing to the best of their abilities and eliminate the use of gasoline powered tools inside caves, acknowledging that best practices will be identified when developing the Code of Conduct.

(180) Australia introduced WP 23 rev.1, *Antarctic Conservation Biogeographic Regions*, jointly prepared with New Zealand and SCAR, which presented the results of recent analyses of the relationships between the best available Antarctic terrestrial biodiversity data, the Environmental Domains adopted under Resolution 3 (2008), and other relevant spatial frameworks. The analyses identified 15 biologically distinct ice-free regions encompassing the Antarctic continent and offshore islands within the Antarctic Treaty area.

(181) Among other potential applications, Australia, New Zealand and SCAR recommended that the Committee endorse the classification represented by the Antarctic Conservation Biogeographic Regions as a dynamic model for identifying ASPAs within a systematic environmental-geographic framework, and also as a basis for managing the risk of transfer of species between locations in Antarctica.

(182) The Russian Federation added that it would make its researchers aware of these analyses with a view to making a contribution to future work on the Antarctic Conservation Biogeographic Regions. The Netherlands highlighted the utility of cross-referencing the map of Antarctic Conservation Biogeographic Regions with other maps, such as those on visitation frequency, in order to identify areas requiring special consideration for management or protection.

(183) In response to queries from China and Argentina about the intended application of the model, Australia explained that the model was not intended

to be prescriptive and was provided as one of a number of tools available for facilitating the designation of ASPAs. It would be most relevant to the designation of examples of major terrestrial ecosystems.

(184) In response to a query from the United States, SCAR informed the Committee that while its current analyses focused on ice-free areas, it intended to include sub-glacial and other ice-covered areas in future analyses. SCAR also referred Members to IP 40 rev.1, *SCAR Products available to support the deliberations of the ATCM*, for a description of the methods used for data collection and management. SCAR remarked that various other studies supported the analyses conducted, but emphasised the need for more data in the future development of Biogeographic Regions. Some Members indicated their national programmes could contribute additional biodiversity data. SCAR encouraged the use of the Antarctic Biodiversity Database.

(185) The Committee congratulated SCAR and the researchers responsible for the study presented in WP 23 rev.1 on their thorough analysis towards a systematic approach to area protection.

(186) The Committee endorsed the recommendations in WP23 rev.1 and

- agreed that the Antarctic Conservation Biogeographic Regions should be used consistently and in conjunction with other tools agreed within the Antarctic Treaty system as a dynamic model for the identification of areas that could be designated as Antarctic Specially Protected Areas within the systematic environmental-geographic framework referred to in Article 3(2) of Annex V of the Protocol;

- requested the Antarctic Treaty Secretariat to make the spatial data layer representing the Antarctic Conservation Biogeographic Regions available via its website;

- reiterated its agreement that Members should encourage the further collection and timely submission of spatially explicit biological data;

- recognised the relevance of the Antarctic Conservation Biogeographic Regions to its work to address non-native species risks, particularly the risk of transfer of species between locations in Antarctica; and

- agreed to incorporate the attached 'Map of Antarctica showing the 15 Antarctic Conservation Biogeographic Regions' into the CEP Non-Native Species Manual, and to identify opportunities to utilise the Antarctic Conservation Biogeographic Regions to manage non-native species risks.

CEP Advice for the ATCM

(187) The Committee recommends that the ATCM adopt the Antarctic Conservation Biogeographic Regions by means of a Resolution.

(188) The Russian Federation introduced WP 35, *Proposals on preparation of revised management plans of Antarctic Specially Protected and Antarctic Specially Managed Areas*, which proposed that, in reviewing any management plans for ASPAs or ASMAs primarily designated to protect living values, the proponent Party should submit to the CEP a report with the results of a scientific monitoring programme on the state of those values.

(189) The Russian Federation expressed the view that scientific monitoring was necessary to enable objective decisions with respect to management plans. In addition to anthropogenic threats, the Antarctic ecosystem was very sensitive and would react to a range of external factors. This necessitated the collection of objective data to detect long-term changes in the biological values being protected and to ensure the initial values continue to warrant protection.

(190) As an example of an existing long-term monitoring plan, the Russian Federation cited CCAMLR's Conservation Measure in relation to marine protected areas, which provided protection for a defined period and which could be extended if an extension was supported by scientific monitoring. The Russian Federation proposed that a similar approach be used by the CEP.

(191) While Members agreed with the need for monitoring of protected areas over the long-term to ensure that protection remained effective, some expressed concern that a compulsory system could compel access to protected areas, which could compromise the values being protected. Some Members also expressed concern that compulsory monitoring might discourage management plan revision, if compliance might be problematic.

(192) The Committee thanked the Russian Federation for its work and reiterated the importance of long-term monitoring of biological values both for the detection of long-term change and to confirm that the values to be protected are still relevant. However, Members expressed concern that in those cases

where remote monitoring may not be feasible visitation may affect the values of the site, requiring monitoring could be counter-productive.

(193) The Russian Federation, acknowledging Members' reservations to its proposal at this stage, expressed its intention to continue work on this matter.

(194) Australia introduced IP 26, *Analyses of the Antarctic Protected Areas System Using Spatial Information*, which updated the CEP on Australia's acquisition of a comprehensive dataset of spatial information representing the boundaries of all ASPAs and ASMAs, and informed the CEP of the availability of this dataset on the Secretariat's website. Australia presented examples of how the dataset could assist in assessing and further developing the Antarctic protected areas system, and support other CEP activities.

(195) The Committee thanked Australia for acquiring the data set and making it freely available and noted the utility of the information for supporting a systematic approach to area protection and management. Members expressed their gratitude to Australia for sharing this dataset, and indicated their intention to use the resource to complement their work. Argentina reserved the right to review nomenclature used on the Secretariat website.

Item 8: Conservation of Antarctic Flora and Fauna

8a) Quarantine and Non-native Species

(196) SCAR introduced WP 5, *Outcomes of the International Polar Year Programme: Aliens in Antarctica*, accompanied by BP 1, *Continent-wide risk assessment for the establishment of non-indigenous species in Antarctica*, which together reported on the assessment of the risks of the establishment of non-native species, and which concluded that the highest current risk is posed to the Western Antarctic Peninsula coast and the islands off the coast of the Peninsula.

(197) The report concluded that by 2100 the risk of the establishment of non-native species would continue to be highest in the Antarctic Peninsula area, but as a result of climate change would also increase substantially in the coastal, ice-free areas to the west of the Amery Ice Shelf and to a lesser extent in the Ross Sea region. SCAR recommended that the CEP: (i) include the spatially explicit, activity-differentiated risk assessments in further development of strategies to mitigate the risks posed by terrestrial

non-native species; (ii) develop a surveillance strategy for areas at high risk of non-native species establishment; and (iii) give additional attention to the risks posed by intra-Antarctic transfer of propagules.

(198) SCAR informed the Committee that research indicated the average seed load during the International Polar Year (IPY) 2007-09 period was 9.5 seeds per person, and approximately 70,000 seeds arrived in Antarctica during the first summer of the IPY, with scientists, science-support and tourism-support personnel having higher loads than tourists.

(199) In response to a question from Norway, SCAR commented that while the current analyses focussed on vascular plants, the assessment had broader implications. SCAR saw value in further research on other biological groups and on methods for identifying natural colonisation.

(200) Several Members informed the Committee of national efforts to mitigate non-native species risks. The United States mentioned that they will report at CEP XVI on their experience in terms of management against intra-continental transfer of non-native species.

(201) IAATO indicated that it would encourage surveillance for non-native species by operators, and said it had launched a communications campaign directed at field staff, who had been identified as major seed carriers.

(202) The Committee thanked SCAR and emphasised that this subject was of major interest to the CEP, including aspects relating to the increasing risks due to climate change, and the further development of the Non-native Species Manual.

(203) The Committee endorsed the recommendations of WP 5, and agreed:

- to include the spatially explicit, activity-differentiated risk assessments in further development of strategies to mitigate the risks posed by terrestrial non-native species;

- in collaboration with SCAR, COMNAP, IAATO, the IUCN and Parties, to develop a surveillance strategy for areas at high risk of non-native species establishment as identified by the Aliens in Antarctica project. Such a strategy should include a mechanism to differentiate natural from anthropogenic colonizations (see Hughes & Convey 2012; ATCM XXXIII WP 15 *Guidance for visitors and environmental managers following the discovery of a suspected non-native species in the terrestrial and freshwater Antarctic environment;* ATCM XXXIII IP 44 *Suggested framework and considerations for scientists attempting to determine the colonisation status of newly discovered terrestrial or freshwater species within the Antarctic Treaty Area*).

- to give additional attention, in collaboration with its partners, to the risks posed by intra-Antarctic transfer of propagules, given that such assessments only formed a small part of the Aliens in Antarctica project.

(204) The Committee warmly welcomed SCAR's WP 6, *Reducing the Risk of Inadvertent Non-Native Species Introductions Associated with Fresh Fruit and Vegetable Importation to Antarctica,* and confirmed that prevention of the introduction of non-native species is a high priority for Members.

(205) The Committee endorsed the two recommendations of WP 6 and agreed to:

- encourage Parties to implement the COMNAP/SCAR checklists for supply chain managers, and

- investigate further methods to reduce the risk of non-native species introductions to Antarctica associated with fresh food.

(206) Australia introduced WP 25 rev.1, *Guidelines to minimise the risks of non-native species and disease associated with Antarctic hydroponics facilities,* jointly submitted with France, which responded to the request by CEP XIV for discussion of best practice in the use of such facilities.

(207) Several Members commended the proposed guidelines. The United Kingdom expressed interest in further information on pests occurring in hydroponic units and in the availability of a risk assessment that takes into consideration the location of the facility and the susceptibility of the surrounding ecosystem to colonisation by common pest species.

(208) Japan also requested that the ATS compile all relevant guidelines, including past guidelines, and make these available to Parties via the website.

(209) Following a suggestion by SCAR, the Committee agreed that the guidelines should be amended to include a reference to floor level insect traps. This minor change was included in the draft guidelines during the meeting.

(210) The Committee agreed to include the proposed revised *Guidelines to minimise the risks of non-native species and disease associated with Antarctic hydroponics facilities* in the Non-Native Species Manual.

(211) Spain presented IP 13, *Colonisation status of the non-native grass* Poa pratensis *at Cierva Point, Danco Coast, Antarctic Peninsula*, jointly prepared with Argentina and the United Kingdom, and noted the need to eradicate this non-native species as soon as possible.

(212) Australia encouraged the authors to report on the success of the attempts to eradicate the plant, noting that their experience may help inform actions to respond to other non-native species introductions, as outlined in IP 29. In response to a query from the Chair regarding the eradication method and the potential existence of other non-native species underneath the roots of the grass, the United Kingdom clarified that they had not yet developed a method of eradication and that other Parties' advice on successful methods would be welcomed.

(213) The United Kingdom presented IP 29, *Colonisation status of known non-native species in the Antarctic terrestrial environment (updated 2012)*, which updated information presented to the CEP in 2010 and 2011 on the colonisation status of known non-native species in the Antarctic terrestrial environment. While the information indicated that there had been no attempts to eradicate any of the known non-native species in the past year, SCAR and South Africa referred to eradication programmes underway in associated and dependent systems in the sub-Antarctic, which may provide useful lessons for the Antarctic.

(214) Several Members and ASOC expressed appreciation for the updated information, expressed their concern that the efforts to date had not halted the introduction of new non-native species or the expansion of those species already established, and reaffirmed the need for Members to increase their collaborative efforts to address this issue. It was also noted that one method of dispersal of non-native species was through their use by native species (eg, skuas using grasses for nests).

(215) Other papers submitted under this Item included:

- BP 1, *Continent-wide risk assessment for the establishment of non-indigenous species in Antarctica.*

8b) Specially Protected Species

(216) No papers were submitted under this Agenda item.

8c) Other Annex II Matters

(217) Germany presented IP 20, *Evaluation of the "Strategic assessment of the risk posed to marine mammals by the use of airguns in the Antarctic Treaty area"*. Germany informed that this evaluation is available at *www. umweltbundesamt.de/antarktis-e/archiv/evaluation_airguns_antarctic.pdf*, and invited Members to comment on this evaluation.

(218) SCAR presented IP 21, *Anthropogenic Sound in the Southern Ocean: an Update*, which responded to the request of CEP XIV for an overview of research developments regarding the potential impacts of anthropogenic sound in the Southern Ocean. SCAR also informed the Committee of publication of a substantial scientific synthesis on the subject by the Subsidiary Body on Scientific and Technological Advice of the Convention on Biological Diversity (*The impacts of underwater noise on marine and coastal biodiversity and habitats*, UNEP/CBD/SBSTTA/16/INF/12).

(219) Germany raised some further points. Noting that SCAR referred to the important Southhall review of 2007 with respect to Temporary Threshold Shift (TTS), it was important to recognise that more recent publications (by Lucke in 2009 and by Popov in 2011) demonstrated that for "high frequency whales" (whales communicating in high frequencies) the thresholds are significantly below those extrapolated by Southall, which therefore requires an exclusion zone for seismic surveys up to several kilometres. So far, no accepted threshold for TTS exists.

(220) In addition the present international focus had changed from injury to disturbance (eg, Second International Conference on Noise on Aquatic Life 2010 in Cork). The third conference will take place in August 2013 in Budapest, Hungary. Moreover, a lot of research has recently dealt with behavioural changes due to acoustic disturbance. For example, for beaked whales, eg, Tyack *et al.* (2011) suggested a disturbance threshold of 142 dB SEL, which is much lower than any value used so far by regulators to define disturbance, Germany suggested that it might be helpful to include an update on the work to the Population Consequences of Acoustic Disturbance (PCAD) model.

(221) In conclusion, Germany emphasised, that anthropogenic sound can have far reaching effects and poorly understood impacts on the marine environment. Germany agreed with SCAR's conclusions that policies for the region of the Antarctic Treaty would benefit very much from further research in the Southern Ocean. Lastly, Germany informed the Members about a new German research project to foster a better understanding of the impact of masking on Antarctic whales, the results of which will be presented to CEP.

(222) ASOC thanked Germany and also SCAR for their documents. In particular, ASOC thanked Germany for consistently bringing the issue of noise in the Antarctic to the attention to the CEP, and also in this instance for using strategic and precautionary perspectives to address risks to marine mammals resulting from the use of airguns. ASOC urged Members to take into consideration the recommendations in IP20 from Germany (regarding appropriate EIAs and consideration of technological alternatives for the collection of seismic measuring data).

(223) The Committee noted with interest the information from Germany and SCAR, and requested regular updates on further research in this area from SCAR and Members.

(224) SCAR agreed to provide updates on this issue, including substantive new data when it is available, to the Committee. In response to a query from the Russian Federation, SCAR suggested the impact of wind turbine noise on humans might be best examined within the joint SCAR-COMNAP Expert Group on Human Biology and Medicine.

(225) SCAR presented IP 35, *Antarctic Conservation for the 21st Century: Background, progress, and future directions*, reporting on initial steps undertaken by SCAR, New Zealand and IUCN on the development of an integrated and comprehensive future strategy for the conservation of Antarctica, and the associated and dependent ecosystems.

(226) In response to a query from the Netherlands, SCAR confirmed that it had taken the question of Antarctic conservation values into consideration within the SCAR Social Science Action Group, and with prominent experts in this area. ASOC noted that the focus of the strategy appeared to be on biodiversity values and hoped that this would be expanded to include non-living elements as they cover a large proportion of the Antarctic area.

(227) The Committee expressed its keen interest in the steps taken to date in this respect, and a number of Members offered to maintain collaborative engagement in the work.

Item 9: Environmental Monitoring and Report

(228) The United Kingdom introduced WP 7, *Remote sensing for monitoring Antarctic Specially Protected Areas: use of multispectral and hyperspectral data for monitoring Antarctic vegetation*, which highlighted ongoing efforts to make wider use of satellite and airborne remote sensing methods to monitor ASPAs and the wider Antarctic environment.

(229) Members expressed strong interest in this technique of data collection and opportunities to exchange information and collaborate. Useful information in this respect could include: the remote sensing data method and knowledge that was used to compile a vegetation map of Japan; Chile's flora research projects in the Antarctic Peninsula region; Norway's remote sensing data on vegetation in the high Arctic; France's remote sensing projects programmes in the Kerguelen Islands, which address validity issues of ground truthing; and Australia's high resolution vegetation remote sensing projects in East Antarctica, specifically moss beds at Casey Station and within ASPA 135.

(230) The United Kingdom welcomed the useful comments and offers of information, and clarified that it was also conducting ground-truthing measurements. Additional queries that could be addressed included China's suggestion that moisture content in soil and vegetation should be kept in mind while collecting hyperspectral data, and India's caution about comparing the data methods to examine Arctic tundra vegetation with those for Eastern Antarctic small lichens and mosses.

(231) The Committee:

i.   Acknowledged the significant value offered by the combination of satellite and aerial monitoring as a new technique for gathering detailed evidence of vegetation change, linked to localised climate change;;

ii. Encouraged Parties with work programmes related to vegetation change to consider collaboration with the UK in further developing and applying these monitoring techniques; in particular to identify particular geographic areas or scientific programmes suitable for these techniques;

    iii. Invited Parties to comment on the methodology and to share their experiences of applying similar techniques.

(232) Germany introduced WP 18, *Penguin monitoring via remote sensing*, and referred to IP 46, *Pilot study on monitoring climate-induced changes in penguin colonies in the Antarctic using satellite images*, referring the Committee to the available study at *www.uba.de/uba-info-medien-e/4283. html*.

(233) Germany also outlined the results of an informal expert meeting held in May 2012 in Germany, which recommended that the further development of penguin monitoring via remote sensing should be a high priority, and should involve relevant programmes such as CCAMLR's Ecosystem Monitoring Programme and the *Southern Ocean Observing System* (SOOS).

(234) China, Japan, Australia, the United States and Argentina shared information on their penguin research and the use of remote sensing.

(235) The Committee agreed that Germany would coordinate and lead an informal intersessional contact group on the topic of remote sensing as an additional tool for monitoring Antarctic penguin populations, which would liaise with CCAMLR and report to the CEP XVI.

(236) New Zealand introduced WP 20, *Establishing a monitoring programme to assess changes in vegetation at two Antarctic Specially Protected Areas*, which reported on simple and fast techniques using GIS analysis for monitoring vegetation changes at fine scales in protected areas, noting that GIS analysis techniques provided a simple and fast method for monitoring of such changes, and which could be expanded to other protected areas. New Zealand noted that this method could assist in monitoring climate change effects on Antarctic species' distribution and abundance, in accordance with ATME (2010) Recommendations 24 and 27.

(237) A number of Members commended New Zealand's use of GIS monitoring techniques as an important method for monitoring the impacts of climate change that had a broad applicability to sites across Antarctica, and looked forward to being informed of future developments.

(238) China, the United States, and the United Kingdom noted that consistency was important when utilising remote sensing and GIS techniques in measuring biological diversity in the Antarctic, and that they would share New Zealand's method with their scientists. China offered to share information on its development of a network of wireless sensors for remote monitoring of flora and fauna. Australia stated that it had a long-term vegetation monitoring vegetation study at ASPA 135, near Casey Station, which could contribute to to a continent-wide network of sites.

(239) In light of the positive response to using GIS techniques in protected areas, Russia referred to its recommendation to make monitoring compulsory when revising management plans of ASPAs, ASMAs, and HSMs (in WP 35). Other Members expressed the view that compulsory monitoring was inappropriate, because some sites were too sensitive or remote.

(240) The Committee:

   i. Acknowledged the potential use of GIS techniques as a method for monitoring changes in species distribution and abundance at fine scales, which could be coupled with remote sensing technologies for monitoring changes at macro scales for both species and the environment;

   ii. Agreed to establish a network of sites for monitoring species distribution and abundance, with priority afforded to ASPAs designated for their flora and/or fauna diversity and abundance, where monitoring can occur during the management plan review process; and

   iii. Recognised the value of applying consistent monitoring methodologies at ASPAs so that changes in species diversity and abundance can be compared continent wide to obtain a more comprehensive understanding of climate change effects in Antarctica.

(241) Chile introduced WP 55, *New records of the Presence of Human Associated Microorganisms in the Antarctic Marine Environment,* informing the Committee of new scientific information on the presence of human associated microorganisms from sewage treatment plant discharges in the Antarctic. Chile referred to research projects which reported the presence of a new case of extended spectrum β-lactamase in the Antarctic Peninsula region and the existence of *E. coli* resistant to antibiotics.

(242) In response to a query from Argentina, Chile confirmed that it may undertake future research into whether human associated microorganisms impacting on Antarctic biodiversity might be brought by other agents.

(243) A number of Members advised that they were also undertaking research relating to the impact of human associated microorganisms from waste water discharge, including the United States, which would report in the future on research concerning seasonal discharge monitoring at McMurdo Station in relation to the number of personnel fluctuation.

(244) The Committee agreed that Members should strengthen their precautionary monitoring of microbial activity in areas near sewage treatment plant discharges, and noted that COMNAP would consider the possibility of reviewing relevant information and guidelines concerning waste water management at its July 2012 Annual General Meeting.

(245) SCAR presented IP 2, *The Southern Ocean Observing System (SOOS)*, which provided an update on progress with the design and implementation of SOOS, a joint initiative of SCAR and the Scientific Committee on Oceanic Research, which had been launched in August 2011.

(246) The Committee expressed its strong support for the programme, noting that it would generate fundamental data to aid understanding of the Southern Ocean, its associated ecosystems relationship with other oceans, and its role in climate change. Several Members indicated their willingness to participate, including Australia, which is supporting the SOOS office in Hobart, and the Russian Federation, whose first stage of a research project to collate data from a large number of sources across all oceans could have synergies with SOOS. India extended an invitation to national programmes to join its annual Southern Ocean Expeditions in the Indian Ocean sector.

(247) The Committee expressed its strong appreciation for the high quality and extremely valuable work of SCAR, and noted its interest in forthcoming results from the SOOS.

(248) SCAR presented IP 40 rev.1, *SCAR Products available to support the deliberations of the ATCM*, prepared in response to a request from CEP XIV, and noted that details of the products can be found at *www.scar.org/ researchgroups/productsandservices/*.

(249) Argentina noted that it regularly used these valuable resources and urged other Members to do so. Norway highlighted that this was an excellent example of the type of information and tools that might be available via the proposed Antarctic Environments Portal. The United Kingdom reaffirmed its commitment to serve as a coordinating body for three of the eleven products listed.

(250) The United States welcomed SCAR's increased involvement in recent years in topics central to the work of the CEP and congratulated SCAR for the high quality of the material produced in response to requests for advice from the CEP.

(251) Chile introduced IP 76, *Antarctic Environmental Monitoring Centre* which presented part of the activities developed by the monitoring project of the Chilean Antarctic Programme.

(252) ASOC presented IP 53, *Antarctic Treaty System Follow-up to Vessel Incidents in Antarctic Waters*, which was concerned with shortcomings in the current vessel incident reporting. Welcoming the information, the Committee noted that the paper would be discussed further under ATCM Agenda Item 10.

Item 10: Inspection Reports

(253) The Russian Federation and the United States presented IP 47, *United States-Russian Federation Report of Inspection*, which provided information on observations and conclusions of joint inspections at Scott Base (New Zealand), Concordia Station (France and Italy), and Mario Zucchelli Station (Italy). This was the first inspection ever undertaken by the Russian Federation Antarctic Programme, and the first joint inspection for the United States. The inspection team appreciated the warm welcomed from station staff, particularly because the process required staff to drop their normal tasks at short notice in order to facilitate the inspection.

(254) The Committee thanked the Russian Federation and the United States for the high quality report, and noted that the inspection mechanism was vital in underpinning the practical application of the Environmental Protocol.

(255) While France and Italy were delighted that Concordia Station was noted as an exemplary model for water treatment measures and for joint management collaboration, they noted their surprise at comments on disparity of salaries between French and Italian support staff, which they considered not relevant

to the application of the Environmental Protocol. In response, the United States remarked that in inspecting the efficiency of operations at jointly operated stations, the issue of salary disparity between national programmes had been raised as a point which caused some tensions.

(256) In response to report comments concerning the implementation of the Environmental Protocol, Italy informed that it was one of the few Parties that had ratified Annex VI, demonstrating its great interest in conservation of Antarctic environmental values. In effect since the beginning of Italian activities in 1986, environmental issues were addressed. Prevention and adequate personnel selection and training were the key tools that helped Italy to be compliant with the requirements set in the Protocol. Italy recognised that a legal difficulty existed and informed the Parties that a working group would be established to reach a satisfactory solution, stressing the fact that, as outlined in the inspection report, compliance was provided.

(257) Concerning the activities in Concordia Station and the questions about EPICA borehole, Italy informed that this borehole is still of high scientific interest and was object of a CEE. The information about the drop of drilling fluid level in the report was incorrect and was a problem in the measurement. The actual level didn't change since the beginning

(258) If needed, Italy could implement, in cooperation with France a monitoring programme. Italy stressed that this issue is likely to concern all the other national Antarctic programmes that are running or ran in the past drilling activities, so a common management procedure could be found.

(259) Speaking in his position as Chairman of the EPICA Project, Prof. Dr. Heinz Miller of Germany clarified that Concordia Station was finished after the completion of the EPICA project, and that the drilling project started in 1995, before the Environmental Protocol entered into force. Therefore, there had been no legal requirement to complete a CEE or EIA. France had, however, completed an EIA, which included the intention to keep the Dome C borehole open for a number of years beyond the completion of the project to facilitate further research of ice sheets. Measurements were taken every two years, and the borehole was accessible to the international community. The fluid used in the Dome C borehole was not kerosene, but the non-toxic and biodegradable solvent EXXOL-D40, and was the same fluid used in the second EPICA borehole in Dronning Maud Land, which had had a CEE considered by the CEP. Freon was also used in the boreholes as it was the

only product available at the time which would allow for drilling down to great depths.

(260) New Zealand thanked the Russian Federation and the United States for inspecting Scott Base, and noted that it would take full account of the report.

(261) ASOC noted that while the inspection had shown the three stations were very efficient and well run, it had also raised some general issues relating to the ageing of facilities and the long-term effects of scientific projects, thus highlighting the need for long-term monitoring of the impacts of all station activities.

(262) The United Kingdom warmly welcomed inspections of its Antarctic research stations by other Parties.

(263) Australian delegate Mr Ewan McIvor, reflecting on his recent visit to Scott Base, congratulated New Zealand for the broad range of environmental initiatives in place, including the wind farm and waste management and waste water treatment practices, and a significant scientific focus on questions of direct relevance to the Committee.

(264) ASOC presented IP 59, *Review of the Implementation of the Environmental Protocol: Inspections by Parties (Article 14)*, prepared jointly with UNEP, which focused on the scope of inspections carried out by Parties under Article 14 of the Environmental Protocol. The analysis reported an overall increase in the number of official inspections and inspected facilities and sites since the Environmental Protocol came into force, while non-active research stations, other land sites, and tourist ships, sites and onsite activities had received few inspections. New Zealand noted the usefulness of such overviews, and encouraged Parties to refer to the analysis when planning future inspections.

(265) Japan and Australia encouraged inspected Parties to report back on measures they had taken in response to recommendations in inspection reports, and in this respect commended India's BP 22, *Measures Adopted at Maitri Station on the Recommendations of Recent Visit of Japanese Inspection Team*.

(266) Belgium emphasised the importance of the inspection mechanism for assessing compliance with the Environmental Protocol, and expressed its willingness to participate in an inspection in the future.

(267) Noting its offer at CEP XIV to provide updates to subsequent meetings, the Russian Federation informed the CEP of progress made in response to inspections of Molodezhnaya Station, Druzhnaya IV Station, Soyuz Station, Leningradskaya Station and Vostok Station carried out by Australia in 2010 and 2011, and reconfirmed its strong commitment to the Environmental Protocol.

(268) The Russian Federation explained that Molodezhnaya Station was the largest Soviet-era station in Antarctica, and that in 1996 it had been converted to a seasonal station where scientific work and environmental protection measures were carried out annually. The Russian Federation had conducted a review in 2010, which considered the future of its national programme through to 2020, and this had concluded Molodezhnaya Station would become an active site in 2014. This meant that from 2014, environmental protection activities would increase.

(269) Regarding the Druzhnaya IV Station, the Russian Federation informed the Committee that it was a summer station, which had existed for twenty years, and environmental issues had accumulated during this time. The Russian Federation was in the process of addressing concerns and planned to bring in additional equipment to accelerate clean-up activities.

(270) The Russian Federation acknowledged environmental issues at Soyuz and Leningradskaya stations, which it planned to address in cooperation with Members. Soyuz Station had been temporarily unoccupied and had suffered wind damage, but would now be re-established. The Russian Federation expressed dismay that Leningradskaya Station had been damaged by unauthorised visits.

(271) Noting concerns about Vostok Station, the Russian Federation informed the CEP that modernisation plans would commence shortly.

(272) In response, Australia reiterated its thanks to the Russian Federation for its cooperation and warm welcome during the inspections, and welcomed the information on the considerable efforts made by the Russian Federation following the inspections, despite the challenges posed by the Antarctic environment.

Item 11: Cooperation with other Organisations

(273) SCAR presented IP 1, *The Scientific Committee on Antarctic Research (SCAR) Annual Report 2011/12.*

(274) COMNAP presented IP 3, *The Annual Report for 2011 of the Council of Managers of National Antarctic Programmes*.

(275) CCAMLR presented IP 28, *Report by the SC-CAMLR Observer to the Fifteenth Meeting of the Committee for Environmental Protection*, which provided an update of discussions in recent CCAMLR forums on the five issues of common interest to the CEP and SC-CAMLR. These were identified in 2009 at the joint CEP/SC-CAMLR workshop as: a) climate change and the Antarctic marine environment, b) biodiversity and non-native species in the Antarctic marine environment, c) Antarctic species requiring special protection, d) spatial marine management and protected areas, and e) ecosystem and environmental monitoring.

(276) CCAMLR also drew the Committee's attention to recent technical workshops on the development of representative systems of MPAs, and forthcoming CCAMLR meetings. He further noted progress on capacity building, with the recent awarding of the first Scientific Scholarship, designed to assist early career scientists to participate in the work of the CCAMLR Scientific Committee and its working groups, and the launch of the collaborative Antarctic and Southern Ocean Internship scheme, which aimed to provide students with an opportunity to gain experience in the work of a multilateral management and conservation organisation.

(277) In light of the relevance of such reports to a range of Committee agenda items, New Zealand and the United States suggested that in future, SCAR, COMNAP and CCAMLR could be invited to present their reports earlier in the Committee meeting.

(278) The Committee welcomed the reports from SCAR, COMNAP and CCAMLR and agreed to put the agenda item 'cooperation with other organisations' on the first day of its meeting agenda next year, given that many of the issues reported were relevant across the committee's agenda.

(279) Dr Polly Penhale, United States, was nominated as CEP Observer to SC-CAMLR-XXXI, Hobart, Australia, 22-26 October, 2012.

(280) Ms Verónica Vallejos, Chile, was nominated as CEP Observer to XXXII SCAR Delegates Meeting, Portland, Oregon, 13-25 July 2012

Item 12: Repair and Remediation of Environmental damage

(281) Australia introduced WP 21, *An Antarctic Clean-Up Manual*, jointly prepared with the United Kingdom, and referred to the supporting information in IP 6. The draft Clean-Up Manual contained guidance to assist Parties to address their obligations under Annex III to the Environmental Protocol to clean up past waste disposal sites on land and abandoned work sites of past activities, and could be regularly updated based on the knowledge and experience of Members and Observers (as is done for the Non-Native Species Manual).

(282) Australia noted that, while many Members had reported to CEP meetings on clean-up activities, there was no central and readily accessible guidance to assist Parties with further efforts to clean-up past waste disposal sites and facilities no longer in use.

(283) Several Members, commenting on their own National Antarctic Programmes' experiences with station clean-ups, welcomed the stimulating papers and expressed their willingness to share lessons learned. Topics that could be useful discussion points during the further development of the draft manual included specific terminology and targets with respect to risk-based management, options for remediation techniques, and the possibility of recycling materials recovered from abandoned sites.

(284) Italy noted that the definition of "clean-up" provided in WP 21 seemed not to include types of accidental contamination other than fuel spill. Italy noted that in other regions risk assessment and environmental quality targets were based on potential impacts on human health.

(285) Italy reminded the Committee that ecotoxicological aspects related to such clean-up activity and their potential impact on human health should be considered.

(286) The United States agreed that the evaluation of associated risks is important and also reminded the Committee that recycling should also be considered in any clean-up operations.

(287) A number of Members considered that the manual prepared by Australia was ready for adoption at this meeting and The Committee reiterated that repair and remediation was of utmost importance.

(288) ASOC thanked Australia and the UK for WP 21 noting that an environmental clean-up manual would help make clean ups more effective and lead to greater compatibility of standards across different Antarctic programmes.

(289) The Committee decided to continue to develop the draft Clean-Up Manual through informal discussion during the intersessional period and to produce an updated document, incorporating comments and suggestions from Members, Observers and Experts, to CEP XVI. The United States noted that, in the interim, Members could use the draft manual when planning and undertaking repair and remediation work.

(290) Australia introduced WP 26, *Examples to illustrate key environmental issues related to the practicality of repair or remediation of environmental damage*, which provided a minor update to a similar submission to ATCM XXXIV (WP 28), addressing ATCM Decision 4 (2010), and referred to supporting information in IP 25. Reflecting on the request from the ATCM for advice on this issue, and the fact that the CEP had made the issue one of the highest priorities in its Five-Year Work Plan, Australia presented eight points for consideration in the CEP's response to the ATCM.

(291) The Committee thanked Australia for its work and for the examples provided in IP 25, and encouraged Members to continue to share their experiences with repair and remediation.

(292) Italy emphasised that, considering the particular sensitivity of the Antarctic environment, it would be a challenge defining acceptable risk levels specific to the Antarctic environment.

(293) In response to Italy's suggestion that other *in situ* remediation technologies were available such as In situ Chemical Oxidation, Australia agreed that *in situ* methods offered various environmental and cost benefits and that other technologies could also be appropriate in addition to the examples of repair and remediation provided in WP 21 and BP 11.

(294) Members agreed that the eight points in WP 26 could be drawn on to guide Members' work, and provided a good starting point for discussion during the intersessional period.

(295) The Committee agreed that an ICG would be a suitable means of advancing its consideration of Decision 4 (2010), with a view to presenting its initial advice to ATCM XXXVI.

(296) The Committee welcomed the offer by Dr Neil Gilbert, New Zealand, to convene the group and agreed the following Terms of Reference:

- Drawing on ATCM XXXV/WP 26 *Environmental issues related to the practicality of repair and remediation of environmental damage* (Australia) and, as appropriate, other papers submitted to CEP XV on the subject of repair and remediation of environmental damage:

  - prepare a draft response to Decision 4 (2010), in which the ATCM requested the CEP to 'consider environmental issues related to the practicality of repair and remediation of environmental damage in the circumstances in Antarctica;

  - where appropriate, seek to identify and present examples to help illustrate matters raised in the draft advice; and

  - report to CEP XVI on the outcomes of this work.

(297) COMNAP introduced WP 62, *Repair or Remediation of Environmental Damage: COMNAP report on its experience*, which summarised the learning outcomes from the 2006 Waste Management in Antarctica Workshop hosted by COMNAP, and reminded the CEP of examples of national programmes clean-up efforts.

(298) COMNAP underlined the important role of recycling and reuse of materials, and encouraged Members to consider possible uses by other national programmes of discarded materials.

(299) In connection with an operation carried out by personnel of Belgrano II Station (77°52'S and 34°37'W), Argentina informed the Committee that the incident occurred due to the incorrect interpretation of operational procedures for waste management. It noted that it had already made plans for the recovery of the drums during the next Antarctic summer season.

(300) ASOC introduced IP 57, *Repair or Remediation of Environmental Damage*, which reviewed key issues associated with the repair or remediation of environmental damage, and concluded that overall there was a general

understanding of what constitutes environmental damage in Antarctica, which includes past activities, ongoing activities, proposed activities and incidents and accidents. ASOC stressed that repair and remediation of environmental damage was a requirement of the Protocol and should be carried out to the maximum extent possible (with assessment and monitoring of damage, suitable recording and reporting as a minimum), while taking into consideration the potential adverse environmental effects. ASOC further noted that the points raised by Australia in WP 28 at ATCM XXXIV covered the most important aspects of repair and remediation of environmental damage.

(301) The Chair thanked ASOC for its contribution to this topic, and noted that the Committee would welcome ASOC's contribution to any further work on this issue.

(302) Other papers submitted under this Item were:

- BP 11, *Clean-up Techniques for Antarctica* (Australia)
- BP 12, *Clean-up of a fuel spill near Lake Dingle, Vestfold Hills* (Australia)
- BP 13, *Development of environmental quality standards for the management of contaminated sites in Antarctica* (Australia)
- BP 14, *Assessment, monitoring and remediation of old Antarctic waste disposal sites: the Thala Valley example at Casey station* (Australia)
- BP 38, *Removal of scrap from Presidente Eduardo Frei Montalva Station, King George Island* (Chile)

Item 13: General Matters

(303) COMNAP presented IP 32, *Survey of National Antarctic Programmes on Oil Spill Contingency Planning,* which included the results of a survey undertaken during the 2011/12 intersessional period, to update a survey carried out in 1996. While most Antarctic stations had oil spill contingency plans in place, many of these had not been updated in recent years. COMNAP noted that this issue would be addressed at their forthcoming meeting in July 2012.

(304) The Committee thanked COMNAP for the survey and urged Parties to continue improving their contingency plans within the framework of their National Antarctic Programmes.

Item 14: Election Officers

(305) The Committee elected Dr Yves Frenot from France for a second two-year term as CEP Chair and congratulated Dr Frenot for his reappointment to the role.

(306) The Committee elected Ms Birgit Njaastad from Norway as Vice-Chair and congratulated Ms Njaastad for her appointment to the role.

(307) The Committee thanked Ewan McIvor from Australia for serving as Vice-Chair for two terms and for convening the SGMP.

Item 15: Preparation for the Next Meeting

(308) The Committee adopted the Provisional Agenda for CEP XVI (Appendix 2).

Item 16: Adoption of the Report

(309) The Committee adopted its Report.

Item 17: Closing of the Meeting

(310) The Chair closed the Meeting on Friday 15th June 2012.

Annex 1

CEP XV Agenda and Summary of Documents

1. OPENING OF THE MEETING	
SP 1 rev. 1	*ATCM XXXV AND CEP XV AGENDA AND SCHEDULE*
SP 15	*CEP XV SUMMARY OF PAPERS*
2. ADOPTION OF THE AGENDA	
3. STRATEGIC DISCUSSION ON THE FUTURE WORK OF THE CEP	
WP 57 New Zealand, Australia & SCAR	*ANTARCTIC ENVIRONMENTS PORTAL.* This paper reports on the development of an online Antarctic Environments Portal, which aims to be the primary source of information on Antarctic environments, as an efficient means to strengthen the link between Antarctic science and policy, enhance the CEP's advisory role to the ATCM, facilitate SCAR's advisory role to the ATCM and CEP and assist in communicating information on Antarctic environments to the public.
4. OPERATION OF THE CEP	
SP 10 Secretariat	*REPORT OF THE INFORMAL CONTACT GROUP ON THE IMPROVEMENT OF THE EIES AND OTHER INFORMATION EXCHANGE MATTERS.* This document contains a report of the ICG on the improvement of the Electronic Information Exchange System convened by the Secretariat, a report on other improvements and on the current usage of the EIES, and unresolved questions concerning the EIES and the Information Exchange requirements which the Secretariat would like to address to the Meeting.
5. CLIMATE CHANGE IMPLICATIONS FOR THE ENVIRONMENT: STRATEGIC approach	
WP 33 Unite Kingdom & Norway	*RACER1 - 'RAPID ASSESSMENT OF CIRCUM-ARCTIC ECOSYSTEM RESILIENCE': A TOOL FROM THE ARCTIC TO ASSESS ECOSYSTEM RESILIENCE AND AREAS OF CONSERVATION IMPORTANCE, AND ITS POSSIBLE APPLICATION TO ANTARCTICA.* Following a recommendation of the ATME on Climate Change, this paper introduces WWF's Rapid Assessment of Circum-Arctic Ecosystem Resilience (RACER), a new tool that is being used in the Arctic to identify and mapping places of conservation importance on the basis of ecosystem resilience, and recommends that work be carried out to test the RACER methodology on a trial area in Antarctica to assess its applicability.

SP 8 Secretariat	*ACTIONS TAKEN BY THE CEP AND THE ATCM ON THE ATME RECOMMENDATIONS ON CLIMATE CHANGE.* This paper presents an update of actions taken by the ATCM and the CEP on the 30 Recommendations on climate Change agreed at the ATME on Climate Change in 2009.
IP 31 COMNAP	*BEST PRACTICE FOR ENERGY MANAGEMENT – GUIDANCE AND RECOMMENDATIONS.* In this IP COMNAP presents the results of a survey of National Antarctic Programmes on the status of implementation of the 2007 COMNAP guidelines for best practices on energy management, as recommended by Rec. 4 of the ATME on Climate Change.
IP 44 SCAR	*COMMUNICATING THE SCIENCE OF CLIMATE CHANGE.* This paper reports on SCAR's climate communications work, with a focus on the elements that need to be considered in the communication of Antarctic climate change science.
IP 45 SCAR	*ANTARCTIC CLIMATE CHANGE AND THE ENVIRONMENT: AN UPDATE.* This paper is the third update report to the ATCM since the publication of the SCAR Antarctic Climate Change and the Environment (ACCE) report (Turner *et al.*, 2009).
IP 58 rev. 1 ASOC, Australia & UK	*EARTH HOUR ANTARCTICA (2013).* In keeping with the objectives of WWF's global Earth Hour initiative, ASOC, Australia and the United Kingdom propose a coordinated continent-wide switch off of all non-essential lights at Antarctic research stations for Earth Hour on 30 March 2013, within all operational and safety constraints.
BP 17 New Zealand	*ENERGY EFFICIENCY AND CARBON REDUCTION INITIATIVES.* This paper provides background information on New Zealand's work on energy efficiency and efforts to reduce the carbon footprint of activities in Antarctica, consistent with the recommendations agreed at the ATME on Climate Change.

6. ENVIRONMENTAL IMPACT ASSESSMENT
a) Draft Comprehensive Environmental Evaluations

b) Other EIA Matters

WP 22 New Zealand	*ENVIRONMENTAL ASPECTS AND IMPACTS OF TOURISM AND NON-GOVERNMENTAL ACTIVITIES IN ANTARCTICA.* This paper presents the key findings and recommendations of the CEP Tourism Study led by New Zealand. It invites the Committee to consider options for forwarding the draft study (presented in IP33) to ATCM XXXV, or to further develop the study ahead of CEP XVI.

IP 33 New Zealand	*ENVIRONMENTAL ASPECTS AND IMPACTS OF TOURISM AND NON-GOVERNMENTAL ACTIVITIES IN ANTARCTICA.* This paper presents the study on the environmental aspects and impacts of tourism and non-governmental activities in Antarctica and supporting tables and data (see WP 22).
WP 34 Russia	*TECHNOLOGY FOR INVESTIGATING THE WATER LAYER OF SUBGLACIAL LAKE VOSTOK THROUGH THE ICE BOREHOLE 5G AT THE RUSSIAN ANTARCTIC VOSTOK STATION.* This paper informs on the methodology and operational steps to be put in place to undertake investigations of water stratums of Lake Vostok, which may commence as early as the 2014-15 season.
WP 53 Brazil	*COMANDANTE FERRAZ STATION: PROPOSED PLAN FOR THE DEMOLITION AND CONSTRUCTION OF ANTARCTIC EMERGENCY MODULES.* This paper outlines Brazil's plan for the construction and operation of Antarctic Emergency Modules (at the same location as the Comandante Ferraz Station). Furthermore, it proposes a plan for the demolition and removal of the main building, which was destroyed by a fire.
SP 6 rev.1 Secretariat	*ANNUAL LIST OF INITIAL ENVIRONMENTAL EVALUATIONS (IEE) AND COMPREHENSIVE ENVIRONMENTAL EVALUATIONS (CEE) PREPARED BETWEEN APRIL 1ST 2011 AND MARCH 31ST 2012.* The Secretariat will report on the list of IEEs and CEEs for the most recent reporting period.
IP 23 Republic of Korea	*FINAL COMPREHENSIVE ENVIRONMENTAL EVALUATION (CEE) FOR THE PROPOSED CONSTRUCTION AND OPERATION OF THE JANG BOGO STATION, TERRA NOVA BAY, ANTARCTICA.* This paper provides information on the Final CEE, including a summary of the responses to significant comments raised by CEP in relation to the Draft CEE and other major improvements and modifications from the Draft CEE.
IP 30 United Kingdom	*THE FINAL COMPREHENSIVE ENVIRONMENTAL EVALUATION (CEE) FOR THE PROPOSED EXPLORATION OF SUBGLACIAL LAKE ELLSWORTH, ANTARCTICA.* This paper notes that the Final CEE prepared by the United Kingdom, addresses comments on the Draft CEE received by the CEP, Parties and experts. A full version of the Final CEE is attached to the paper.
IP 41 Italy	*STARTING A FEASIBILITY STUDY FOR THE REALIZATION OF A GRAVEL RUNWAY NEAR MARIO ZUCCHELLI STATION.* Italy informs that this year it is starting a study aimed to assess the technical, economical and environmental feasibility of a gravel runway in the vicinity of Mario Zuccheli Station. The paper reports that this runway would be an important facility which could also be helpful in supporting other National Antarctic Programmes in the area.

IP 43 India	ESTABLISHMENT AND OPERATION OF NEW INDIAN RESEARCH STATION *"BHARATI" AT LARSEMANN HILLS.* India informs that the second phase of the construction of Bharati Station started in November 2011, and that it was formally made operational on 18 March 2012. This paper describes the second and final phase of construction activities carried out during the austral summer of 2011-12.
IP 74 Russia	RESULTS OF RUSSIAN ACTIVITY FOR PENETRATING SUBGLACIAL LAKE VOSTOK IN THE SEASON *2011–12.* Russia informs on details of penetrating activity at Lake Vostok during the last summer season and the main results obtained. The paper informs that theoretical suggestions of Russian specialists about the physics of the processes at the drill contact with the lake water layer considered in the CEE process were confirmed in practice.
BP 36 Ecuador	SUMMARY OF AN ENVIRONMENTAL AUDIT AT THE ECUADORIAN STATION *VICENTE MALDONADO.* This paper informs on an environmental assessment process at Maldonado Station during the 2011-12 seasons.

7. AREA PROTECTION AND MANAGEMENT

a) Management Plans

i.   Draft management plans which had been reviewed by the Subsidiary Group on Management Plans

WP 14 Australia	SUBSIDIARY GROUP ON MANAGEMENT PLANS – REPORT ON *2011/12 INTERSESSIONAL WORK.* This paper reports on the work of the SGMP in accordance with the TORs #1 to #3 and recommends that the Committee approve the revised version of ASPA 140 *Parts of Deception Island* which is attached to this document.

ii.   Draft revised management plans which had not been reviewed by the Subsidiary Group on Management Plans

WP 2 Poland	REVISED MANAGEMENT PLAN FOR ANTARCTIC SPECIALLY PROTECTED AREA *(ASPA) No. 151 LIONS RUMP, KING GEORGE ISLAND, SOUTH SHETLAND ISLANDS.* Poland has conducted a review of the management plan for ASPA 151 and has determined that only minor amendments are required. Poland recommends that the CEP approve the revised management plan.
WP 3 Poland	REVISED MANAGEMENT PLAN FOR ANTARCTIC SPECIALLY PROTECTED AREA *(ASPA) No. 128 WESTERN SHORE OF ADMIRALTY BAY, KING GEORGE ISLAND, SOUTH SHETLAND ISLANDS.* Poland has conducted a review of the management plan for ASPA 128 and has determined that only minor amendments are required. Poland recommends that the CEP approve the revised management plan.

WP 8 United Kingdom	REVISION OF THE MANAGEMENT PLAN FOR ANTARCTIC SPECIALLY PRO- TECTED AREA (ASPA) NO. 129 ROTHERA POINT, ADELAIDE ISLAND. The UK has undertaken a review of the Management Plan for ASPA 129. It recommends that the CEP ask the SGMP to undertake an intersessional review and to report back to CEP XVI.
WP 9 United Kingdom	REVISION OF THE MANAGEMENT PLAN FOR ANTARCTIC SPECIALLY PROTECTED AREA (ASPA) NO. 109 MOE ISLAND, SOUTH ORKNEY ISLANDS. The UK has undertaken a review of the Management Plan for ASPA 109. It recommends that the CEP ask the SGMP to undertake an intersessional review and to report back to CEP XVI.
WP 10 United Kingdom	REVISION OF THE MANAGEMENT PLAN FOR ANTARCTIC SPECIALLY PROTECTED AREA (ASPA) NO. 111 SOUTHERN POWELL ISLAND AND ADJACENT ISLANDS, SOUTH ORKNEY ISLANDS. The UK has undertaken a major review of the Management Plan for ASPA 111. It recommends that the CEP ask the SGMP to undertake an intersessional review and to report back to CEP XVI.
WP 11 United Kingdom	REVISION OF THE MANAGEMENT PLAN FOR ANTARCTIC SPECIALLY PROTECTED AREA (ASPA) NO. 115 LAGOTELLERIE ISLAND, MARGUERITE BAY, GRAHAM LAND. The United Kingdom has undertaken a major review of the Management Plan for ASPA 115. It recommends that the CEP ask the SGMP to undertake an intersessional review and to report back to CEP XVI.
WP 12 United Kingdom	REVISION OF THE MANAGEMENT PLAN FOR ANTARCTIC SPECIALLY PROTECTED AREA (ASPA) NO. 110 LYNCH ISLAND, SOUTH ORKNEY ISLANDS. The UK has undertaken a review of the Management Plan for ASPA 110. It recommends that the CEP ask the SGMP to undertake an intersessional review and to report back to CEP XVI.
WP 42 Argentina, Chile, Norway, Spain, UK & USA	REVIEW OF THE MANAGEMENT PLAN FOR ASMA NO. 4: DECEPTION ISLAND. The Deception Island Management Group has conducted its first five-yearly review of the Management Plan for ASMA 4. The Group recommends that the CEP approve the attached revised Management Plans for these Areas.
WP 44 Argentina	REVISED MANAGEMENT PLAN FOR ANTARCTIC SPECIALLY PROTECTED AREA (ASPA) NO. 132 POTTER PENINSULA. Argentina has undertaken the review of the Management Plan for ASPA 132. Changes include minor adjustments to the boundaries, a more precise map and an updating in the description of the Area. Argentina asks that the CEP consider the review and decide if the revised version can be adopted at the meeting or if it needs to be considered intersessionally by the SGMP.

WP 52 Argentina & Chile	*REVIEW OF THE MANAGEMENT PLAN OF ANTARCTIC SPECIALLY PROTECTED AREA (ASPA) No. 133 HARMONY POINT.* Argentina and Chile have undertaken the review of ASPA 133. Changes include minor adjustments to the boundaries, a more precise map and an updating in the description of the Area. Argentina and Chile ask that the CEP consider the review and decide if the revised version can be adopted at the meeting or if it needs to be considered intersessionally by the SGMP.
WP 54 Chile	*REVISED MANAGEMENT PLAN FOR ANTARCTIC SPECIALLY PROTECTED AREA (ASPA) No. 145 PORT FOSTER, DECEPTION ISLAND, SOUTH SHETLAND ISLANDS.* Chile has conducted the first review of the Management Plan for ASPA 145, after the entry into force of Annex V to the Protocol. In view of the extensive modifications proposed to the revised plan, Chile requires of the SGMP a more detailed examination of the revised plan in the intersessional period.
WP 58 Chile	*MANAGEMENT PLAN FOR ANTARCTIC SPECIALLY PROTECTED AREA (ASPA) No. 112 COPPERMINE PENINSULA, ROBERT ISLAND, SOUTH SHETLAND ISLANDS.* Chile presents the Management Plan for ASPA 112 according to the format required by Annex V to the Protocol. Chile recommends that the Management Plan be considered by the SGMP during the intersessional period.
WP 60 Chile	*MANAGEMENT PLAN FOR ANTARCTIC SPECIALLY PROTECTED AREA (ASPA) No. 146 SOUTH BAY, DOUMER ISLAND, PALMER ARCHIPELAGO.* Chile presents the Management Plan for ASPA 146 according to the format required by Annex V to the Protocol. Chile recommends that the Management Plan be considered by the SGMP during the intersessional period.
WP 61 Chile	*MANAGEMENT PLAN FOR ANTARCTIC SPECIALLY PROTECTED AREA (ASPA) No. 144 'CHILE BAY' (DISCOVERY BAY), GREENWICH ISLAND, SOUTH SHETLAND ISLANDS.* Chile presents the Management Plan for ASPA 144 according to the format required by Annex V to the Protocol. Chile recommends that the Management Plan be considered by the SGMP during the intersessional period. (See also WP 42)

iii.   New draft management plans for protected/managed areas

WP 19 New Zealand	*THE PROPOSED DESIGNATION OF AN ANTARCTIC SPECIALLY PROTECTED AREA FOR HIGH ALTITUDE GEOTHERMAL AREAS OF THE ROSS SEA REGION.* New Zealand proposes the designation of a new ASPA comprising all high altitude geothermal areas in the Ross Sea region (at Mount Erebus, Mount Melbourne and Mount Rittmann). The proposal aims to represent a more strategic approach to protecting a rare environment type in Antarctica and to apply consistent measures to protect the highly sensitive and unique species assemblages to the same high standard in a single management plan.

WP 40 Italy & United States	PROPOSAL FOR A NEW ANTARCTIC SPECIALLY PROTECTED AREA AT CAPE WASHINGTON AND SILVERFISH BAY TERRA NOVA BAY, ROSS SEA. Italy and the United States propose the designation of a new ASPA in the northern part of Terra Nova Bay.
WP 41 United States	PROPOSAL FOR A NEW ANTARCTIC SPECIALLY PROTECTED AREA AT TAYLOR GLACIER AND BLOOD FALLS, TAYLOR VALLEY, MCMURDO DRY VALLEYS VICTORIA LAND. The United States proposes the establishment of a new ASPA at Taylor Glacier and Blood Falls to protect the area's unique biological and physical characteristics and high scientific and educational values. Increasing activity on the Taylor Glacier and recent ice-core drilling projects have highlighted the need to protect the Blood Falls environment as these activities have the potential to influence the unique microbial community and chemistry of the feature.

iv.　　Other matters relating to management plans for protected/managed areas

WP 14 Australia	SUBSIDIARY GROUP ON MANAGEMENT PLANS – REPORT ON 2011/12 INTERSESSIONAL WORK. This paper reports on the work of the SGMP in accordance with the TORs #4 and #5. The SGMP would welcome advice from the CEP regarding work to develop guidance for establishing ASMAs and for preparing and reviewing ASMA management plans. In accordance with the arrangements agreed by ATCM XXXI, the Committee may wish to consider appointing a new SGMP convener to serve in the role on the conclusion of CEP XV.
SP 7 Secretariat	STATUS OF ANTARCTIC SPECIALLY PROTECTED AREA AND ANTARCTIC SPECIALLY MANAGED AREA MANAGEMENT PLANS. This paper presents information on the status of ASPA and ASMA management plans according to the review requirements of Annex V to the Protocol.
IP 24 Republic of Korea	MANAGEMENT REPORT OF NARĘBSKI POINT (ASPA 171) AND ARDLEY ISLAND (ASPA 150) DURING THE 2011/2012 PERIOD. This paper presents a survey summary on ASPA 171 and its vicinity and ASPA 150 to achieve the objectives and principles of the ASPAs' management plans during the 2011/2012 period.
IP 38 IAATO	ESTABLISHING IAATO SAFETY ADVISORIES. This paper describes IAATO's establishment of a formalised internal Safety Advisory system. The Advisories are intended to enhance safety for operators in the Antarctic, thus ensuring that there is a readily accessible, searchable bank of 'local knowledge' information on both general matters and site-specific advice.

IP 61 Australia, India China, Romania & Russia	REPORT OF THE LARSEMANN HILLS ANTARCTIC SPECIALLY MANAGED AREA (ASMA) MANAGEMENT GROUP. Following the adoption of ASMA the Parties active in the ASMA established a Management Group to oversee the implementation of the Management Plan. This paper gives a brief report on the Management Group's activities during 2011-12.
IP 66 Brazil	WORKING PLAN PROPOSAL FOR THE REVIEW OF THE ADMIRALTY BAY ANTARCTIC SPECIALLY MANAGED AREA MANAGEMENT PLAN (ASMA No. 1). In this paper Brazil, as coordinator of the ASMA 1 Management Plan for a 5 year period, outlines the proposed working plan for the review of the ASMA 1 Management Plan.
IP 78 United States	AMUNDSEN-SCOTT SOUTH POLE STATION, SOUTH POLE ANTARCTICA SPECIALLY MANAGED AREA (ASMA No. 5) 2012 MANAGEMENT REPORT. This paper summarises the continuing challenges in managing diverse activities in ASMA 5. It discusses the implementation of the newly positioned primary camping area and the secondary (or overflow) camping area and the implementation of a Visitor Centre.
IP 82 Argentina, Chile, Norway, Spain, UK & USA	DECEPTION ISLAND SPECIALLY MANAGED AREA (ASMA) MANAGEMENT GROUP REPORT. This paper summarises the activities undertaken within the Deception ASMA, and the work of the Management Group to fulfil the objectives and principles of ASMA No. 4 Management Plan during the intersessional period 2011-12.

b) Historic Sites and Monuments	
WP 36 Russia	PROPOSAL ON REVISION OF HISTORIC SITES AND MONUMENTS UNDER MANAGEMENT OF THE RUSSIAN FEDERATION. This paper proposes amendments and updates in the description of several HSMs under Russian management.
WP 46 Argentina	FINAL REPORT OF THE INFORMAL DISCUSSIONS ON HISTORIC SITES AND MONUMENTS. This paper presents the final report of informal discussions on Historic Sites and Monuments, led by Argentina during the intersessional periods 2010-2011 and 2011-2012.
WP 56 rev.1 Chile	PROPOSAL FOR MODIFICATION OF HISTORIC SITE No 37. This paper proposes the addition of new structures and elements to HSM 37, a statue erected of Bernardo O'Higgins at O'Higgins Station. Chile proposes to modify the HSM by adding the structures of the old O'Higgins Station, a plaque and a grotto.
IP 14 China	BRIEF INTRODUCTION OF THE MAINTENANCE AND CONSERVATION PROJECT OF No.1 BUILDING AT GREAT WALL STATION. This paper reports on the Maintenance and Conservation Project of No.1 Building at Great Wall Station (HSM 86) planned to be completed during the following two or three years. The Building is expected to be a HSM displaying the history of China's Antarctic research.

BP 41 New Zealand	*ANTARCTIC HERITAGE TRUST CONSERVATION UPDATE.* This paper provides information on the Antarctic Heritage Trust's Ross Sea Heritage Restoration Project being undertaken at ASPAs at Ross Island and at Cape Adare, related to the expedition bases built by the *Southern Cross* Expedition (1898-1900) led by Carsten Borchgrevink; the *Discovery* Expedition (1901-1904) and the *Terra Nova* Expedition (1910-1913) both led by Robert Falcon Scott; and the *Nimrod* Expedition (1907-1909) led by Ernest Shackleton.

c) Site Guidelines

WP 15 UK , Argentina & USA	*SITE GUIDELINES FOR D'HAINAUT ISLAND, MIKKELSEN HARBOUR, TRINITY ISLAND.* This document proposes the adoption of site guidelines for D'Hainaut Island because the site is recognised for its historical importance and contains the remains of a whalers' water boat and large pile of whale bones. The site also has important environmental values. The proponents recommend that the CEP submit the site guidelines for adoption by the ATCM.
WP 16 Argentina, France, Ukraine, UK & USA	*SITE GUIDELINES FOR PORT CHARCOT, BOOTH ISLAND.* This paper proposes the adoption of site guidelines for Port Charcot because the site is recognised for its historical importance and contains the remains of the base used to over-winter by the French Antarctic Expedition, led by Dr. Jean Baptiste Charcot, in 1904. The site also has important environmental values including floral species and the fact that a number of bird species breed in the area and several seal and penguin species use the beach as a resting place.
WP 45 Argentina, Chile, Norway, Spain, UK & USA	*SITE GUIDELINES FOR VISITORS, PENDULUM COVE, DECEPTION ISLAND, SOUTH SHETLAND ISLANDS.* This paper proposes the adoption of site guidelines which aim to minimise the risk of visitor related pressures at this site of outstanding natural and historic value, as well as to safeguard visitor safety.
WP 59 Ecuador & Spain	*REVIEW OF THE SITE VISITOR GUIDELINES FOR AITCHO ISLANDS.* This paper proposes a review of the site guidelines for Aitcho Islands, adopted in 2005. Based on monitoring activities during the last years, the paper proposes modifications in the guidelines related to anchorage areas, routes and maps of the current version of the guidelines.
IP 37 IAATO	*REPORT ON IAATO OPERATOR USE OF ANTARCTIC PENINSULA LANDING SITES AND ATCM VISITOR SITE GUIDELINES, 2011-2012 SEASON.* IAATO reports on the levels of tourism in Antarctica and on the use of site guidelines or National Programme management in sites visited in the proximity of stations.

BP 3 Unites States	ANTARCTIC SITE INVENTORY: 1994-2012. This paper provides an update on results of the Antarctic Site Inventory project through February 2012, which has collected biological data and site-descriptive information in the Antarctic Peninsula since 1994.

d) Human footprint and wilderness values

WP 50 New Zealand & Netherlands	CONCEPTS FOR WILDERNESS PROTECTION IN ANTARCTICA USING TOOLS IN THE PROTOCOL. Considering the context of a significantly changing Antarctic environment and increasing human activity in Antarctica, this paper proposes the development of practical guidance material to support the protection of wilderness values when applying the EIA and area protection tools of Annex I and Annex V of the Protocol. (See also IP 60.)
IP 52 ASOC	DATA SOURCES FOR MAPPING THE HUMAN FOOTPRINT IN ANTARCTICA. This paper suggests that the compilation of information on human activity in Antarctica from the different information repositories in a common format and in one place, would be a useful step in constructing a model of the human footprint in Antarctica and the Southern Ocean.
IP 60 New Zealand & Netherlands	FURTHER INFORMATION ABOUT WILDERNESS PROTECTION IN ANTARCTICA AND USE OF TOOLS IN THE PROTOCOL. Acknowledging the inherent difficulties in the management of wilderness, this Information Paper provides supporting information for the WP on the development of practical guidance material to support the protection of wilderness values when applying the EIA and area protection tools of Annex I and Annex V of the Protocol.

e) Marine Spatial Protection and Management

IP 34 IUCN	USING ASMAS AND ASPAS WHEN NECESSARY TO COMPLEMENT CCAMLR MPAS. IUCN considers that some CCAMLR MPAs may require additional management and protection efforts and that it is therefore important that the ATCM, taking into account the recommendations from C-CAMLR, consider whether there is a possible need or not to establish ASMAs or ASPAs, partly or fully, in the area of a CCAMLR MPA.
IP 50 ASOC	ANTARCTIC OCEAN LEGACY: A MARINE RESERVE FOR THE ROSS SEA. This paper summarises a publication y the Antarctic Ocean Alliance (AOA), of which ASOC is a member. The Alliance is calling for the creation of a network of marine protected areas and no-take marine reserves in the Southern Ocean.

IP 51 ASOC	*ANTARCTIC OCEAN LEGACY: A VISION FOR CIRCUMPOLAR PROTECTION.* This paper summarises the report "Antarctic Ocean Legacy: A Vision for Circumpolar Protection" published by the Antarctic Ocean Alliance (AOA).
IP 54 ASOC	*IMPLICATIONS OF ANTARCTIC KRILL FISHING IN ASMA No. 1 - ADMIRALTY BAY.* ASOC informs that the 2011 meeting of WG-EMM noted that in 2009/10, the krill fishery operated in ASMA 1. Fishing was not identified or envisaged when the management plan was adopted by the ATCM following its approval by CCAMLR. ASOC offers a series of recommendations in order to prevent similar future events.
IP 68 Ukraine	*PROGRESS OF UKRAINE ON DESIGNATION OF BROAD-SCALE MANAGEMENT SYSTEM IN THE VERNADSKY STATION AREA.* Given the increasing scientific, logistic and tourist activities around Verdnasky Station and the surrounding islands in recent years, Ukraine is proposing to prepare a broad-scale and comprehensive management system for the area and invites all interested Parties to take part in further discussion on strategic views of environmental protection and possible management for this area.
IP 80 CCAMLR	*REPORT OF THE CEP OBSERVER TO THE CCAMLR WORKSHOP ON MARINE PROTECTED AREAS. BREST, FRANCE, 29 AUGUST TO 2 SEPTEMBER 2011.* This paper provides a synopsis of those aspects of the workshop of particular relevance to the ongoing collaboration between the CEP and SC-CAMLR. A full version is available online at the CCAMLR website.

f) Other Annex V Matters	
WP 23 rev.1 Australia, New Zealand & SCAR	*ANTARCTIC CONSERVATION BIOGEOGRAPHIC REGIONS.* This paper presents the results of recent analyses of the relationships between the best available Antarctic terrestrial biodiversity data, the Environmental Domains and other relevant spatial frameworks. The authors recommend that the Committee endorse the 'Antarctic Conservation Biogeographic Regions' as a dynamic model for the identification of ASPAs within a systematic environmental-geographic framework, and as a basis for ongoing work to address non-native species risks. A draft Resolution is provided for consideration by the Committee.
WP 35 Russia	*PROPOSALS ON PREPARATION OF REVISED MANAGEMENT PLANS OF ANTARCTIC SPECIALLY PROTECTED AND ANTARCTIC SPECIALLY MANAGED AREAS.* This paper proposes that, in reviewing ASPA and ASMA management plans in which representatives of living Antarctic nature are designated as the main values to be protected, the proponent Party should submit to the CEP a report with the results of a monitoring programme on the state of those values. A draft Measure is attached to the paper.

WP 38 USA & New Zealand	DEVELOPING PROTECTION FOR A GEOTHERMAL AREA; VOLCANIC ICE CAVES AT MOUNT EREBUS, ROSS ISLAND. This paper proposes a strategy to protect the unique environments of geothermal areas of Mount Erebus recommending the interested Parties and SCAR to develop an inventory on ice cave features and a code of conduct and adopt a temporary moratorium on visits to the area.
IP 26 Australia	ANALYSES OF THE ANTARCTIC PROTECTED AREAS SYSTEM USING SPATIAL INFORMATION. Australia has acquired a comprehensive dataset of spatial information representing the boundaries of all ASPAs and ASMAs. This dataset is now freely available, via the Secretariat, for use in accordance with basic terms and conditions. This paper presents examples of how the dataset can assist in assessing and further developing the Antarctic protected areas system as well as support other CEP activities.
IP 49 ASOC	ANNEX V INVIOLATE AND REFERENCE AREAS: CURRENT MANAGEMENT PRACTICES INFORMATION. ASOC considers that the designation of closed and inviolate areas of significant size can make multiple contributions towards meeting the objectives of the Protocol, and that it is a tool already in the toolbox of Antarctic environmental management practices which can be used more widely to complement existing environmental management activities.

8. CONSERVATION OF ANTARCTIC FLORA AND FAUNA

a) Quarantine and Non-native Species

WP 5 SCAR	OUTCOMES OF THE INTERNATIONAL POLAR YEAR PROGRAMME: ALIENS IN ANTARCTICA. This paper reports on the findings of the IPY project *Aliens in Antarctica* related to a spatially explicit, activity-differentiated assessment of the risks of establishment of terrestrial non-native species across Antarctica, both currently and with climate change. SCAR recommends the CEP to include this assessment in further development of strategies to mitigate the risks posed by terrestrial non-native species, to develop a surveillance strategy and to give additional attention to the risks posed by intra-Antarctic transfer of propagules.
WP 6 SCAR	REDUCING THE RISK OF INADVERTENT NON-NATIVE SPECIES INTRODUCTIONS ASSOCIATED WITH FRESH FRUIT AND VEGETABLE IMPORTATION TO ANTARCTICA. SCAR reviews the science concerning the risk of non-native species introductions associated with the importation of fresh fruits and vegetables to the Antarctic region. SCAR recommends that the CEP encourage Parties to implement the recommendations of the COMNAP/SCAR *checklists for supply chain managers*; and encourages Parties and/or COMNAP to further investigate practical, cost effective methods of reducing the risk of non-native species introductions associated with fresh foods.

WP 25 rev.1 Australia & France	GUIDELINES TO MINIMISE THE RISKS OF NON-NATIVE SPECIES AND DISEASE AS-SOCIATED WITH ANTARCTIC HYDROPONICS FACILITIES. This paper presents suggested *Guidelines to minimise the risks of non-native species and disease associated with Antarctic hydroponics facilities.* Australia and France recommend that the guidelines be included in the CEP Non-native Species Manual for reference, as appropriate, by those using or planning to use hydroponics facilities.
IP 13 Spain, Argentina & United Kingdom	COLONISATION STATUS OF THE NON-NATIVE GRASS *POA PRATENSIS* AT *CIERVA POINT, DANCO COAST, ANTARCTIC PENINSULA.* This paper proposes that, given that climate change may increase and following the procedures proposed in the CEP Non-native Species Manual, it would be desirable to eradicate this species, which was accidentally introduced in Cierva Point, Antarctic Peninsula, in 1954.
IP 29 United Kingdom	COLONISATION STATUS OF KNOWN NON-NATIVE SPECIES IN THE ANTARCTIC TER-RESTRIAL ENVIRONMENT (UPDATED *2012*). This paper updates the information presented to the CEP in 2010 and 2011 on the colonisation status of known non-native species in the Antarctic terrestrial environment. The paper reports that no attempts have been made to eradicate any of the known non-native species in the past year.
BP 1 SCAR	CONTINENT-WIDE RISK ASSESSMENT FOR THE ESTABLISHMENT OF NONINDIG-ENOUS SPECIES IN ANTARCTICA. This scientific publication presents an evidence-based assessment demonstrating which parts of Antarctica are at growing risk from alien species that may become invasive, and provides the means to mitigate this threat now and into the future as the continent's climate changes.

b)   Specially Protected Species

c)   Other Annex II Matters

IP 20 Germany	EVALUATION OF THE "STRATEGIC ASSESSMENT OF THE RISK POSED TO MARINE MAMMALS BY THE USE OF AIRGUNS IN THE ANTARCTIC TREATY AREA". This paper presents an assessment, undertaken by the Federal Environment Agency of Germany, of the Alfred Wegner Institute's analysis of risks posed to marine mammals by the use of airguns. Germany notes that all aspects of the risk analysis were thoroughly assessed and special emphasis is placed on hazard identification, level of protection and corresponding safety zones for the assets to be protected.
IP 21 SCAR	ANTHROPOGENIC SOUND IN THE SOUTHERN OCEAN: AN UPDATE . This paper forms the basis of a response to a request from CEP XIV, and presents a summary of new information on anthropogenic sound in the Southern Ocean.

IP 35 SCAR, IUCN & New Zealand	*ANTARCTIC CONSERVATION FOR THE 21ST CENTURY: BACKGROUND, PROGRESS, AND FUTURE DIRECTIONS.* Recognizing the need for an integrated, comprehensive and dynamic plan for the conservation of Antarctica and associated and dependent ecosystems, this paper describes developments to date and plans for the further development of an Antarctic Conservation Strategy (ACS).

9. ENVIRONMENTAL MONITORING AND REPORTING

WP 7 United Kingdom	*REMOTE SENSING FOR MONITORING ANTARCTIC SPECIALLY PROTECTED AREAS: USE OF MULTISPECTRAL AND HYPERSPECTRAL DATA FOR MONITORING ANTARCTIC VEGETATION.* This paper describes the development and application of new remote sensing techniques in Antarctica to monitor vegetation. The UK recommends that the CEP consider further the value and application of the methodology, and encourage future collaboration in the development and application of these techniques for monitoring of ASPAs and the wider environment.
WP 18 Germany	*PENGUIN MONITORING VIA REMOTE SENSING.* Taking into account the calling of ATCM XXXIV to Parties to intensify their efforts in using remote sensing techniques for improved monitoring of environment and climate changes in the Antarctic, and informal discussions at the CEP and on scientific forums on the possibilities of penguin monitoring in the Antarctic based on remote sensing techniques, this paper proposes the establishment of an ICG to discuss this matter intersessionally.
IP 46 Germany	*PILOT STUDY ON MONITORING CLIMATE-INDUCED CHANGES IN PENGUIN COLONIES IN THE ANTARCTIC USING SATELLITE IMAGES.* This paper reports on a feasibility study on penguin monitoring using remote sensing techniques carried out by Germany. (See also WP 18.)
WP 20 New Zealand	*ESTABLISHING A MONITORING PROGRAMME TO ASSESS CHANGES IN VEGETATION AT TWO ANTARCTIC SPECIALLY PROTECTED AREAS.* New Zealand established a monitoring programme at two ASPAs using GIS techniques to monitor changes in vegetation cover. This paper invites the CEP to consider how this method may be used for monitoring climate change effects on Antarctic species distribution and abundance.
WP 55 Chile	*NEW RECORDS OF THE PRESENCE OF HUMAN ASSOCIATED MICROORGANISMS IN THE ANTARCTIC MARINE ENVIRONMENT.* Chile informs on new records of presence of human associated microorganisms in the Antarctic marine environment and suggests that the CEP recommend that COMNAP develop monitor activities to study the presence of these microorganisms in the vicinity of the stations and to evaluate the existing precautions and sewage treatments that the National Programmes have established to avoid the incidental introduction of microorganisms due to human activities in the Antarctic environment.

IP 2 SCAR	*The Southern Ocean Observing System (SOOS).* This paper presents an update on progress with the design and implementation of a Southern Ocean Observing System (SOOS) over the last year.
IP 40 rev. 1 SCAR	*SCAR Products available to support the deliberations of the ATCM.* Following a request from the CEP, this paper lists the SCAR products which provide scientific information useful to scientists and others, such as meteorological data, biodiversity data in a more easily usable form, and information on bathymetry in the Southern Ocean.
IP 53 ASOC	*Antarctic Treaty System Follow-up to Vessel Incidents in Antarctic Waters.* This paper undertakes a preliminary assessment of reporting following a vessel incident. It addresses comprehensiveness of reporting, reporting of impact of the pollution produced from an incident and implementation of lessons learned and recommendations arising. It identifies a number of shortcomings in the current system and recommends that the ATCM and CCAMLR address these as a matter of urgency.
IP 76 Chile	*Antarctic Environmental Monitoring Centre.* This document presents part of the activities developed by the monitoring project of the Chilean Antarctic Programme, aimed to aid the decision making process with the support of scientific environmental information, to optimise the use of resources and to encourage the creation of specialised technical skills to maintain a continuous monitoring programme.
BP 10 Australia	*Assessment of Environmental impacts arising from sewage discharge at Davis Station.* This paper informs on a comprehensive study undertaken by Australia to assess the environmental impacts of wastewater disposal into the coastal marine environment at Davis Station.
BP 15 Poland	*Summary information on improvements and modernizations done on Polish Antarctic Station "Arctowski".* This paper informs on the important changes made at Arctowski Station aimed to reduce the potentially adverse human impacts on the Antarctic environment, to modernise the Station, to reduce energy demand and to improve the safety of its logistical operations.

10. Inspection reports

IP 47 USA & Russia	*United States-Russian Federation Report of Inspection.* The United States and the Russian Federation conducted an inspection under the Antarctic Treaty from 23-28January 2012. The report attached to this IP describes the observations and conclusions of Joint Antarctic Inspection Team. A summary of overall conclusions is included.

IP 59 UNEP & ASOC	REVIEW OF THE IMPLEMENTATION OF THE MADRID PROTOCOL: INSPECTIONS BY PARTIES (ARTICLE 14). This paper reviews the practice of inspections undertaken by Parties carried out under Article 14 of the Madrid Protocol.
BP 22 India	MEASURES ADOPTED AT MAITRI STATION ON THE RECOMMENDATIONS OF RECENT VISIT OF JAPANESE INSPECTION TEAM. This paper reports on the measures already adopted or being implemented with regard to observations made by a Japanese inspection team in 2010 on improvements in the conditions of some systems at Maitri Station.

11. COOPERATION WITH OTHER ORGANISATIONS

IP 1 SCAR	THE SCIENTIFIC COMMITTEE ON ANTARCTIC RESEARCH (SCAR) ANNUAL REPORT 2011/12. This paper summarises past SCAR highlights and future meetings of interest to Treaty Parties.
IP 3 COMNAP	THE ANNUAL REPORT FOR 2011 OF THE COUNCIL OF MANAGERS OF NATIONAL ANTARCTIC PROGRAMMES (COMNAP). This document presents COMNAP highlights and achievements as well as products and tools developed in 2011.
IP 28 CCAMLR	REPORT BY THE SC-CAMLR OBSERVER TO THE FIFTEENTH MEETING OF THE COMMITTEE FOR ENVIRONMENTAL PROTECTION. This paper reports on matters of common interest between the SC-CAMLR and the CEP, discussed at the last SC-CAMLR Meeting.

12. REPAIR AND REMEDIATION OF ENVIRONMENTAL DAMAGE

WP 21 Australia & United Kingdom	AN ANTARCTIC CLEAN-UP MANUAL. This paper proposes that the Committee agree to develop a Clean-Up Manual containing guidance to assist Parties in addressing their obligations under Annex III to clean up past waste disposal sites on land and abandoned work sites of past activities. A draft Resolution and proposed first version of a Clean-Up Manual area attached. The paper further proposes that the Committee encourage interested Members and Observers to develop practical guidelines and supporting resources for inclusion in the Clean-Up Manual.
WP 26 Australia	ENVIRONMENTAL ISSUES RELATED TO THE PRACTICALITY OF REPAIR OR REMEDIATION OF ENVIRONMENTAL DAMAGE. This paper is an update of ATCM XXXIV - WP 28 on environmental issues related to the practicality of repair or remediation of environmental damage, and should be read in conjunction with Australia's IP 25.
IP 25 Australia	EXAMPLES TO ILLUSTRATE KEY ENVIRONMENTAL ISSUES RELATED TO THE PRACTICALITY OF REPAIR OR REMEDIATION OF ENVIRONMENTAL DAMAGE. In support of WP 26 this paper presents examples to illustrate the points that Australia suggests could be considered by the Committee when addressing Decision 4 (2010).

WP 62 COMNAP	REPAIR OR REMEDIATION OF ENVIRONMENTAL DAMAGE: **COMNAP** REPORT ON ITS EXPERIENCE. COMNAP reports on the results of a Waste Management in Antarctica Workshop organised by its Environmental Experts Group, and provides several examples of remediation activities by various National Antarctic Programmes.
IP 6 Australia	TOPIC SUMMARY: **CEP** DISCUSSIONS ON CLEAN-UP. This paper supports WP 21 and presents a summary of CEP meeting documents that have addressed the clean-up of waste disposal sites on land, abandoned work sites of Antarctic activities and sites contaminated by fuel spills.
IP 57 ASOC	REPAIR OR REMEDIATION OF ENVIRONMENTAL DAMAGE. This paper reviews some of the key issues associated with the repair or remediation of environmental damage and comments on the various points suggested by Australia in WP 28 at ATCM XXXIV.
BP 11 Australia	CLEAN-UP TECHNIQUES FOR ANTARCTICA. This report relates that the Australian Antarctic programme is developing techniques suitable for the clean-up of contaminated sites in Antarctica and that the results of this work may be beneficial in managing other Antarctic contaminated sites.
BP 12 Australia	CLEAN-UP OF A FUEL SPILL NEAR LAKE DINGLE, VESTFOLD HILLS. This paper relates Australia's experience from a recent fuel spill in the Vestfold Hills and illustrates how environmental risk assessment, following a simple risk-based decision tree, was instrumental in choosing the most appropriate remediation plan.
BP 13 Australia	DEVELOPMENT OF ENVIRONMENTAL QUALITY STANDARDS FOR THE MANAGE-MENT OF CONTAMINATED SITES IN ANTARCTICA. In this paper Australia presents information on research to develop environmental quality standards based on the sensitivity of Antarctic species to metals and fuel contaminants.
BP 14 Australia	ASSESSMENT, MONITORING AND REMEDIATION OF OLD ANTARCTIC WASTE DIS-POSAL SITES: THE THALA VALLEY EXAMPLE AT CASEY STATION. This paper describes the approach to impact assessment and monitoring that was developed at the Thala Valley waste disposal site at Casey station as an integral part of the clean-up project, to ensure that all obligations under the Protocol were satisfied.
BP 38 Chile	REMOVAL OF SCRAP FROM PRESIDENTE EDUARDO FREI MONTALVA STATION, KING GEORGE ISLAND. This paper reports that during the 2011-12 seasons, an important amount of scrap was removed from the station by Chile in conjunction with the assistance of a private company.

13. GENERAL MATTERS	
IP 32 COMNAP	***COMNAP** SURVEY OF NATIONAL ANTARCTIC PROGRAMMES ON OIL SPILL CONTINGENCY PLANNING.* This paper presents the results of a new COMNAP survey undertaken during the 2011/2012 intersessional period as an update of a survey carried out in 1996 on best practice in the event of an accident or oil spill.

14. ELECTION OF OFFICERS

15. PREPARATION FOR NEXT MEETING

16. ADOPTION OF THE REPORT

17. CLOSING OF THE MEETING

Appendix 1

CEP Five Year Work Plan

Issue / Environmental Pressure Actions	CEP Priority	Intersessional Period	CEP XVI 2013	Intersessional Period	CEP XVII 2014	Intersessional Period	CEP XVIII 2015	Intersessional Period	CEP XIX 2016	Intersessional Period	CEP XX 2017
Introduction of non-native species	1	Interested Members, experts, NAPs work on monitoring measures.	Discuss further monitoring measures for inclusion in NSS manual, including a surveillance strategy for areas at high risk of establishment	Interested members, experts, NAPs work on response measures and eradication.	Discuss further response measures for inclusion in NNS manual	Prepare for review of manual-consider informal discussion group	Review non-native species manual				
Actions:											
1. Continue developing practical guidelines & resources for all Antarctic operators.											
2. Continue advancing recommendations from climate change ATME.		Update the NNS manual with the guidelines for hydroponic facilities and ABCR.									
3. Consider the spatially explicit, activity-differentiated risk assessments to mitigate the risks posed by terrestrial non-native species.		Incorporate the map of Antarctica showing the 15 ACBR (refer to recommendation 5 in WP23), and incorporate the guidelines to minimise the risks of non-native species and disease associated with Antarctic hydroponics facilities (refer to WP 25).									
4. Develop a surveillance strategy for areas at high risk of non-native species establishment.											
5. Give additional attention to the risks posed by intra-Antarctic transfer of propagules.											
Tourism and NGO activities	1	Dependant on ATCM reaction	Respond to ATCM request.								
Actions:											
1. Provide advice to ATCM as requested.											
2. Advance recommendations from ship-borne tourism ATME.											

155

Issue / Environmental Pressure Actions	CEP Priority	Intersessional Period	CEP XVI 2013	Intersessional Period	CEP XVII 2014	Intersessional Period	CEP XVIII 2015	Intersessional Period	CEP XIX 2016	Intersessional Period	CEP XX 2017
Global Pressure: Climate Change	1	Continue to advance recommendations from ATME	Standing agenda item. SCAR provides yearly update	Continue to advance recommendations from ATME	Standing agenda item. SCAR provides update	Continue to advance recommendations from ATME	Standing agenda item. SCAR provides update	Continue to advance recommendations from ATME	Standing agenda item. SCAR provides update	Continue to advance recommendations from ATME	Standing agenda item. SCAR provides update
Actions: 1. Consider implications of climate change for management of Antarctic environment. 2. Advance recommendations from climate change ATME.											
Processing new and revised protected / managed area management plans	1	SGMP / conducts work as per agreed work plan. Review draft management plans referred by CEP for intersessional review and provide advice to proponents. Work with relevant Parties to ensure progress on review of management plans overdue for five-yearly review.	Consideration of SGMP / report. Review and update SGMP work plan	SGMP / conducts work as per agreed work plan	Consideration of SGMP / report	SGMP / conducts work as per agreed work plan	Consideration of SGMP / report	SGMP / conducts work as per agreed work plan	Consideration of SGMP / report		
Actions: 1. Refine the process for reviewing new and revised management plans. 2. Update existing guidelines. 3. Advance recommendations from climate change ATME. 4. Develop guidelines to ASMAs preparation.											
Marine spatial protection and management	1	Revision and discussion of ASMA 1, and ASPAs with marine component, work progressed in conjunction with SC-CCAMLR	Review outcome of CCAMLR MPA decisions and review SC-CAMLR Plan of Work for further co-ordination								
Actions: 1. Cooperate with CCAMLR on Southern Ocean bioregionalisation and other common interests and agreed principles. 2. Identify and apply processes for spatial marine protection. Advance recommendations from climate change ATME.											

Issue / Environmental Pressure Actions	CEP Priority	Intersessional Period	CEP XVI 2013	Intersessional Period	CEP XVII 2014	Intersessional Period	CEP XVIII 2015	Intersessional Period	CEP XIX 2016	Intersessional Period	CEP XX 2017
Operation of the CEP and Strategic Planning	1		Standing item Review and revise work plan as appropriate		Standing item Review and revise work plan as appropriate		Standing item Review and revise work plan as appropriate		25th anniversary of Protocol. Review and revise work plan as appropriate		
Actions: 1. Keep the 5 year plan up to date based on changing circumstances and ATCM requirements. 2. Identify opportunities for improving the effectiveness of the CEP. 3. Consider long-term objectives for Antarctica (50-100 years time).											
Repair or Remediation of Environmental Damage	1	ICG to prepare draft advice on Decision 4 (2010).	Consider ICG Report and, as appropriate, provide advice to the ATCM.	Consider further request by the ATCM							
Actions: 1. Develop advice in response to request from ATCM Decision 4 (2010) in order to assist the ATCM in adopting an informed decision in 2015 on the resumption of negociations on liability arising from environmental damage. 2. Establish Antarctic-wide inventory of sites of past activity. 3. Consider guidelines for repair and remediation. 4. Prepare manual of clean-up guidance		Members prepare further papers. Informal discussion to consider draft clean-up manual.	As required, establish ICG to respond to further ATCM request Consider revised Clean-up Manual	Possible ICG to develop further advice on Decision 4 (2010)			Secretariat requested to develop and maintain an inventory				
Human footprint / wilderness management	2	Discussion in an informal group by interested Parties, using CEP forum.	Report to the CEP. Discussion of guidance material to assist Parties assessing and protecting wilderness values.								
Actions: 1. Develop an agreed understanding of the terms "footprint" and "wilderness". 2. Develop methods for improved protection of wilderness under Annexes I and V.											

Issue / Environmental Pressure Actions	CEP Priority	Intersessional Period	CEP XVI 2013	Intersessional Period	CEP XVII 2014	Intersessional Period	CEP XVIII 2015	Intersessional Period	CEP XIX 2016	Intersessional Period	CEP XX 2017
Monitoring and state of the environment reporting	2		Report to the CEP as appropriate								
Actions: 1. Identify key environmental indicators and tools. 2. Establish a process for reporting to the ATCM. 3. Advance recommendations from climate change ATME. 4. COMNAP to review its information from the Waste Management Workshop, as first step. 5. SCAR to support information to COMNAP and CEP.											
Biodiversity knowledge	2										
Actions: 1. Maintain awareness of threats to existing biodiversity. 2. Advance recommendations from climate change ATME							Discussion of SCAR update on underwater noise.				
Site specific guidelines for tourist-visited sites	2	Further research at Barrientos Island, Aitcho Islands, including effects of closure of track across closed area. Parties are encourage to continue the review of site guidelines.	Standing agenda item; Parties to report on their reviews of site guidelines. Report to the CEP with Barrientos Island, Aitcho Islands, monitoring results. Consider re-naming this issue as 'Visitor Site Management'.		Standing agenda item; Parties to report on their reviews of site guidelines		Standing agenda item; Parties to report on their reviews of site guidelines		Standing agenda item; Parties to report on their reviews of site guidelines		Standing agenda item; Parties to report on their reviews of site guidelines
Actions: 1. Review site specific guidelines as required. 2. Provide advice to ATCM as required.											

Issue / Environmental Pressure Actions	CEP Priority	Intersessional Period	CEP XVI 2013	Intersessional Period	CEP XVII 2014	Intersessional Period	CEP XVIII 2015	Intersessional Period	CEP XIX 2016	Intersessional Period	CEP XX 2017
Overview of the protected areas system **Actions:** 1. Apply the Environmental Domains Analysis (EDA) and Antarctic Conservation Biogeographic Regions (ACBR) to enhance the protected areas system. 2. Advance recommendations from climate change ATME. 3. Maintain and develop Protected Area database.	2	Secretariat to make available the ACBR via Protected Areas Data Base.	Discussion of environmental monitoring for ASPAs and ASMAs.		Discuss possible implications of an updated gap analysis based on EDA and ACBR.						
Maintain the list of Historic Sites and Monuments **Actions:** 1. Maintain the list and consider new proposals as they arise. 2. Consider strategic issues as necessary.	3	Secretariat update list of HSMs. Secretariat to publish the agreed list of the complete information in the list of HSM.	Standing item	Secretariate update list of HSMs	Standing item	Secretariate update list of HSMs	Standing item	Secretariate update list of HSMs	Standing item	Secretariate update list of HSMs	Standing item
Exchange of Information **Actions:** 1. Assign to the Secretariat. 2. Monitor and facilitate easy use of the EIES.	3	Continue informal discussions to improved EIES and Secretariate put refinements in place.	Secretariat Report		Secretariat Report		Secretariat Report		Secretariat Report		Secretariat Report

Issue / Environmental Pressure Actions	CEP Priority	Intersessional Period	CEP XVI 2013	Intersessional Period	CEP XVII 2014	Intersessional Period	CEP XVIII 2015	Intersessional Period	CEP XIX 2016	Intersessional Period	CEP XX 2017
Implementing and Improving the EIA provisions of Annex I	3	Establish ICG to review draft CEEs as required	Consideration of ICG reports on draft CEE, as required	Establish ICG to review draft CEEs as required	Consideration of ICG reports on draft CEE, as required	Establish ICG to review draft CEEs as required	Consideration of ICG reports on draft CEE, as required	Establish ICG to review draft CEEs as required	Consideration of ICG reports on draft CEE, as required	Establish ICG to review draft CEEs as required	Consideration of ICG reports on draft CEE, as required
Actions: 1. Refine the process for considering CEEs and advising the ATCM accordingly. 2. Develop guidelines for assessing cumulative impacts. 3. Keep the EIA Guidelines under review. 4. Consider application of strategic environmental assessment in Antarctica. 5. Advance recommendations from climate change ATME											
Specially protected species	3		Consider proposal as required		Consider proposal as required						
Actions: 1. Consider proposals related to specially protected species.											
Emergency response action and contingency planning	3	Discuss Work	ICG	Discussion	ICG	Discussion	ICG	Final Recs to the ATCM			
Actions: 1. Advance recommendations from ship-borne tourism ATME.											
Updating the Protocol and reviewing Annexes	3		Requires CEP discussion on the need and aims for reviewing Protocol annexes								
Actions: 1. Prepare a prioritised timetable for the review of the remaining annexes.											
Inspections (Article 14 of the Protocol)	3		Standing item		Standing item		Standing item		Standing item		Standing item
Actions: 1. Review inspection reports as required.											

Issue / Environmental Pressure Actions	CEP Priority	Intersessional Period	CEP XVI 2013	Intersessional Period	CEP XVII 2014	Intersessional Period	CEP XVIII 2015	Intersessional Period	CEP XIX 2016	Intersessional Period	CEP XX 2017
Waste	3										
Actions:											
1. Develop guidelines for best practice disposal of waste including human waste.					COMNAP reviews information from 2006 waste management workshop						
Energy management	4										
Actions:											
1. Develop best-practice guidelines for energy management at stations and bases.											
Outreach and education	4		Dedicated time for discussion.								
Actions:											
1. Review current examples and identify opportunities for greater education and outreach. 2. Encourage Members to exchange information regarding their experiences in this area.			Members to produce documents for the Meeting.								

161

Appendix 2

Provisional Agenda for CEP XVI

1. Opening of the Meeting
2. Adoption of the Agenda
3. Strategic Discussions on the Future Work of the CEP
4. Operation of the CEP
5. Cooperation with other Organisations
6. Repair and Remediation of Environment Damage
7. Climate Change Implications for the Environment: Strategic approach
8. Environmental Impact Assessment (EIA)
    a. Draft Comprehensive Environmental Evaluations
    b. Other EIA Matters
9. Area Protection and Management Plans
    a. Management Plans
    b. Historic Sites and Monuments
    c. Site Guidelines
    d. Human footprint and wilderness values
    e. Marine Spatial Protection and Management
    f. Other Annex V Matters
10. Conservation of Antarctic Flora and Fauna
    a. Quarantine and Non-native Species
    b. Specially Protected Species
    c. Other Annex II Matters
11. Environmental Monitoring and Reporting
12. Inspection Reports
13. General Matters
14. Election of Officers
15. Preparation for Next Meeting
16. Adoption of the Report
17. Closing of the Meeting

3. Appendices

ATCM XXXV Communiqué

The Antarctic Treaty Consultative Meeting XXXV (ATCM) was held in Hobart, Australia, for the first time in an eight day format from 11-20 June 2012 in conjunction with the Committee for Environmental Protection XV. The ATCM is the premier international forum on Antarctica through which Antarctic Treaty Parties come together annually to discuss and decide on measures to realise their vision for Antarctica as a natural reserve devoted to peace and science. The outcomes of ATCM XXXV reinforce and advance this vision. This year marks the centenary of the Amundsen and Scott expeditions to the South Pole and, for the host country of Australia, the centenary of its first Antarctic expedition led by Douglas Mawson.

Over 250 representatives from the Antarctic Treaty Parties, experts and observers, attended. The Meeting welcomed Malaysia and Pakistan as Parties to the Antarctic Treaty, taking to 50 the number of Parties.

The Parties recalled that, while they were meeting, in Antarctica national science programme personnel were working in the middle of winter. They also recalled the spirit of community in Antarctica and expressed their condolences at the tragic loss of life at the Brazilian station Comandante Ferraz.

The following outcomes were among the highlights of the Meeting.

The ATCM continued to focus on understanding and addressing implications of climate change for Antarctica, including by identifying areas of conservation importance on account of their resilience to climate change. Parties reaffirmed their commitment to undertake and promote scientific research in Antarctica, to enhance understanding of global climate change and its implications for our planet.

The Meeting agreed on a number of actions to ensure that tourism activities in Antarctica are conducted safely and in a manner that protects the environment. The Meeting adopted check-lists for assessing land-based expeditions and for supporting inspections of tourist activities ashore. The Parties adopted three further guidelines for sites visited by tourists and revised the existing guidelines for one site. The first comprehensive study on the environmental aspects and impacts of tourism in Antarctica was considered and will provide a basis for future management decisions.

The ATCM agreed guidelines on the planning of safe and environmentally responsible yacht expeditions in Antarctic waters. Parties confirmed their commitment to promote safety in those waters, given recent serious incidents involving vessels in the Antarctic Treaty area. Parties decided to focus on steps to further enhance search and rescue coordination by bringing together experts at a special session during ATCM XXXVI.

Parties agreed to initiate discussion aimed at promoting broader Antarctic cooperation.

Parties also agreed to start discussion on issues relating to the exercise of jurisdiction in the Antarctic Treaty area.

Parties discussed ways to enhance their scientific cooperation in Antarctica. Parties also shared information on major research activities – including Russia's achievement in accessing Lake Vostok, the world's largest sub-glacial lake located almost four kilometres below the ice, and the United Kingdom's final plans to drill into sub-glacial Lake Ellsworth for scientific research.

Recognising that the introduction of non-native species is one of the biggest threats to Antarctic ecosystems, particularly in a warming climate, the ATCM welcomed groundbreaking scientific research on non-native species and biogeographic regions, which will enable Parties to better manage the risks of non-native species and support further development of the protected areas system in Antarctica.

The ATCM welcomed news regarding India's recently completed research station and the Republic of Korea's final plans to construct a new research station. These facilities will use state-of-the-art technology to minimise environmental impacts and will provide additional capacity for globally significant science.

The ATCM agreed to develop a manual by 2013 on practical approaches to dealing with the cleanup of sites of past activity arising from the era before the Protocol on Environmental Protection to the Antarctic Treaty (Madrid Protocol), such as waste disposal sites and abandoned facilities. The ATCM also agreed to work intersessionally on approaches to repair and remediation of sites that may be subject to environmental damage.

Parties conduct inspections of Antarctic facilities as a vital part of promoting compliance with rules established in the Antarctic Treaty system. Parties welcomed the report on joint inspections conducted by the United States and the Russian Federation since ATCM XXXIV.

The ATCM designated a new Antarctic Specially Protected Area at Blood Falls in the McMurdo Dry Valleys. This brings the number of protected areas across the continent to 72. Parties also agreed on improvements to the ongoing management of several existing specially protected areas and one specially managed area.

Parties shared progress on implementing, and reaffirmed their commitment to ratifying, Annex VI of the Madrid Protocol, covering Liability Arising from Environmental Emergencies. The ATCM continued to encourage Parties to the Antarctic Treaty that are not yet Parties to the Madrid Protocol to accede. The Madrid Protocol provides for comprehensive protection of the Antarctic environment, including by prohibiting mining and providing a framework to assess the environmental impacts of activities in the Antarctic Treaty area (the area south of 60 degrees South Latitude).

The Meeting agreed to complement its existing agenda by developing a Multi-Year Strategic Work Plan.

Consistent with the Parties' commitment to protect the Antarctic environment, host country arrangements for the ATCM included actions to reduce its environmental impact, such as paper and waste minimisation and carbon offsets.

Parties reaffirmed their commitment to continue to work together in these and other areas. The next ATCM will be hosted by Belgium from 20-29 May 2013.

Parties expressed their gratitude for the generosity of the Australian Government and their great appreciation for the excellent facilities provided for the meeting in the beautiful and historic city of Hobart. Parties also expressed their warmest thanks to the Government and people of Tasmania.

Hobart, 20 June 2012

Preliminary Agenda for ATCM XXXVI

1. Opening of the Meeting

2. Election of Officers and Creation of Working Groups

3. Adoption of the Agenda and Allocation of Items

4. Operation of the Antarctic Treaty System: Reports by Parties, Observers and Experts

5. Operation of the Antarctic Treaty System: General Matters

6. Operation of the Antarctic Treaty System: Review of the Secretariat's Situation

7. Development of a Multi-Year Strategic Work Plan

8. Report of the Committee for Environmental Protection

9. Liability: Implementation of Decision 4 (2010)

10. Safety and Operations in Antarctica, including Search and Rescue

11. Tourism and Non-Governmental Activities in the Antarctic Treaty Area

12. Inspections under the Antarctic Treaty and the Environment Protocol

13. Science Issues, Scientific Cooperation and Facilitation

14. Implications of Climate Change for Management of the Antarctic Treaty Area

15. Education Issues

16. Exchange of Information

17. Biological Prospecting in Antarctica

18. Preparation of the 37th Meeting

19. Any Other Business

20. Adoption of the Final Report

21. Close of the meeting

PART II

Measures, Decisions and Resolutions

1. Measures

Antarctic Specially Protected Area No 109
(Moe Island, South Orkney Islands): Revised Management Plan

The Representatives,

Recalling Articles 3, 5 and 6 of Annex V to the Protocol on Environmental Protection to the Antarctic Treaty, providing for the designation of Antarctic Specially Protected Areas ("ASPA") and approval of Management Plans for those Areas;

Recalling

- Recommendation IV-13 (1966), which designated Moe Island, South Orkney Islands as Specially Protected Area ("SPA") No 13 and annexed a map of the Area;

- Recommendation XVI-6 (1991), which annexed a revised description of SPA 13 and a Management Plan for the Area;

- Measure 1 (1995), which annexed a revised description and a revised Management Plan for SPA 13;

- Resolution 9 (1995), which recommended that the structure of the Management Plan for SPA 13 annexed to Measure 1 (1995) be regarded as a model for all new and revised Management Plans for protected areas for the purposes of Annex V;

- Decision 1 (2002), which renamed and renumbered SPA 13 as ASPA 109;

- Measure 1 (2007), which adopted a revised Management Plan for ASPA 109;

Recalling that Recommendation IV-13 (1966) was designated as no longer current by Decision 1 (2011);

Recalling that Recommendation XVI-6 (1991) and Measure 1 (1995) have not become effective;

Recalling that Resolution 9 (1995) was designated as no longer current by Resolution 1 (2008);

Noting that the Committee for Environmental Protection has endorsed a revised Management Plan for ASPA 109;

Desiring to replace the existing Management Plan for ASPA 109 with the revised Management Plan;

Recommend to their Governments the following Measure for approval in accordance with Paragraph 1 of Article 6 of Annex V to the Protocol on Environmental Protection to the Antarctic Treaty:

That:

1. the revised Management Plan for Antarctic Specially Protected Area No 109 (Moe Island, South Orkney Islands), which is annexed to this Measure, be approved; and

2. the Management Plan for ASPA 109 annexed to Measure 1 (2007) shall cease to be effective.

Antarctic Specially Protected Area No 110
(Lynch Island, South Orkney Islands):
Revised Management Plan

The Representatives,

Recalling Articles 3, 5 and 6 of Annex V to the Protocol on Environmental Protection to the Antarctic Treaty, providing for the designation of Antarctic Specially Protected Areas ("ASPA") and approval of Management Plans for those Areas;

Recalling

- Recommendation IV-14 (1966), which designated Lynch Island, South Orkney Islands as Specially Protected Area ("SPA") No 14 and annexed a map of the Area;

- Recommendation XVI-6 (1991), which annexed a Management Plan for the Area;

- Resolution 1 (1998), which allocates responsibility among Consultative Parties for the revision of Management Plans for protected areas;

- Measure 1 (2000), which annexed a revised Management Plan for SPA 14;

- Decision 1 (2002), which renamed and renumbered SPA 14 as ASPA 110;

Recalling that Recommendation XVI-6 (1991) and Measure 1 (2000) have not become effective;

Noting that the Committee for Environmental Protection has endorsed a revised Management Plan for ASPA 110;

Desiring to replace the existing Management Plan for ASPA 110 with the revised Management Plan;

Recommend to their Governments the following Measure for approval in accordance with Paragraph 1 of Article 6 of Annex V to the Protocol on Environmental Protection to the Antarctic Treaty

That:

1. the revised Management Plan for Antarctic Specially Protected Area No 110 (Lynch Island, South Orkney Islands), which is annexed to this Measure, be approved; and

2. the Management Plan for SPA 14 annexed to Measure 1 (2000), which has not become effective, be withdrawn.

Antarctic Specially Protected Area No 111
(Southern Powell Island and adjacent islands, South Orkney Islands): Revised Management Plan

The Representatives,

Recalling Articles 3, 5 and 6 of Annex V to the Protocol on Environmental Protection to the Antarctic Treaty, providing for the designation of Antarctic Specially Protected Areas ("ASPA") and approval of Management Plans for those Areas;

Recalling

- Recommendation IV-15 (1966), which designated Southern Powell Island and adjacent islands, South Orkney Islands as Specially Protected Area ("SPA") No 15 and annexed a map of the Area;

- Recommendation XVI-6 (1991), which annexed a Management Plan for SPA 15;

- Measure 1 (1995), which annexed a modified description and a revised Management Plan for SPA 15;

- Decision 1 (2002), which renamed and renumbered SPA 15 as ASPA 111;

Recalling that Recommendation XVI-6 (1991) and Measure 1 (1995) have not become effective;

Noting that the Committee for Environmental Protection has endorsed a revised Management Plan for ASPA 111;

Desiring to replace the existing Management Plan for ASPA 111 with the revised Management Plan;

Recommend to their Governments the following Measure for approval in accordance with Paragraph 1 of Article 6 of Annex V to the Protocol on Environmental Protection to the Antarctic Treaty:

That:

1. the revised Management Plan for Antarctic Specially Protected Area No 111 (Southern Powell Island and adjacent islands, South Orkney Islands), which is annexed to this Measure, be approved; and

2. the Management Plans for SPA 15 annexed to Recommendation XVI-6 (1991) and Measure 1 (1995), which have not become effective, be withdrawn.

Antarctic Specially Protected Area No 112
(Coppermine Peninsula, Robert Island, South Shetland Islands): Revised Management Plan

The Representatives,

Recalling Articles 3, 5 and 6 of Annex V to the Protocol on Environmental Protection to the Antarctic Treaty, providing for the designation of Antarctic Specially Protected Areas ("ASPA") and approval of Management Plans for those Areas;

Recalling

- Recommendation VI-10 (1970), which designated Coppermine Peninsula, Robert Island, South Shetland Islands as Specially Protected Area ("SPA") No 16 and annexed a map of the Area;

- Resolution XVI-6 (1991), which adopted a Management Plan for SPA 16;

- Resolution 1 (1998), which allocates responsibility among Consultative Parties for the revision of Management Plans for protected areas;

- Decision 1 (2002), which renamed and renumbered SPA 16 as ASPA 112;

Recalling that Resolution XVI-6 (1991) has not become effective;

Noting that the Committee for Environmental Protection has endorsed a revised Management Plan for ASPA 112;

Desiring to replace the existing Management Plan for ASPA 112 with the revised Management Plan;

Recommend to their Governments the following Measure for approval in accordance with paragraph 1 of Article 6 of Annex V to the Protocol on Environmental Protection to the Antarctic Treaty:

That:

1. the revised Management Plan for Antarctic Specially Protected Area No 112 (Coppermine Peninsula, Robert Point, South Shetland Islands), which is annexed to this Measure, be approved; and

2. the Management Plan for SPA 16 annexed to Resolution XVI-6 (1991), which has not become effective, be withdrawn.

Antarctic Specially Protected Area No 115
(Lagotellerie Island, Marguerite Bay, Graham Land):
Revised Management Plan

The Representatives,

Recalling Articles 3, 5 and 6 of Annex V to the Protocol on Environmental Protection to the Antarctic Treaty, providing for the designation of Antarctic Specially Protected Areas ("ASPA") and approval of Management Plans for those Areas;

Recalling

- Recommendation XIII-11 (1985), which designated Lagotellerie Island, Marguerite Bay, Graham Land as Specially Protected Area ("SPA") No 19 and annexed a map of the Area;

- Recommendation XVI-6 (1991), which annexed a Management Plan for the Area;

- Resolution 1 (1998), which allocates responsibility among Consultative Parties for the revision of Management Plans for protected areas;

- Measure 1 (2000), which annexed a revised Management Plan for SPA 19;

- Decision 1 (2002), which renamed and renumbered SPA 19 as ASPA 115;

Recalling that Recommendation XVI-6 (1991) and Measure 1 (2000) have not become effective;

Noting that the Committee for Environmental Protection has endorsed a revised Management Plan for ASPA 115;

Desiring to replace the existing Management Plan for ASPA 115 with the revised Management Plan;

Recommend to their Governments the following Measure for approval in accordance with Paragraph 1 of Article 6 of Annex V to the Protocol on Environmental Protection to the Antarctic Treaty:

That:

1. the revised Management Plan for Antarctic Specially Protected Area No 115 (Lagotellerie Island, Marguerite Bay, Graham Land), which is annexed to this Measure, be approved; and

2. the Management Plan for SPA 19 annexed to Measure 1 (2000), which has not become effective, be withdrawn.

Antarctic Specially Protected Area No 129
(Rothera Point, Adelaide Island): Revised Management Plan

The Representatives,

Recalling Articles 3, 5 and 6 of Annex V to the Protocol on Environmental Protection to the Antarctic Treaty, providing for the designation of Antarctic Specially Protected Areas ("ASPA") and approval of Management Plans for those Areas;

Recalling

- Recommendation XIII-8 (1985), which designated Rothera Point, Adelaide Island as Site of

  Special Scientific Interest ("SSSI") No 9 and annexed a Management Plan for the site;

- Resolution 7 (1995), which extended the expiry date of SSSI 9;

- Measure 1 (1996), which annexed a revised description and a revised Management Plan for SSSI 9;

- Decision 1 (2002), which renamed and renumbered SSSI 9 as ASPA 129;

- Measure 1 (2007), which adopted a revised Management Plan for ASPA 129 and revised its boundaries;

Recalling that Resolution 7 (1995) was designated as no longer current by Decision 1 (2011);

Recalling that Measure 1 (1996) has not become effective and was withdrawn by Measure 10 (2008);

Noting that the Committee for Environmental Protection has endorsed a revised Management Plan for ASPA 129;

Desiring to replace the existing Management Plan for ASPA 129 with the revised Management Plan;

Recommend to their Governments the following Measure for approval in accordance with Paragraph 1 of Article 6 of Annex V to the Protocol on Environmental Protection to the Antarctic Treaty:

That:

1. the revised Management Plan for Antarctic Specially Protected Area No 129 (Rothera Point, Adelaide Island), which is annexed to this Measure, be approved; and

2. the Management Plan for ASPA 129 annexed to Measure 1 (2007) shall cease to be effective.

Antarctic Specially Protected Area No 133
(Harmony Point, Nelson Island, South Shetland Islands): Revised Management Plan

The Representatives,

Recalling Articles 3, 5 and 6 of Annex V to the Protocol on Environmental Protection to the Antarctic Treaty, providing for the designation of Antarctic Specially Protected Areas ("ASPA") and approval of Management Plans for those Areas;

Recalling

- Recommendation XIII-8 (1985), which designated Harmony Point, Nelson Island, South Shetland Islands as Site of Special Scientific Interest ("SSSI") No 14;

- Resolution 7 (1995), which extended the expiry date for SSSI 14;

- Measure 3 (1997), which adopted a revised Management Plan for SSSI 14; Decision 1 (2002), which renamed and renumbered SSSI 14 as ASPA 133;

- Measure 2 (2005), which annexed a revised Management Plan for ASPA 133;

Recalling that Resolution 7 (1995) was designated as no longer current by Decision 1 (2011);

Recalling that Measure 3 (1997) has not become effective;

Noting that the Committee for Environmental Protection has endorsed a revised Management Plan for ASPA 133;

Desiring to replace the existing Management Plan for ASPA 133 with the revised Management Plan;

Recommend to their Governments the following Measure for approval in accordance with Paragraph 1 of Article 6 of Annex V to the Protocol on Environmental Protection to the Antarctic Treaty:

That:

1. the revised Management Plan for Antarctic Specially Protected Area No 133 (Harmony Point, Nelson Island, South Shetland Islands), which is annexed to this Measure, be approved; and

2. the Management Plan for ASPA 133 annexed to Measure 2 (2005) shall cease to be effective.

Antarctic Specially Protected Area No 140
(Parts of Deception Island): Revised Management Plan

The Representatives,

Recalling Articles 3, 5 and 6 of Annex V to the Protocol on Environmental Protection to the Antarctic Treaty, providing for the designation of Antarctic Specially Protected Areas ("ASPA") and approval of Management Plans for those Areas;

Recalling

- Recommendation XIII-8 (1985), which designated Shores of Port Foster, Deception Island, South Shetland Islands as Site of Special Scientific Interest ("SSSI") No 21 and annexed a Management Plan for the site;

- Resolution 7 (1995), which extended the expiry date for SSSI 21;

- Resolution 1 (1998), which allocates responsibility among Consultative Parties for the revision of Management Plans for protected areas;

- Measure 2 (2000), which extended the expiry date for SSSI 21;

- Decision 1 (2002), which renamed and renumbered SSSI 21 as ASPA 140;

- Measure 3 (2005), which adopted a revised Management Plan for ASPA 140;

Recalling that Resolution 7 (1995) was designated as no longer current by Decision 1 (2011);

Recalling that Measure 2 (2000) has not become effective and was withdrawn by Measure 5 (2009);

Noting that the Committee for Environmental Protection has endorsed a revised Management Plan for ASPA 140;

Desiring to replace the existing Management Plan for ASPA 140 with the revised Management Plan;

Recommend to their Governments the following Measure for approval in accordance with Paragraph 1 of Article 6 of Annex V to the Protocol on Environmental Protection to the Antarctic Treaty:

That:

1. the revised Management Plan for Antarctic Specially Protected Area No 140 (Parts of Deception Island), which is annexed to this Measure, be approved; and

2. the Management Plan for ASPA 140 annexed to Measure 3 (2005) shall cease to be effective.

Antarctic Specially Protected Area No 172
(Lower Taylor Glacier and Blood Falls, Taylor Valley, McMurdo Dry Valleys, Victoria Land): Management Plan

The Representatives,

Recalling Articles 3, 5 and 6 of Annex V to the Protocol on Environmental Protection to the Antarctic Treaty providing for the designation of Antarctic Specially Protected Areas ("ASPA") and approval of Management Plans for those Areas;

Recalling Measure 1 (2004), which designated McMurdo Dry Valleys, Southern Victoria Land as Antarctic Specially Managed Area ("ASMA") No 2 and annexed a Management Plan for the Area;

Noting that the Committee for Environmental Protection has endorsed a Proposal for a new ASPA at Lower Taylor Glacier and Blood Falls, Taylor Valley, McMurdo Dry Valleys, Victoria Land, lying within ASMA 2, and endorsed the Management Plan annexed to this Measure;

Recognising that this area supports outstanding environmental, scientific, historic, aesthetic or wilderness values, or ongoing or planned scientific research, and would benefit from special protection;

Desiring to designate Lower Taylor Glacier and Blood Falls, Taylor Valley, McMurdo Dry Valleys, Victoria Land as an ASPA and to approve the Management Plan for this Area;

Recommend to their Governments the following Measure for approval in accordance with paragraph 1 of Article 6 of Annex V to the Protocol on Environmental Protection to the Antarctic Treaty:

That:

1. Lower Taylor Glacier and Blood Falls, Taylor Valley, McMurdo Dry Valleys, Victoria Land be designated as Antarctic Specially Protected Area No 172; and

2. the Management Plan, which is annexed to this Measure, be approved.

Antarctic Specially Managed Area No 4
(Deception Island): Revised Management Plan

The Representatives,

Recalling Articles 4, 5 and 6 of Annex V to the Protocol on Environmental Protection to the Antarctic Treaty, providing for the designation of Antarctic Specially Managed Areas ("ASMA") and the approval of Management Plans for those Areas;

Recalling Measure 3 (2005), which designated Deception Island as ASMA No 4 and adopted a Management Plan for the Area;

Noting that the Committee for Environmental Protection has endorsed a revised Management Plan for ASMA 4;

Desiring to replace the existing Management Plan for ASMA 4 with the revised Management Plan;

Recommend to their Governments the following Measure for approval in accordance with Paragraph 1 of Article 6 of Annex V to the Protocol on Environmental Protection to the Antarctic Treaty:

That:

1. the revised Management Plan for Antarctic Specially Managed Area No 4 (Deception Island), which is annexed to this Measure, be approved; and

2. the Management Plan for ASMA 4 annexed to Measure 3 (2005) shall cease to be effective.

Antarctic Historic Sites and Monuments:
No 4 Pole of Inaccessibility Station building
No 7 Ivan Khmara's Stone
No 8 Anatoly Shcheglov's Monument
No 9 Buromsky Island Cemetery
No 10 Soviet Oasis Station Observatory
No 11 Vostok Station Tractor
No 37 O'Higgins Historic Site

The Representatives,

Recalling the requirements of Article 8 of Annex V to the Protocol on Environmental Protection to the Antarctic Treaty that a list of current Historic Sites and Monuments be maintained, and that such sites shall not be damaged, removed or destroyed;

Recalling

- Recommendation VII-9 (1972), which annexed a revised and updated "List of Historic Sites and Monuments";

- Measure 3 (2003), which revised and updated the "List of Historic Sites and Monuments";

Desiring to change the description of several Historic Sites and Monuments;

Recommend to their Governments the following Measure for approval in accordance with Paragraph 2 of Article 8 of Annex V to the Protocol on Environmental Protection to the Antarctic Treaty:

1. the description of Historic Site and Monument No 4 (Recommendation VII-9 (1972)) be changed to read as follows:

"No 4: Pole of Inaccessibility Station building

Station building to which a bust of V.I. Lenin is fixed, together with a plaque in memory of the conquest of the Pole of Inaccessibility by Soviet Antarctic explorers in 1958. As of 2007 the station building was covered by snow. The bust of Lenin is erected on the wooden stand mounted on the building roof at about 1.5 m high above the snow surface."

Location: 82°06'42"S, 55°01'57"E

Original proposing Party: Russia

Party undertaking management: Russia.

2. the description of Historic Site and Monument No 7 (Recommendation VII-9 (1972)) be changed to read as follows:

"No 7: Ivan Khmara's Stone

Stone with inscribed plaque erected at Buromsky island in memory of Ivan Khmara, driver-mechanic, the member of the 1st Complex Antarctic Expedition of the USSR (1st Soviet Antarctic Expedition) who perished on fast ice in the performance of duties on 21.01.1956. Initially the stone was erected at Mabus Point, Mirny observatory. In 1974, 19th SAE, the stone was moved to Buromsky Island because of construction activity."

Location: 66°32'04"S, 92°59'57"E

Original proposing Party: Russia

Party undertaking management: Russia

3. the description of Historic Site and Monument No 8 (Recommendation VII-9 (1972)) be changed to read as follows:

"No 8: Anatoly Shcheglov's Monument

Metal stele with plaque in memory of Anatoly Shcheglov, driver-mechanic who perished in the performance of duties, erected on sledge on the Mirny – Vostok route, at 2 km from Mirny station."

Location: 66°34'43"S, 92°58'23"E

Original proposing Party: Russia

Party undertaking management: Russia

4. the description of Historic Site and Monument No 9 (Recommendation VII-9 (1972)) be changed to read as follows:

"No 9: Buromsky Island Cemetery

Cemetery on Buromsky Island, near Mirny Observatory in which are buried citizens of the USSR (Russian Federation), Czechoslovakia, GDR and Switzerland (members of the Soviet and Russian Antarctic Expeditions) who perished in the performance of their duties."

Location: 66°32'04"S, 93°00'E

Original proposing Party: Russia

Party undertaking management: Russia

5. the description of Historic Site and Monument No 10 (Recommendation VII-9 (1972)) be changed to read as follows:

"No 10: Soviet Oasis Station Observatory

Magnetic observatory building at Dobrowolsky station (a part of the former Soviet station Oasis transferred to Poland) at Bunger Hills with a plaque in memory of the opening of Oasis station in 1956."

Location: 66°16'30"S, 100°45'03"E

Original proposing Party: Russia

Party undertaking management: Russia

6. the description of Historic Site and MonumentNo 11 (Recommendation VII-9 (1972)) be changed to read as follows:

"No 11: Vostok Station Tractor
Heavy tractor ATT 11 at Vostok station which participated in the first traverse to the Earth Geomagnetic Pole, with plaque in memory of the opening of the Station in 1957."

Location: 78°27'48" S, 106°50'06" E

Original proposing Party: Russia

Party undertaking management: Russia

> 7. the description of Historic Site and Monument No 37 (Recommendation VII-9 (1972)) be changed to read as follows:

"No 37: O'Higgins Historic Site located on Cape Legoupil, Antarctic Peninsula and comprising the following structures of historical value:

- "Capitán General Bernardo O′Higgins Riquelme" Bust, erected in 1948 opposite the Base known under the same name. General O′Higgins was the first ruler of Chile to recognise the importance of Antarctica. It has a symbolic meaning in the history of Antarctic exploration since it was during his government that the vessel Dragon landed on the coast of the Antarctic Peninsula in 1820. This monument is also representative of pre-IGY activities in Antarctica. (63°19'14.3" S / 57°53'53.9"W)

- Former "Capitán General Bernardo O'Higgins Riquelme" Antarctic Base, unveiled on 18th February, 1948 by the President of the Republic of Chile, Gabriel González Videla, the first President in the world to visit Antarctica. It is considered as a model pioneering base in the modern period of Antarctic exploration. (63°19' S, 57°54'W)

- Plaque in memory of Lieutenants Oscar Inostroza Contreras and Sergio Ponce Torrealba, who perished in the Antarctic Continent for the sake of peace and science, on 12th August, 1957. (63°19'15.4" S / 57°53'52.9"W)

- Virgen del Carmen Grotto, located in the surroundings of the base, built approximately forty years ago. It has served as a place of spiritual withdrawal for the staff of the different Antarctic stations and expeditions. (63°19'15.9" S / 57°54'03.2"W)"

Location: 63°19' S, 57°54'W

Original proposing Party: Chile

Party undertaking management: Chile

2. Decisions

Measures on Operational Matters designated as no longer current

The Representatives,

Recalling Decision 3 (2002), Decision 1 (2007) and Decision 1 (2011), which established lists of measures* that were designated as spent or no longer current;

Having reviewed a number of measures on the subject of operational matters;

Recognising that the measures listed in the Annex to this Decision are no longer current;

Decide:

1. that the measures listed in the Annex to this Decision require no further action by the Parties; and

2. to request the Secretariat of the Antarctic Treaty to post the text of the measures that appear in the Annex to this Decision on its website in a way that makes clear that these measures are no longer current and that the Parties do not need to take any further action with respect to them.

*Note: measures previously adopted under Article IX of the Antarctic Treaty were described as Recommendations up to ATCM XIX (1995) and were divided into Measures, Decisions and Resolutions by Decision 1 (1995). te: measures previously adopted under Article IX of the Antarctic Treaty were described as Recommendations up to ATCM XIX (1995) and were divided into Measures, Decisions and Resolutions by Decision 1 (1995).

Measures on Operational Matters designated as no longer current

1. Telecommunications

- Recommendation III-V
- Recommendation VI-2

2. Logistics

- Recommendation IX-4

3. Shipping regulations

- Decision 2 (1999)
- Decision 8 (2005)
- Decision 2 (2006)
- Resolution 8 (2009)

Secretariat Report, Programme and Budget

The Representatives,

Recalling Measure 1 (2003) on the establishment of the Secretariat of the Antarctic Treaty (the Secretariat);

Bearing in mind the Financial Regulations for the Secretariat annexed to Decision 4 (2003);

Decide:

1. to approve the audited Financial Report for 2010/11, annexed to this Decision (Annex 1);

2. to take note of the Secretariat Report 2011/12 (SP 2 rev.1), which includes the Estimate of Income and Expenditures 2011/12, annexed to this Decision (Annex 2);

3. to approve the Secretariat Programme (SP 3 rev.1), including the Budget for 2012/13 and the Forecast Budget for 2013/14, annexed to this Decision (Annex 3);

4. to establish an open-ended Intersessional Contact Group ("ICG") on financial issues to be convened by the host country of the next Antarctic Treaty Consultative Meeting ("ATCM"). The ICG will:

   a) provide guidance, at the request of the Executive Secretary, on the implementation of the budget adopted at this ATCM;

   b) take account of the quarterly report of budget implementation, to be provided by the Executive Secretary;

   c) provide guidance to the Executive Secretary on the draft budget to be submitted to the next ATCM;

d) undertake any other tasks assigned to it by the ATCM; and

e) report on its work to the next ATCM;

and

5. to request the Executive Secretary to open the ATCM forum for the ICG and to provide assistance to the ICG.

AUDITOR'S REPORT

XXXV Antarctic Treaty Consultative Meeting 2012, Hobart, Australia

1. Report on Financial Statements

We have audited the attached Financial Statements of the Antarctic Treaty Secretariat, which include the following: Statement of Income and Expenditure, Statement of Financial Position, Statement of Net Capital Assets, Statement of Origin and Application of Funds and Explanatory Notes for the period commencing 1st April 2010 and ending 31st March 2011.

2. Management Responsibility for Financial Statements

The Antarctic Treaty Secretariat is responsible for the preparation and reasonable presentation of these Financial Statements according to International Accounting Standards and the specific rules of the Antarctic Treaty Consultative Meetings. Such responsibility includes: the design, implementation and maintenance of internal controls for the preparation and presentation of the Financial Statements, such that they are free of misstatements due to error or fraud; the selection and implementation of appropriate accounting policies, and the preparation of accounting estimates which are reasonable under the circumstances.

3. Auditor's Responsibility

Our responsibility is to express an opinion on these Financial Statements based on the audit conducted. The audit was conducted in accordance with International Auditing Standards and the Annex to Decision 3 (2008) of the XXXI Antarctic Treaty Consultative Meeting, which describes the tasks to be carried out by the external audit.

These rule require compliance with ethical requirements, and planning and execution of the audit so as to provide reasonable assurance that the Financial Statements are free of misstatements.

An audit includes the execution of procedures in order to obtain evidence on the amounts and the exposure reflected in the Financial Statements. Relevant procedures are selected based on the auditor's judgement, including an assessment of the risks of material misstatement in the Financial Statements, either by fraud or error. On conducting such assessment of risks, the auditor considers the internal control relevant to the preparation and reasonable presentation of the financial statements by the organisation, in order to design suitable procedures that are appropriate to the circumstances.

An audit also includes an assessment of appropriateness, of the accounting principles used, an opinion on whether the accounting estimates made by Management are reasonable, as well as an assessment of the general presentation of the Financial Statements.

We believe that the audited evidence we have obtained is sufficient and appropriate to provide a basis for our opinion as auditors.

4. Opinion

In our opinion, the Financial Statements audited present fairly, in all material aspects, the financial position of the Antarctic Treaty Secretariat as at 31st March 2011 and its financial performance for the period ending on such date in accordance with International Accounting Standards and the specific rules of the Antarctic Treaty Consultative Meetings.

Dr. Edgardo de Rose
  Public Accountant
  Registered with the Professional Council
  of Economic Science for the City of Buenos
  Aires (CPCECABA) in Book No. 182,
Page No. 195

Buenos Aires, 18th April 2012

Sindicatura General de la Nación
Av. Corrientes 389, Buenos Aires
Argentine Republic

Final Report 2010/2011

1. Statement of Income and Expenditure for all Funds for the Period 1st April 2010 to 31st March 2011

INCOME	31/03/2010	Budget	31/03/2011
Contributions	$ 840,740	$ 899,942	$ 899,942
Special contributions	$ 0	$ 0	$ 0
Other income (Note 2)	$ 1,364	$ 1,000	$ 528
Total Income	**$ 842,104**	**$ 900,942**	**$ 900,470**

EXPENDITURE			
Salaries	$ 403,363	$ 466,419	$ 469,948
Translation and interpreting services	$ 232,876	$ 212,670	$ 159,270
Travel an accommodation	$ 56,843	$ 68,800	$ 61,325
IT	$ 35,523	$ 38,700	$ 37,615
Printing, editing and copying	$ 13,581	$ 11,500	$ 15,964
General services	$ 33,147	$ 34,060	$ 38,886
Communications	$ 10,708	$ 12,500	$ 12,207
Office expenses	$ 12,220	$ 10,200	$ 8,217
Administration	$ 4,786	$ 3,500	$ 4,582
Representation	$ 2,802	$ 2,000	$ 3,143
Financing	$ 5,117	$ 0	$ 8,477
Total Expenditure	**$ 810,966**	**$ 860,349**	**$ 819,635**

Fund appropriation			
Staff Termination Fund	$ 15,662	$ 25,974	$ 25,974
Staff Replacement Fund	$ 0	$ 8,333	$ 8,333
Working Capital Fund	$ 2,475	$ 62,260	$ 62,260
Future Meeting Fund	$ 13,001	$ 0	$ 0
Total Fund appropriation	**$ 31,138**	**$ 96,567**	**$ 96,567**

Total Expenses & appropriation	**$ 842,104**	**$956,916**	**$916,202**

(Deficit) / Surplus for the period	**$ 0**	**($ 55,974)**	**($ 15,732)**

This statement should be read in conjunction with NOTES 1 to 10 attached.

2. Statement of Financial Position as at 31st March 2011

ASSETS		31/03/2010	31/03/2011
Current assets			
Cash and banks (Note 3)	$	876,024	$ 818,991
Contributions owed (Note 9)	$	70,159	$ 23,257
Other debtors (Note 4)	$	12,780	$ 23,606
Other current assets (Note 5)	$	34,818	$ 26,658
Total current assets	**$**	**993,781**	**$ 892,512**
Non-current assets			
Fixed assets (Note 1.5 and 6)	$	66,297	$ 68,727
Total non-current assets	**$**	**66,297**	**$ 68,727**
Total Assets		**$ 1,060,078**	**$ 961,239**

LIABILITIES		31/03/2010	31/03/2011
Current liabilities			
payables (Note 7)	$	31,357	$ 26,345
Contributions received in advance (Note 1.2 and 9)	$	407,572	$ 618,929
Salaries and social contributions payables(Note 8)	$	22,080	$ 11,298
Total current liabilities		**$ 461,009**	**$ 656,572**
Non-current liabilities			
Staff Replacement Fund (Note 1.7)	$	23,421	$ 26,510
Staff Termination Fund (Note 1.6)	$	38,781	$ 64,755
Fixed Assets Replacement Fund (Note 1.10)	$	0	$ 2,430
Total Non-current liabilities		**$ 62,202**	**$ 93,696**
Total Liabilities		**$ 523,211**	**$ 750,268**
NET ASSETS		**$ 536,867**	**$ 210,971**

This statement should be read in conjunction with NOTES 1 to 10 attached.

3. Statement of changes in Net Assets as at 31st March 2011

Represented by	Net assets 01-04-2010	Income	Expenses and appropriation	Net assets 31-03-2010
General Fund	$ 35,051	$ 899,942	($ 915,675)	$ 19,319
Working Capital Fund (Note 1.8)	$ 129,392		$ 62,260	$ 191,652
Future Meeting Fund (Note 1.9)	$ 372,424		($ 372,424)	$ 0
Net Assets	**$ 536,867**	**$ 899,942**	**($ 1,225,839)**	**$ 210,971**

This statement should be read in conjunction with NOTES 1 to 10 attached.

4. Cash Flow Statement for the period 1st April 2010 to 31st March 2011

Variation in cash & cash equivalents

Cash & cash equivalent at beginning of the year	$ 876,024
Cash & cash equivalent at year end	$ 818,991
Net decrease in cash and cash equivalents	($ 57,033)

Causes for the variations in cash & cash equivalents

Operating activities

Contributions received	$ 539,272	
Payment of salaries	($ 469,948)	
Payment of translation services	($ 531,694)	
Payment of travel and accommodation	($ 61,325)	
Printing, editing and copying	($ 15,964)	
Relocation expenses	($ 5,244)	
Other payments	($ 86,449)	
Net cash & cash equivalents from operating activities		($ 631,353)

Investment activities

Purchase of fixed assets	($ 17,253)	
Other	$ 0	
Net cash & cash equivalents from investment activities		($ 17,253)

Financing activities

Contributions received in advance	$ 618,929	
Collection pt. 5.6 of Staff Regulations	$ 82,371	
Payment pt. 5.6 of Staff Regulations	($ 93,197)	
Pre paid expenses ATCM XXXIV	($ 9,538)	
Net cash & cash equivalents from financing activities		$ 598,564

Foreign currency activities

Net loss	($ 6,992)	
Net cash & cash equivalents from foreign currency activities	($ 6,992)	
Net decrease of cash & cash equivalents		($ 57,033)

This statement should be read in conjunction with NOTES 1 to 10 attached.

NOTES TO THE FINANCIAL STATEMENTS AS AT 31 MARCH 2011

1. BASIS FOR PREPARATION OF FINANCIAL STATEMENTS

1.1 Historical Cost

The accounts are drawn up in accordance with the convention of historical cost , except where otherwise indicated.

1.2 Accrual Basis

Financial Statements are prepared on an accrual basis in accordance with International Accounting Standards (IAS).

1.3 Currency

All Financial Statements transactions are prepared in US dollar

1.4 Premises

The Secretariat Offices are provided by the Ministry of Foreign Affairs, International Trade and Cult of the Argentine Republic. Premises are free of rent and common expenses.

1.5 Fixed Assets

All items are valued at historical cost, less accumulated depreciation. Depreciation is calculated on a straight-line basis at annual rates appropriate to their estimated useful life. The aggregate residual value of fixed assets does not exceed their use value.

1.6 Executive Staff Termination Fund

Pursuant to Section 10.4 of the Staff Regulations, this fund shall be sufficiently funded to compensate executive staff members at a rate of one month base pay for each year of service. As at 31st March, 2011 the Fund is underfunded by $ 11,561.42 (eleven thousand, five hundred and sixty-one dollars with forty-two cents).

1.7 Staff Replacement Fund

This fund is used to cover Secretariat executive staff relocation expenses to and from the Secretariat Head Office.

1.8 Working Capital Fund

Pursuant to Financial Regulations 6.2 (a), the fund shall stand at one-sixth (1/6) of the budget for the current financial year.

1.9 Future Meeting Fund

Pursuant to Decision 7 (2005), this Fund was created to cover the Interpreting and Translation expenses. Once Measure 1 (2003) becomes effective, such fund shall be renamed Translation Contingency Fund. The Measure became effective on 31st August 2009.

1.10 Fixed Asset Replacement Fund

Pursuant to IAS, assets with a useful life beyond the current financial year shall be reflected as an asset in the Statement of Financial Position. To date, the offseting entry was reflected as an adjustment to the General Fund. From now on, the offseting entry shall be reflected as a liability under such heading.

NOTES TO THE FINANCIAL STATEMENTS AS AT 31st MARCH 2011

	31/03/2010	31/03/2011
Note 2 Other Income		
Earned interest	$ 1,135	$ 255
Discounts obtained	$ 229	$ 273
	$ 1,364	$ 528
Note 3 Cash and banks		
Cash US Dollars	$ 2,731	$ 1,338
Cash Argentine Pesos	$ 680	$ 544
BNA US Dollar account	$ 868,933	$ 755,882
BNA Argentine Peso account	$ 3,679	$ 61,227
Total	$ 876,024	$ 818,991
Note 4 Others debtors		
Staff Regulations pt. 5.6	$ 12,780	$ 23,606
	$ 12,780	$ 23,606
Note 5 Other current assets		
Advance payments	$ 28,481	$ 13,676
VAT refund	$ 6,338	$ 12,726
Other recoverable expenses	$ 0	$ 256
Total	$ 34,819	$ 26,658
Note 6 Fixed Assets		
Books & subscriptions	$ 2,877	$ 4,515
Machines	$ 28,307	$ 30,787
Furniture	$ 24,374	$ 23,092
IT equipment and software	$ 39,747	$ 54,164
Total original cost	$ 95,305	$112,558
Accumulated depreciation	($ 29,008)	($ 43,831)
Total Net Fixed Assets	$ 66,297	$ 68,727

Note 7 Payables

Business	$ 3,483	$ 7,700
Accrued expenses	$ 27,197	$ 17,978
Other	$ 677	$ 667
	$ 31,357	$ 26,345

Note 8 Salaries and social contributions

Salaries	$ 10,800	$ 0
Social contributions	$ 11,280	$ 11,298
	$ 22,080	$ 11,298

NOTES TO THE FINANCIAL STATEMENTS AS AT 31st MARCH 2011

Note 9 Contributions

Breakdown of contributions owed and received:

Financial Year	2009/10	2010/11		2011/12	
Received	Owed	Pledged	Received	Receivable	In advance
Argentina		$ 40,540	$ 40,540		
Australia		$ 40,540	$ 40,540		$ 60,346
Belgium	$ 18	$ 26,946	$ 26,929	$ 36	
Brazil	$ 9,557	$ 26,946	$ 36,491	$ 12	
Bulgaria		$ 22,868	$ 22,868		
Chile	$ 17,859	$ 31,024	$ 48,883		
China		$ 31,024	$ 31,024		
Ecuador		$ 22,868	$ 22,868		
Finland		$ 26,946	$ 26,946		
France		$ 40,540	$ 40,540		
Germany	$ 30	$ 35,102	$ 35,070	$ 62	$ 52,281
India	$ 62	$ 31,024	$ 30,962	$ 124	
Italy		$ 35,102	$ 35,102		
Japan	($ 1)	$ 40,540	$ 40,540	($ 1)	
Korea		$ 26,946	$ 26,946		$ 40,110
Netherlands		$ 31,024	$ 31,024		$ 46,181
New Zealand		$ 40,540	$ 40,540		$ 60,320
Norway	$ 30	$ 40,540	$ 40,540	$ 30	$ 60,346
Peru		$ 22,868		$ 22,868	
Poland		$ 26,946	$ 26,946		$ 40,110
Russia		$ 31,024	$ 31,024		$ 46,181
South Africa		$ 31,024	$ 31,024		$ 46,181

Financial Year	2009/10		2010/11		2011/12	
Received	Owed	Pledged	Received	Receivable	In advance
Spain		$ 115	$ 31,024	$ 31,024	$ 115	
Sweden			$ 31,024	$ 31,024		$ 46,181
Ukraine		$ 42,490	$ 26,946	$ 69,424	$ 12	
United Kingdom			$ 40,540	$ 40,540		$ 60,346
United States			$ 40,540	$ 40,540		$ 60,346
Uruguay			$ 26,946	$ 26,946		
TOTAL		$ 70,160	$ 899,942	$ 946,845	$ 23,258	$ 618,929

NOTES TO THE FINANCIAL STATEMENTS AS AT 31st MARCH 2011

Note 10 Statement of Income and Expenditure for all Funds for the period 1st April 2010 to 31st March 2011 (old format)

INCOME	31/03/2010	Budget	31/03/2011
Contributions	$ 840,740	$ 899,942	$ 899,942
Other income/ (expenditure)	($ 3,754)	$ 1,000	($ 7,950)
Total Income	**$ 836,986**	**$ 900,942**	**$ 891,992**

EXPENDITURE			
Salaries			
Executive Staff	$ 232,425	$ 247,974	$ 250,104
General Service Staff	$ 167,876	$ 218,445	$ 219,845
Total Salaries	**$ 400,301**	**$ 466,419**	**$ 469,948**

Goods and services			
Audit	$ 9,248	$ 9,360	$ 9,299
Data entry	$ 0	$ 0	$ 0
Documentation services	$ 3,062	$ 0	$ 0
Legal advisory	$ 3,600	$ 4,200	$ 4,360
Miscellaneous	$ 9,950	$ 8,500	$ 10,008
Office expenses	$ 10,950	$ 11,700	$ 12,141
Post	$ 1,483	$ 2,500	$ 1,871
Printing, editing and copying	$ 13,581	$ 11,500	$ 15,964
Representation	$ 2,802	$ 2,000	$ 3,143
Telecommunications	$ 11,720	$ 13,000	$ 12,689
Training	$ 5,504	$ 4,100	$ 8,208
Translation, editing	$ 232,876	$ 212,670	$ 159,270

Travel an accommodation	$ 56,843	$ 68,800	$ 61,325
Total Goods and services	**$ 361,619**	**$ 348,330**	**$ 298,278**

Equipment

Documentation	$ 1,762	$ 1,900	$ 1,137
Office furniture	$ 6,643	$ 5,000	$ 4,179
IT Equipment	$ 23,729	$ 23,600	$ 21,796
Development	$ 11,794	$ 15,100	$ 15,820
Total Equipment	**$ 43,928**	**$ 45,600**	**$ 42,931**

Fund appropriation

Working Capital Fund (Note 1.8)	$ 2,475	$ 62,260	$ 62,260
Staff Replacement Fund (Note 1.7)	$ 0	$ 8,333	$ 8,333
Staff Termination Fund (Note 1.6)	$ 15,662	$ 25,974	$ 25,974
Future Meeting Fund (Note 1.9)	$ 13,001	$ 0	$ 0
Total Fund appropriation	**$ 31,138**	**$ 96,567**	**$ 96,567**

TOTAL EXPENDITURE	**$ 836,986**	**$ 956,916**	**$ 907,725**

(Deficit) / Surplus	**$**	**($ 55,974)**	**($ 15,733)**

Dr. Manfred Reinke   Roberto A. Fennell
Executive Secretary   Finance Officer

Estimate of Income and Expenditures 2011/2012

**Estimate of Income and Expenditure for all Funds
for the Period 1 April 2011 to 31 March 2012**

	Statement 2010/11		Budget 2011/12		Provisional Statement 2011/12	
INCOME						
General Contributions	$	899,942	$	1,339,600	$	1,339,600
Other income	$	528	$	70	$	1,506
Total Income	$	900,470	$	1,339,670	$	1,341,106
EXPENDITURE						
Salaries	$	469,948	$	578,101	$	577,637
Translation Services	$	159,270	$	365,825	$	367,846
Travel & Lodging	$	61,325	$	52,815	$	52,533
Information Technology	$	37,615	$	42,500	$	40,949
Printing, Editing & Copying	$	15,964	$	14,000	$	26,301
General Services	$	38,886	$	44,060	$	46,598
Comunications	$	12,207	$	13,368	$	13,568
Office expenses	$	8,217	$	11,983	$	13,269
General administration	$	4,582	$	4,698	$	9,879
Representation	$	3,143	$	4,500	$	5,446
Financing	$	8,477	$	0	$	7,518
Relocation	$	0	$	50,000	$	38,641
Total Expenditure	$	**819,634**	$	**1,181,850**	$	**1,200,185**
FUNDS APPROPIATfON						
Working capital fund	$	62,260	$	67,072	$	44,930
Staff termination fund	$	25,974	$	42,502	$	42,502
Staff replacement fund	$	8,333	$	18,246	$	23,490
Translation Contingency Fund	$	0	$	30,000	$	30,000
Total Funds Appropiation	$	**96,567**	$	**157,820**	$	**140,922**
Total Expenses & Appropiations	$	**916,201**	$	**1,339,670**	$	**1,341,106**
(Deficit) / Surplus for the period	$	**(15,731)**	$	**0**	$	**(0)**

	Statement 2010/11		Budget 2011/12		Provisional Statement 2011/12
MOVING					
Specific Contribution Argentina					53,800
Moving expenses					53,831
Total Moving					**-31**

	Statement 2010/11		Budget 2011/12		Provisional Statement 2011/12
Summary of Funds					
Working capital fund	$	210,917	$	277,989	$	255,847
Staff termination fund	$	64,755	$	107,257	$	107,257
Staff replacement fund	$	26,510	$	50,000	$	50,000
Translation Contingency Fund	$	0	$	30,000	$	30,000

Secretariat Programme 2012/13

Introduction

This work programme outlines the activities proposed for the Secretariat in the Financial Year 2012/13 (1 April 2012 to 31 March 2013). The main areas of activity of the Secretariat are treated in the first three chapters, which are followed by a section on management and a forecast of the programme for the financial year 2012/13.

The draft budget for 2012/13, the forecast budget for 2013/14, and the accompanying contribution and salary scales are included in the appendices.

The programme and the accompanying budget figures for 2012/13 are based on the Forecast Budget for 2012/13 (Decision 3 (2011), Annex 3, Appendix 1).

The programme focuses on the regular activities, such as preparation of the ATCM XXXV and ATCM XXXVI, publication of Final Reports, and the various specific tasks assigned to the Secretariat under Measure 1 (2003).

Contents:

1. ATCM/CEP support
2. Information Exchange
3. Documentation
4. Public Information
5. Management
6. Forecast Programme

1. ATCM/CEP Support

ATCM XXXV

The Secretariat will support ATCM XXXV by gathering and collating the documents for the meeting and publishing them in a restricted section of the Secretariat website. The Delegates section will also provide online registration for delegates and a downloadable, up-to-date list of delegates.

The Secretariat will support the functioning of the ATCM through the production of Secretariat Papers, a Manual for Delegates, and summaries of papers for the ATCM, the CEP, and the ATCM Working Groups.

Coordination and contact

Aside from maintaining constant contact via email, telephone and other means with the Parties and international institutions of the Antarctic Treaty System, attendance at meetings is an important tool to maintain coordination and contact.

The Secretariat is already in close contact with the Government of Belgium in connection with the preparation of the ATCM XXXVI in 2013, and will maintain contact with the Government of Brazil regarding the preparation of the ATCM XXXVII.

Development of the Secretariat website

The website will continue to be improved to make it more concise and easier to use, and to increase the visibility of the most relevant sections and information. The searching facilities of the website databases, especially the Meeting Document database, will be further developed. The Protected Areas database will be enhanced by including new fields and geographical information in a joint project with Australia.

Support of intersessional activities

During recent years both the CEP and the ATCM have produced an important amount of intersessional work, mainly through Intersessional Contact Groups (ICG). The Secretariat will provide technical support for the online establishment of the ICGs agreed at the ATCM XXXV and CEP XV and by producing specific documents if required by the ATCM or the CEP.

The Secretariat will update the website with the measures adopted by the ATCM and with the information produced by the CEP and the ATCM.

Printing

The Secretariat will publish and distribute the Final Report and its Annexes of the ATCM XXXV in the four Treaty languages. The text of the Final Report will be printed, while the annexes will be published as a CD attached to the printed report. The full text of the Final Report will be available in book form through online retailers.

Intersessional Contact Group (ICG) on Financial Issus

The Secretariat will cooperate in all important financial issues with the ICG on Financial Issues.

2. Information Exchange

General

The Secretariat will continue to assist Parties in posting their information exchange materials, as well as integrating information on EIAs in the EIA database.

Electronic Information Exchange System

During the next operational season and depending on the decisions of the ATCM XXXV, the Secretariat will continue to make adjustments necessary to facilitate the use of the electronic system for the Parties, as well as develop tools to compile and present summarised reports.

3. Records and Documents

Documents of the ATCM

The Secretariat will continue its efforts to complete its archive of the Final Reports and other records of the ATCM and other meetings of the Antarctic Treaty System in the four Treaty languages. Assistance from the Parties in searching for their archives will be essential in achieving a complete archive. The Secretariat expects a set of Working Papers from ATCMs between 1961 and 1998 from a joint project with the Scott Polar Research Institute (Cambridge, UK) and will incorporate them into the Antarctic Treaty Database. This involves the scanning, proofreading, and data entry of the documents.

Antarctic Treaty database

The database of the Recommendations, Measures, Decisions and Resolutions of the ATCM is at present complete in English and almost complete in Spanish and French, although the Secretariat still lacks various Final Report copies in those languages. In Russian more Final Reports are lacking, and materials that have been received are being proofread and converted into electronic formats.

4. Public Information

The Secretariat and its website will continue to function as a clearinghouse for information on the Parties' activities and relevant developments in Antarctica.

5. Management

Personnel

On 1 April 2012 the Secretariat staff consisted of the following personnel:

Executive staff

Name	Position	Since	Rank
Manfred Reinke	Executive Secretary	1-09-2009	E1
José María Acero	Assistant Executive Secretary	1-01-2005	E3

General staff

José Luis Agraz	Information Officer	1-11-2004	G1
Diego Wydler	Information Technology Officer	1-02-2006	G1
Roberto Alan Fennell	Accountant (part time 25h/week)	1-12-2008	G2
Pablo Wainschenker	Editor	1-02-2006	G3
Ms. Violeta Antinarelli	Librarian (part time)	1-04-2007	G3
Ms. Gloria Fontán	Office Manager	1-12-2004	G5
Ms. Anna Balok	Data Entry Assistant (part time 20h/week)	1-10-2010	G5

Financial Matters

The Budget for 2012/13 and the Forecast Budget for 2013/14 are shown in Appendix 1. The budget will be implemented after consultations with the Parties when necessary.

Translation and Interpretation

In 2010, in cooperation with Argentina and Australia, the hosts of the ATCMs XXXIV and XXXV, the Secretariat had prepared an international call for proposals for translation and interpretation services for the ATCMs XXXIV and XXXV. Costs for translation and interpretation were budgeted for the ATCM XXXIV at 365,825 US$ and for the ATCM XXXV at 361,000 US$.

The Secretariat is preparing a new call for proposals for translation and interpretation for the ATCM XXXVI (2013 Brussels), ATCM XXXVI (Brazil) and ATCM XXXVII (Bulgaria). It has already contacted various companies in the market. Seven companies have expressed their willingness to participate in a call for proposals for the next ATCMs.

Salaries, IT, Publishing, Administrative and Travel Costs in FY 2012/13

The Executive Secretary proposes that the General Staff receives a raise of 14%, to compensate for the rise on the cost of living. Authorisation to implement this raise is subject to the guidance of the Intersessional Contact Group (ICG) on Financial Issues, to be provided by end of August 2012. The Executive Staff will not receive any such compensation. Staff members shall receive annual step increases, subject to satisfactory performance of their duties due to Staff Regulation 5.7. The salary scheme for the FY 2012/13 is shown in SP3 Appendix 3.

Regulation 5.10 of the Staff Regulations requires compensating staff members in the general category when they have to work more than 40 hours during one week. Overtime is requested during the ATCMs.

To compensate for the rise in travel costs, the Executive Secretary will reduce the daily subsistence allowance (DSA) rates to 80% of the DSA rates from the International Civil Service for the staff of the Secretariat.

Funds

Working Capital Fund

According to the Financial Regulation 6.2 (a), the Working Capital Fund has to be maintained at 1/6 of the Secretariat's budget of 223,433 US$ in the upcoming year.

Appropriation Lines

The ATCM XXXIV agreed that the budget should be presented with a new set of budget lines developed in cooperation with the external auditor *Sindicatura General de la Nación* (SIGEN) to better demonstrate how the Secretariat spent the contributions.

The new appropriation lines are:

- *Salaries*: this would include not only the salaries approved in the budget for ATS direct staff, but also those who assist the Secretariat in the meetings and the overtime for the general staff during the ATCM
- *Translation and Interpretation*: all costs for translation before, during and after the ATCM annual meeting and interpretation during the meeting (includes air fares, lodging and sundry)
- *Information technology*: all the investments in equipment, software development, and IT maintenance and security
- *Printing, editing and copying*: for the printed Final Report and electronic support
- *General services:* all local support services, such as legal, auditing, banking, training
- *Communications*: includes telephone, internet, WEB hosting, postage
- *Office:* stationary, books, insurance, maintenance
- *Administrative:* local transport, supplies
- *Financing:* net exchange gain or loss

The budget of FY 2012/13 and the forecast budget of FY 2013/14 are presented on this basis (Appendix 1).

Contributions for the Financial Year 2013/14

There will be a zero nominal increase of the contributions compared to the FY 2010/11 and FY 2011/12.

Contributions are shown in Appendix 2b.

6. Forecast Programme

It is expected that most of the ongoing activities of the Secretariat will be continued in 2013/14 and therefore, unless the programme undergoes major changes, no change in staff positions is foreseen for the following years.

Appendix 1

Provisional Report 2011/12, Budget 2012/13 and Forecast 2013/14

APPROPRIATION LINES	Prov. State-ment 2011/12	Forecast 2012/13	Budget 2012/13	Forecast 2013/14
INCOME				
CONTRIBUTIONS needed	**$ -1,339,600**	**$ -1,339,600**	**$ -1,339,600**	**$ -1,339,600**
Interest Income Investments	$ -1,506	$ -1,000	$ -1,000	$ -1,000
Total Income	**$ -1,341,106**	**$ -1,340,600**	**$ -1,340,600**	**$ -1,340,600**
EXPENDITURE				
SALARIES				
Executive	$ 305,654	$ 342,332	$ 311,323	$ 317,001
General Staff	$ 241,159	$ 277,333	$ 294,966	$ 306,860
ATCM Support Staff	$ 11,561	$ 12,139	$ 12,750	$ 12,750
Trainee	$ 4,800	$ 4,800	$ 4,800	$ 4,800
Overtime	$ 14,926	$ 11,565	$ 10,000	$ 10,000
	$ 577,637	**$ 648,169**	**$ 633,839**	**$ 651,411**
TRANSLATION AND INTERPRETATION				
Translation and Interpretation	**$ 367,846**	**$ 358,002**	**$ 361,000**	**$ 400,000**
TRAVEL				
Travel	**$ 52,533**	**$ 110,380**	**$ 90,000**	**$ 80,000**
INFORMATION TECHNOLOGY				
Hardware	$ 11,785	$ 13,000	$ 10,000	$ 10,000
Software	$ 2,823	$ 3,500	$ 3,000	$ 3,000
Development	$ 15,892	$ 18,400	$ 16,500	$ 16,500
Support	$ 10,449	$ 10,000	$ 13,000	$ 13,000
	$ 40,949	**$ 44,900**	**$ 42,500**	**$ 42,500**
PRINTING, EDITING & COPYING				
Final report	$ 26,301	$ 15,400	$ 16,500	$ 18,975
Site guidelines	$ 0	$ 0	$ 2,500	$ 2,875
	$ 26,301	**$ 15,400**	**$ 19,000**	**$ 21,850**

	Prov. State-ment 2011/12	Forecast 2012/13	Budget 2012/13	Forecast 2013/14
GENERAL SERVICES				
Legal advice	$ 8,400	$ 9,900	$ 4,000	$ 4,600
External audit	$ 10,764	$ 10,764	$ 10,764	$ 12,379
Cleaning, maintenance & security	$ 11,433	$ 11,385	$ 25,093	$ 16,207
Training	$ 6,979	$ 8,000	$ 6,000	$ 6,000
Banking	$ 4,890	$ 5,940	$ 5,624	$ 6,467
Rental of equipment	$ 4,132	$ 2,550	$ 4,752	$ 5,465
	$ 46,598	**$ 48,539**	**$ 56,232**	**$ 51,117**
COMMUNICATION				
Telephone	$ 3,180	$ 3,360	$ 3,864	$ 4,444
Internet	$ 1,879	$ 1,879	$ 2,161	$ 2,485
Web hosting	$ 5,995	$ 6,675	$ 6,894	$ 7,928
Postage	$ 2,514	$ 2,814	$ 2,471	$ 2,842
	$ 13,568	**$ 14,728**	**$ 15,390**	**$ 17,699**
OFFICE				
Stationery & supplies	$ 2,208	$ 2,200	$ 2,200	$ 2,530
Books & subscriptions	$ 1,650	$ 1,650	$ 5,898	$ 6,782
Insurance	$ 2,283	$ 2,280	$ 1,958	$ 2,252
Furniture	$ 999	$ 800	$ 800	$ 800
Office equipment	$ 4,560	$ 4,610	$ 4,000	$ 4,600
Maintenance	$ 1,952	$ 1,961	$ 2,000	$ 2,300
	$ 13,652	**$ 13,501**	**$ 16,856**	**$ 19,264**
ADMINISTRATIVE				
Supplies	$ 1,920	$ 1,920	$ 2,000	$ 2,300
Local transport	$ 730	$ 800	$ 1,000	$ 1,150
Miscellaneous	$ 2,534	$ 2,534	$ 2,500	$ 2,875
Utilities (Energy)	$ 4,695	$ 0	$ 8,000	$ 10,400
	$ 9,879	**$ 5,254**	**$ 13,500**	**$ 16,725**
REPRESENTATION				
Representation	**$ 5,446**	**$ 3,500**	**$ 3,000**	**$ 3,000**
FINANCING				
Exchange loss	**$ 7,518**	**$ 930**	**$ 5,000**	**$ 5,000**
SUBTOTAL APPROPRIATIONS	**$ 1,200,185**	**$ 1,263,304**	**$ 1,256,318**	**$ 1,308,566**

	Prov. State-ment 2011/12	Forecast 2012/13	Budget 2012/13	Forecast 2013/14
ALLOCATION TO FUNDS				
Translation Contingency Fund	$ 30,000	$ 0	$ 0	$ 0
Staff Replacement Fund	$ 23,490	$ 0	$ 0	$ 0
Staff Termination Fund	$ 42,501	$ 32,778	$ 28,403	$ 28,880
Working Capital Fund	$ 12,516	$ 0	$ 0	$ 0
	$ 108,507	**$ 32,778**	**$ 28,403**	**$ 28,880**

TOTAL APPROPRIATIONS	**$ 1,308,692**	**$ 1,296,082**	**$ 1,284,721**	**$ 1,337,446**

BALANCE	**$ 32,414**	**$ 44,518**	**$ 55,879**	**$ 3,154**

TOTAL EXPENDITURES	**$ 1,341,106**	**$ 1,340,600**	**$ 1,340,600**	**$ 1,340,600**

Summary of Funds

Translation Contingency Fund	$ 30,000	$ 30,000	$ 30,000	$ 30,000
Staff Replacement Fund	$ 50,000	$ 50,000	$ 50,000	$ 50,000
Staff Termination Fund	$ 107,257	$ 140,035	$ 135,660	$ 164,064
Working Capital Fund	$ 223,433	$ 223,433	$ 223,433	$ 223,433
General Fund	$ 32,414	$ 76,932	$ 88,293	$ 91,447
Maximum Required Amount Working Capital Fund (Fin, Reg, 6,2)	$ 223,433	$ 223,433	$ 223,433	$ 223,433

Appendix 2

Contribution Scale 2013/14

2013/14	Cat.	Mult.	Variable	Fixed	Total
Argentina	A	3.6	$ 36,424.17	$ 23,921.43	$60,346
Australia	A	3.6	$ 36,424.17	$ 23,921.43	$60,346
Belgium	D	1.6	$ 16,188.52	$ 23,921.43	$40,110
Brazil	D	1.6	$ 16,188.52	$ 23,921.43	$40,110
Bulgaria	E	1.0	$ 10,117.82	$ 23,921.43	$34,039
Chile	C	2.2	$ 22,259.21	$ 23,921.43	$46,181
China	C	2.2	$ 22,259.21	$ 23,921.43	$46,181
Ecuador	E	1.0	$ 10,117.82	$ 23,921.43	$34,039
Finland	D	1.6	$ 16,188.52	$ 23,921.43	$40,110
France	A	3.6	$ 36,424.17	$ 23,921.43	$60,346
Germany	B	2.8	$ 28,329.91	$ 23,921.43	$52,251
India	C	2.2	$ 22,259.21	$ 23,921.43	$46,181
Italy	B	2.8	$ 28,329.91	$ 23,921.43	$52,251
Japan	A	3.6	$ 36,424.17	$ 23,921.43	$60,346
Korea	D	1.6	$ 16,188.52	$ 23,921.43	$40,110
Netherlands	C	2.2	$ 22,259.21	$ 23,921.43	$46,181
New Zealand	A	3.6	$ 36,424.17	$ 23,921.43	$60,346
Norway	A	3.6	$ 36,424.17	$ 23,921.43	$60,346
Peru	E	1.0	$ 10,117.82	$ 23,921.43	$34,039
Poland	D	1.6	$ 16,188.52	$ 23,921.43	$40,110
Russia	C	2.2	$ 22,259.21	$ 23,921.43	$46,181
South Africa	C	2.2	$ 22,259.21	$ 23,921.43	$46,181
Spain	C	2.2	$ 22,259.21	$ 23,921.43	$46,181
Sweden	C	2.2	$ 22,259.21	$ 23,921.43	$46,181
Ukraine	D	1.6	$ 16,188.52	$ 23,921.43	$40,110
United Kingdom	A	3.6	$ 36,424.17	$ 23,921.43	$60,346
United States	A	3.6	$ 36,424.17	$ 23,921.43	$60,346
Uruguay	D	1.6	$ 16,188.52	$ 23,921.43	$40,110
		66.2	$ 669,800.00	$ 669,800.00	**$1,339,600**

Budget amount $1,339,600
Base rate $10,118

Appendix 3

Salary Scale 2012/13

Schedule A

SALARY SCALE FOR THE EXECUTIVE STAFF CATEGORY

(United States dollars)

2012/13 Level		STEPS														
		I	II	III	IV	V	VI	VII	VIII	IX	X	XI	XII	XIII	XIV	XV
E1	A	$133,830	$136,320	$138,810	$141,301	$143,791	$146,281	$148,771	$151,262							
E1	B	$167,287	$170,400	$173,512	$176,626	$179,739	$182,851	$185,964	$189,078							
E2	A	$112,692	$114,812	$116,931	$119,050	$121,168	$123,286	$125,404	$127,524	$129,643	$131,761	$133,880	$134,120	$136,210		
E2	B	$140,865	$143,515	$146,164	$148,812	$151,460	$154,107	$156,755	$159,405	$162,054	$164,702	$167,349	$167,650	$170,263		
E3	A	$93,973	$96,016	$98,061	$100,106	$102,151	$104,195	$106,240	$108,285	$110,328	$112,372	$114,417	$114,852	$116,869	$118,886	$120,901
E3	B	$117,466	$120,020	$122,577	$125,133	$127,689	$130,243	$132,800	$135,356	$137,910	$140,465	$143,021	$143,565	$146,086	$148,607	$151,126
E4	A	$77,922	$79,815	$81,710	$83,599	$85,494	$87,386	$89,275	$91,171	$93,065	$94,955	$96,849	$97,377	$99,244	$101,110	$102,977
E4	B	$97,403	$99,768	$102,138	$104,498	$106,868	$109,232	$111,594	$113,964	$116,332	$118,694	$121,062	$121,722	$124,055	$126,388	$128,721
E5	A	$64,604	$66,299	$67,992	$69,685	$71,377	$73,070	$74,763	$76,452	$78,147	$79,841	$81,530	$82,078			
E5	B	$80,755	$82,874	$84,989	$87,106	$89,222	$91,337	$93,454	$95,565	$97,684	$99,801	$101,913	$102,597			
E6	A	$51,143	$52,771	$54,396	$56,025	$57,650	$59,276	$60,905	$62,531	$64,156	$65,146	$65,784				
E6	B	$63,929	$65,963	$67,994	$70,031	$72,062	$74,095	$76,131	$78,164	$80,195	$81,432	$82,230				

Note: Row B is the base salary (shown in Row A) with an additional 25% for salary on-costs (retirement fund and insurance premiums, installation and repatriation grants, education allowances etc.)
and is the total salary entitlement for executive staff in accordance with regulation 5.1

Schedule B

SALARY SCALE FOR THE GENERAL STAFF CATEGORY

(United States dollars)

Level	STEPS														
	I	II	III	IV	V	VI	VII	VIII	IX	X	XI	XII	XIII	XIV	XV
G1	$60,439	$63,258	$66,079	$68,897	$71,836	$74,901									
G2	$50,366	$52,715	$55,066	$57,415	$59,864	$62,417									
G3	$41,970	$43,928	$45,887	$47,845	$49,887	$52,016									
G4	$34,976	$36,608	$38,240	$39,871	$41,573	$43,346									
G5	$28,893	$30,242	$31,590	$32,939	$34,346	$35,814									
G6	$23,684	$24,787	$25,893	$26,998	$28,151	$29,353									

The Development of a Multi-Year Strategic Work Plan for the Antarctic Treaty Consultative Meeting

The Representatives,

Reaffirming the values, objectives and principles contained in the Antarctic Treaty and its Protocol on Environmental Protection;

Considering that a Multi-Year Strategic Work Plan (Plan) may contribute positively to the Antarctic Treaty Consultative Meeting ("ATCM"), so that the ATCM focuses on matters of priority and timely importance, operates more effectively and efficiently and schedules its work appropriately;

Bearing in mind that the Plan is complementary to the ATCM agenda and that the Antarctic Treaty Parties and other ATCM participants are encouraged to contribute as usual to other matters on the ATCM agenda;

Recalling ATCM XXXII in Baltimore (2009), where Parties expressed support for a Plan;

Decide:

1. to develop a Multi-Year Strategic Work Plan within existing resources;

2. to adopt the principles annexed to this Decision (Annex 1) to guide the completion of the Plan;

3. to establish an open-ended Intersessional Contact Group, co-convened by Australia and Belgium, as the Chairs of Antarctic Treaty Consultative Meetings XXXV and XXXVI respectively, to coordinate the further development of the Plan; and

4. to hold a workshop immediately prior to ATCM XXXVI, with the following terms of reference:

a) develop a draft Plan for consideration at ATCM XXXVI; and

b) report to ATCM XXXVI on the outcomes of this workshop.

Antarctic Treaty Consultative Meeting
Multi-Year Strategic Work Plan – Principles

1. The Multi-Year Strategic Work Plan (Plan) will reflect the objectives and principles of the Antarctic Treaty and its Protocol on Environmental Protection.

2. Consistent with the operation of the Antarctic Treaty Consultative Meeting ("ATCM"), adoption of the Plan, inclusion of items on the Plan and decisions regarding the Plan, will be made by consensus.

3. The purpose of the Plan is to complement the agenda by assisting the ATCM to identify a limited number of priority issues and to operate more effectively and efficiently.

4. The Antarctic Treaty Parties and other ATCM participants are encouraged to contribute as usual to other matters on the ATCM agenda.

5. The Plan will cover a rolling multi-year period to be determined, and should be reviewed at each ATCM and updated as necessary to reflect work still to be completed, new issues and changing priorities.

6. The Plan will be dynamic and flexible and will incorporate emerging issues as they arise.

7. The Plan will identify issues that require the collective attention of the ATCM, and that require discussion and/or decisions by the ATCM.

8. The Plan should not interfere with the regular development of the ATCM agenda.

Electronic Information Exchange System

The Representatives,

Recalling the obligation of the Parties on information sharing under Article III(1) (a) and Article VII(5) of the Antarctic Treaty as well as Article 17 of the Protocol on Environmental Protection to the Antarctic Treaty and its annexes;

Recalling particularly Recommendation VIII-6 (1975), Recommendation XIII-3 (1985) and other improvements that have been made by the Parties to keep each other informed through regular or occasional exchanges;

Recalling Decision 10 (2005) on the creation of an Electronic Information Exchange System ("EIES") and Resolution 6 (2010) on improving the co-ordination of maritime search and rescue in the Antarctic Treaty area;

Emphasising that prompt, easily accessible and complete expedition information for all Parties ensures better supervision of human activities in Antarctic Treaty area and reduces the risks to the environment and safety;

Noting the development and operation of the EIES by the Antarctic Treaty Secretariat, which takes into account observations made by the Parties during the trial period;

Desiring to ensure that the exchange of information between the Parties takes place in the most efficient and timely possible manner, and that the Antarctic Treaty Consultative Meeting and the Committee on Environmental Protection have access to the most complete and reliable information on Antarctica;

Decide:

1. that Parties use the Electronic Information Exchange System to exchange information in accordance with the Antarctic Treaty and the Protocol on Environmental Protection to the Antarctic Treaty and its annexes;

2. that the EIES be modified in order to give Parties, as applicable, the option to:

    a) include the denial of authorisations to operators; and

    b) identify activities cancelled by an operator after meeting Parties' regulatory requirements;

3. that relevant sections of the EIES be updated regularly throughout the year by the Parties, and at a minimum in accordance with Resolution 6 (2001), in order that such information be known and accessible and made available to Parties as soon as practicable;

4. that, wherever practicable, required information shall be entered directly and completely in the EIES, rather than in the form of links to websites or files outside of the EIES; and

5. that Parties continue to work with the Antarctic Treaty Secretariat to refine and improve EIES.

3. Resolutions

Strengthening Support for the Protocol on Environmental Protection to the Antarctic Treaty

The Representatives,

Recalling Resolution 1 (2011), which recorded the Parties' agreement that the achievement of the objective and principles of the Protocol on Environmental Protection to the Antarctic Treaty (the Protocol) would be better ensured if the Protocol was supported by a larger number of States;

Recalling further that Resolution 1 (2011) recommended that all Parties appeal to States that are Antarctic Treaty Parties but not yet Party to the Protocol to become Party to the Protocol, accept the offer by Australia, France and Spain to coordinate with other Consultative Parties on representations to these States and invited Australia, France and Spain to report on the outcome of these representations at Antarctic Treaty Consultative Meeting ("ATCM") XXXV;;

Welcoming the commitment by several Parties to accede to the Protocol;

Recommend that:

1. the Antarctic Treaty Consultative Meeting remain seized of the need to appeal to States that are Antarctic Treaty Parties, but not yet Party to the Protocol on Environmental Protection to the Antarctic Treaty, to accede to the Protocol;

2. further representations are required in following up activities conducted in the 2011-2012 ATCM intersessional period to make progress towards increasing the number of Parties to the Protocol;

3. Consultative Parties be invited to update future ATCMs, as appropriate, on this matter; and the Antarctic Treaty Secretariat post the text of Resolution 1 (2011) on its website ia way that makes clear that it is no longer current.

Cooperation on questions related to the exercise of jurisdiction in the Antarctic Treaty area

The Representatives,

Recalling Article IX(1)(e) of the Antarctic Treaty, which provides that Contracting Parties consult on "questions relating to the exercise of jurisdiction in Antarctica";

Convinced of the necessity to consider such questions with respect to human activities and incidents occurring in the Antarctic Treaty area;

Noting the increase of human activities in the Antarctic Treaty area;

Acknowledging the need to promote compliance with law in the Antarctic Treaty area;

Recognising the unique challenges, both practical and legal, of law enforcement in the Antarctic Treaty area;

Recommend that:

the Parties cooperate to institute discussion on issues related to the exercise of jurisdiction in the Antarctic Treaty area.

Improving Cooperation in Antarctica

The Representatives,

Recalling the centrality of scientific cooperation in the Antarctic Treaty and its Protocol on Environmental Protection;

Recognising, with appreciation, the contributions of the Scientific Committee on Antarctic Research and the Council of Managers of National Antarctic Programmes to scientific and logistical cooperation among the Antarctic Treaty Parties;

Convinced of the need to promote broader Antarctic cooperation beyond scientific and logistical cooperation to facilitate and strengthen the work of the Parties in the implementation of the Antarctic Treaty system;

Convinced that sharing of knowledge, experience and technical support will help Parties at an earlier stage in their Antarctic development to achieve a higher level of compliance with their obligations;

Acknowledging that further cooperation will better equip Parties to respond to the multiple challenges posed by Antarctic activities;

Recommend that:

the Parties and other Antarctic Treaty Consultative Meeting participants conduct a discussion on promoting broader Antarctic cooperation.

Site Guidelines for visitors

The Representatives,

Recalling Recalling Resolution 5 (2005), Resolution 2 (2006), Resolution 1 (2007), Resolution 2 (2008), Resolution 4 (2009) and Resolution 1 (2010), which adopted lists of sites subject to Site Guidelines;

Recalling Resolution 4 (2011), which provided that any proposed amendment to existing Site Guidelines be discussed by the Committee for Environmental Protection, which should advise the Antarctic Treaty Consultative Meeting ("ATCM") accordingly, and that if such advice is endorsed by the ATCM, the Antarctic Treaty Secretariat (the Secretariat) should make the necessary changes to the texts of Site Guidelines on its website;

Believing that Site Guidelines enhance the provisions set out in Recommendation XVIII-1 (1994) *(Guidance for those organising and conducting tourism and non-Governmental activities in the Antarctic);*

Confirming that the term "visitors" does not include scientists conducting research within such sites, or individuals engaged in official governmental activities;

Noting that the Site Guidelines have been developed based on the current levels and types of visits at each specific site, and aware that the Site Guidelines would require review if there were any significant changes to the levels or types of visits to a site;

Believing that the Site Guidelines for each site must be reviewed and revised promptly in response to changes in the levels and types of visits, or in any demonstrable or likely environmental impacts;

Desiring to increase the number of Site Guidelines developed for visited sites and to keep existing Site Guidelines up to date;

Recommend that:

1. the list of sites subject to Site Guidelines that have been adopted by the Antarctic Treaty Consultative Meeting be extended to include a further three new sites (D'Hainaut Island, Mikkelsen Harbour, Trinity Island; Port Charcot, Booth Island; Pendulum Cove, Deception Island, South Shetland Islands), and that the full list of sites subject to Site Guidelines be replaced by the one annexed to this Resolution;

2. the Antarctic Treaty Secretariat place the full list and the modified Site Guidelines, as adopted by the ATCM, on its website;

3. their Governments urge all those intending to visit such sites to ensure that they are fully conversant with, and adhere to, the advice in the relevant Site Guidelines as published by the Secretariat;

4. any proposed amendment to existing Site Guidelines be discussed by the Committee for Environmental Protection, which should advise the ATCM accordingly, and that if such advice is endorsed by the ATCM, the Secretariat should make the necessary changes to the Site Guidelines on the website; and

5. the Secretariat post the text of Resolution 4 (2011) on its website in a way that makes clear that it is no longer current.

List of Sites subject to Site Guidelines

1. Penguin Island (Lat. 62° 06' S, Long. 57° 54' W);
2. Barrientos Island - Aitcho Islands (Lat. 62° 24' S, Long. 59° 47' W);
3. Cuverville Island (Lat. 64° 41' S, Long. 62° 38' W);
4. Jougla Point (Lat 64° 49' S, Long 63° 30' W);

5. Goudier Island, Port Lockroy (Lat 64° 49' S, Long 63° 29' W);
6. Hannah Point (Lat. 62° 39' S, Long. 60° 37' W);
7. Neko Harbour (Lat. 64° 50' S, Long. 62° 33' W);
8. Paulet Island (Lat. 63° 35' S, Long. 55° 47' W);
9. Petermann Island (Lat. 65° 10' S, Long. 64° 10' W);
10. Pleneau Island (Lat. 65° 06' S, Long. 64° 04' W);
11. Turret Point (Lat. 62° 05' S, Long. 57° 55' W);
12. Yankee Harbour (Lat. 62° 32' S, Long. 59° 47' W);

13. Brown Bluff, Tabarin Peninsula (Lat. 63° 32' S, Long. 56° 55' W);
14. Snow Hill (Lat. 64° 22' S, Long. 56° 59' W);
15. Shingle Cove, Coronation Island (Lat. 60° 39' S, Long. 45° 34' W);
16. Devil Island, Vega Island (Lat. 63° 48' S, Long. 57° 16.7' W);
17. Whalers Bay, Deception Island, South Shetland Islands (Lat. 62° 59' S, Long. 60° 34' W);
18. Half Moon Island, South Shetland Islands (Lat. 60° 36' S, Long. 59° 55' W);

19. Baily Head, Deception Island, South Shetland Islands (Lat. 62° 58' S, Long. 60° 30' W);
20. Telefon Bay, Deception Island, South Shetland Islands (Lat. 62° 55' S, Long. 60° 40' W);
21. Cape Royds, Ross Island (Lat. 77° 33' 10.7" S, Long. 166° 10' 6.5" E);
22. Wordie House, Winter Island, Argentine Islands (Lat. 65° 15' S, Long. 64° 16' W);
23. Stonington Island, Marguerite Bay, Antarctic Peninsula (Lat. 68° 11' S, Long. 67° 00' W);
24. Horseshoe Island, Antarctic Peninsula (Lat. 67° 49' S, Long. 67° 18' W);
25. Detaille Island, Antarctic Peninsula (Lat. 66° 52' S, Long. 66° 48' W);
26. Torgersen Island, Arthur Harbour, Southwest Anvers Island (Lat. 64° 46' S, Long. 64° 04' W);

27. Danco Island, Errera Channel, Antarctic Peninsula (Lat. 64° 43' S, Long. 62° 36' W);

28. Seabee Hook, Cape Hallett, Northern Victoria Land, Ross Sea, Visitor Site A and Visitor Site B (Lat. 72° 19' S, Long. 170° 13' E);

29. Damoy Point, Wiencke Island, Antarctic Peninsula (Lat. 64° 49' S, Long. 63° 31' W);

30. Taylor Valley Visitor Zone, Southern Victoria Land (Lat. 77° 37.59' S, Long. 163° 03.42' E);

31. North-east beach of Ardley Island (Lat. 62° 13' S; Long. 58° 54' W);

32. Mawson's Huts and Cape Denison, East Antarctica (Lat. 67° 01' S; Long. 142 ° 40' E);

33. D'Hainaut Island, Mikkelsen Harbour, Trinity Island (Lat. 63° 54' S, Long. 60° 47' W);

34. Port Charcot, Booth Island (Lat. 65° 04'S, Long. 64 °02'W);

35. Pendulum Cove, Deception Island, South Shetland Islands (Lat. 62°56'S, Long. 60°36' W).

Barrientos Island – Aitcho Islands visitor Site Guidelines

The Representatives,

Recalling Resolution 5 (2005), which adopted Site Guidelines for Barrientos Island – Aitcho Islands;

Concerned at the significant damage that has occurred to important moss beds on Barrientos Island - Aitcho Islands as a result of repeated foot traffic;

Noting the flexibility afforded by the site guidelines mechanism to be able to respond quickly to changing environmental and management circumstances;

Welcoming the research and monitoring effort that is being undertaken at the site that will help inform future management options;

Recognising that the International Association of Antarctica Tour Operators will apply a moratorium on visitation to the central part of Barrientos Island - Aitcho Island among its members at least for the 2012/13 season;

Desiring, on the advice of the Committee for Environmental Protection, to take actions that will provide the best opportunity for recovery of the moss beds and the best possible management outcomes;

Recommend that:

- Parties take appropriate steps within their own legal and administrative systems to restrict access to the central part of Barrientos Island - Aitcho Islands (Closed Area B) by their nationals and operators, other than for reasons of scientific research and monitoring related to the recovery of the site;

- the Site Guidelines for Barrientos Island – Aitcho Islands be replaced by the modified Site Guidelines;

- Parties active in the area cooperate in designing and implementing appropriate surveys, research and monitoring plans that will help inform decisions on future management actions, and bring information from such efforts to the 16th meeting of the Committee for Environmental Protection (CEP XVI);

- the Committee for Environmental Protection further reviews the situation at CEP XVI; and

- the Antarctic Treaty Secretariat place the modified Site Guidelines on its website.

Antarctic Conservation Biogeographic Regions

The Representatives,

Recalling Article 3 of Annex V to the Protocol on Environmental Protection to the Antarctic Treaty (the Protocol) which provides for the designation of Antarctic Specially Protected Areas;

Recalling further that Article 3(2) of Annex V states that Parties shall seek to identify such areas within a systematic environmental-geographic framework;

Recalling also that Resolution 3 (2008) recommended that the 'Environmental Domains Analysis of the Antarctic Continent' annexed to that Resolution be used consistently and in conjunction with other tools agreed within the Antarctic Treaty system as a dynamic model for the identification of areas that could be designated as Antarctic Specially Protected Areas within the systematic environmental-geographical framework referred to in Article 3(2) of Annex V of the Protocol;

Welcoming the classification of the ice-free areas of the Antarctic continent and close lying islands within the Antarctic Treaty area into 15 biologically distinct Antarctic Conservation Biogeographic Regions, based on analyses of spatially explicit biodiversity data available from the Scientific Committee on Antarctic Research (SCAR) Biodiversity Database;

Recommend that:

the Antarctic Conservation Biogeographic Regions annexed to this Resolution be used in conjunction with the Environmental Domains Analysis and other tools agreed within the Antarctic Treaty system to support activities relevant to the interests of the Parties, including as a dynamic model for the identification of areas that could be designated as Antarctic Specially Protected Areas within the systematic environmental-geographic framework referred to in Article 3(2) of Annex V to the Environmental Protocol.

Antarctic Conservation Biogeographic Regions

The use of quantitative analyses to combine spatially explicit Antarctic terrestrial biodiversity data with other relevant spatial frameworks (a grid of 200 km x 200 km squares, the nine ice-free domains identified in the Environmental Domains Analysis for the Antarctic continent, and 22 bioregions identified by the SCAR SCAR Regional Sensitivity to Climate Change (RiSCC) Programme) has identified 15 biologically distinct ice-free regions encompassing the Antarctic continent and close-lying islands within the Antarctic Treaty area (see Table 1). A full description of the methods employed is presented in Terauds *et al.* (2012). The Antarctic Conservation Biogeographic Regions illustrated in Figure 1 represent the best classification of Antarctic terrestrial biodiversity based on data currently available from the SCAR Biodiversity Database.

The spatial data layer representing the regions is publicly available for download from the Australian Antarctic Data Centre: *http://data.aad.gov.au/aadc/portal/download_file. cfm?file_id=3420.*

Reference

Terauds, A., Chown, S., Morgan, F., Peat, H., Watts, D., Keys, H., Convey, P. & Bergstrom, D. (2012) Conservation biogeography of the Antarctic. *Diversity and Distributions*, 22 May 2012, DOI: 10.1111/j.1472-4642.2012.00925.x.

Table 1 – Descriptions of Antarctic Conservation Biogeographic Regions

Region	Name	Area (km²)
1	North-east Antarctic Peninsula	1142
2	South Orkney Islands	148
3	North-west Antarctic Peninsula	5081
4	Central south Antarctic Peninsula	4959
5	Enderby Land	2152
6	Dronning Maud Land	5502
7	East Antarctica	1360
8	North Victoria Land	9522
9	South Victoria Land	10368
10	Transantarctic Mountains	19347
11	Ellsworth Mountains	2965
12	Marie Byrd Land	1158
13	Adelie Land	178
14	Ellsworth Land	220
15	South Antarctic Peninsula	2990

Figure 1 – Map of Antarctica showing the 15 Antarctic Conservation Biogeographic Regions

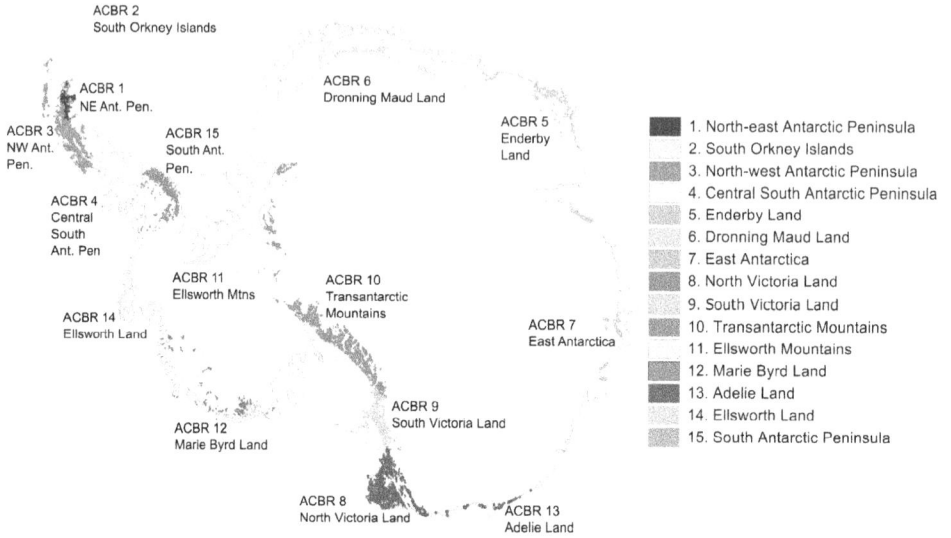

Source: Terauds *et al.* (2012).

Vessel Safety in the Antarctic Treaty Area

The Representatives,

Recalling the Protocol on Environmental Protection to the Antarctic Treaty and Resolution 1 (2004), which strongly supported "the progress achieved by CCAMLR Resolution 20/XXII urging its Members, which are harvesting in high Antarctic latitudes, to license only those fishing vessels with at least an ice classification standard of ICE-1C";

Convinced of the continuing need for comprehensive protection of the Antarctic environment and dependent and associated ecosystems;

Registering concern about the continued occurrence of incidents involving stricken fishing vessels licensed by Members of the Commission for the Conservation of Antarctic Marine Living Resources ("CCAMLR") in the Antarctic region;

Noting the role of the International Maritime Organization ("IMO") with regard to vessel safety internationally;

Further recalling actions taken by CCAMLR to support the IMO in relation to the activities of fishing vessels operating in the Southern Ocean;

Reaffirming the role of the Antarctic Treaty Consultative Meeting to promote the protection of the Antarctic environment in the Antarctic Treaty area;

Recommend that:

1. continue to work on the International Maritime Organization mandatory code for ships operating in Polar waters and participate in the forthcoming negotiations on the Agreement on the Torremolinos Protocol ;

2. consider appropriate measures to enhance the safety standards of fishing vessels that are flagged to Parties and that operate in the Antarctic Treaty area;

3. report annually to the Committee for Environmental Protection on responses to environmental emergencies involving vessels that are flagged to Parties and that operate in the Antarctic Treaty area in accordance with Article 17 of the Protocol on Environmental Protection to the Antarctic Treaty;

4. remind the operators of their flagged fishing vessels of the IMO Global Search and Rescue Plan and, specifically, to urge Members of the Commission for the Conservation of Antarctic Marine Living Resources to provide or encourage fishing vessels under their flag to make available their contact details and other relevant information to the responsible Maritime Rescue Coordination Centre in advance of entering the Antarctic Treaty area in line with CCAMLR Resolution 33/XXX; and

5. encourage CCAMLR Members to implement CCAMLR Resolution 20/ XXII, which calls on Members to license only those fishing vessels with a minimum ice classification standard ICE-1C to operate within the Antarctic Treaty area.

Improved Coordination of Maritime, Aeronautical and Land-Based Search and Rescue

The Representatives,

Concerned about the tragic loss of life in several vessel casualties in the Ross Sea and Southern Ocean in recent years;

Mindful that anticipated increases in human activity in the Antarctic have the potential to add substantially to the challenges and risks associated with Antarctic Search and Rescue ("SAR") operations;

Conscious of the need to continue efforts to prevent incidents;

Recalling the commitment of Parties to the 1979 International Convention on Maritime Search and Rescue and the 1944 Convention on International Civil Aviation, Annex 12 – Search and Rescue to cooperate in the execution SAR missions and activities;

Desiring to increase the success and efficiency of SAR operations in the Antarctic;

Believing that discussions by the Antarctic Treaty Consultative Parties of means to improve Antarctic SAR coordination could promote marine, aeronautical and land-based safety in Antarctica;

Recommend that the Parties:

1. convene a special working group to meet for one full day on the second day (currently scheduled for Thursday, 23 May 2013) of Antarctic Treaty Consultative Meeting ("ATCM") XXXVI to discuss means of improving Search and Rescue coordination in Antarctica, including, *inter alia,*

    a) risk assessment and contingency planning;

b) international coordination of maritime, aeronautical and land-based SAR; and

c) best practices or other arrangements;

and to evaluate whether further work on this topic should be undertaken by the ATCM, and what the nature of that work would be;

2. include relevant experts on SAR in addition to national Antarctic programme personnel in their delegations participating in the special working group; and

3. invite the Council of Managers of National Antarctic Programmes ("COMNAP") to provide an update on actions resulting from the two COMNAP SAR workshops, "Towards Improved Search and Rescue Coordination and Response in the Antarctic" (Valparaiso, 2008 and Buenos Aires, 2009).

The Assessment of Land-Based Expeditionary Activities

The Representatives,

Concerned that poorly planned and executed land-based activities, particularly those undertaken in remote areas of Antarctica, have the potential to present risks to safety of life;

Concerned also to ensure that activities in remote and less well-studied areas of Antarctica do not have any adverse impacts on unique environmental attributes;

Recalling the Environmental Principles contained in Article 3 of the Protocol on Environmental Protection to the Antarctic Treaty;

Recalling also Resolution 3 (2004), Resolution 4 (2004), Resolution 5 (2007) and Resolution 7 (2009);

Noting the increasing interest in land-based expeditionary activities, particularly as a result of the recent centenaries of Amundsen and Scott's expeditions to the South Pole of 1911/12;

Desiring to ensure that all such activities are assessed in a consistent and thorough way, in respect of their environmental, safety and operational procedures;

Recommend that:

the Parties, consistent with their national law and as they consider appropriate, utilise the attached *Questions to consider as part of the authorisation or comparable regulatory process for non-Governmental land-based activities in Antarctica* when assessing proposed land-based expeditionary activities to be undertaken in Antarctica.

Questions to consider as part of the authorisation process for non-Governmental land-based activities in Antarctica

In undertaking domestic procedures to assess potential non-Governmental land-based activities in Antarctica, Competent Authorities may find it helpful to consider the following list of questions. The overall aim of the list is to underpin the consideration of land-based activities to ensure full compliance with the Protocol on Environmental Protection and other relevant ATCM instruments, including Measure 4(2004), Resolution 4(2004), Resolution 7(2009) and Resolution 3(2011), as appropriate.

The list of questions is neither exhaustive nor prescriptive and is intended for guidance purposes only. Not all of the questions will be relevant to every land-based activity, and the requirements of those operating regularly in Antarctica will clearly be different to those conducting one-off activities. Each Party's Competent Authority will determine how it wishes to utilise this list of questions to consider in each case.

General Environmental Issues

Overarching issues, likely relevant to all land-based activities:

- Are the proposed activities, in terms of scale (eg, number of participants, duration and extent of operational area) and type (ie, what is specifically planned), consistent with the Environmental Principles set out in Article 3 of the Environmental Protocol?

- Has the Environmental Impact Assessment (EIA) been developed in accordance with the Guidelines appended to Resolution 4(2005) and does it cover all of the activities to be undertaken whilst in Antarctica, including those of any other operator contracted to, or working with, the organisers of the activities, where these other operators are not already authorised by another Treaty Party? Does the EIA include any alternative activities that may be offered because of weather restrictions etc? In all cases, have the environmental risks been identified and appropriate mitigation measures planned?

- Does the Environmental Impact Assessment specify clearly defined geographic boundaries within which all of the proposed activities will take place, taking into account contingency plans and potential alternative operating areas (including the location of any field camps, storage facilities or depots, or the route of any traverses)? Are the organisers (or the Competent Authority) aware of what other activities might also be planned to take place simultaneously in this area, and how will any potential cumulative effects be assessed and considered? Are activities known to have previously taken place in the area or is it, as far as known, a pristine area? Is the proposed activity a one-off event or is it likely to be repeated in the foreseeable future in the same location?

- Can the organisers of the proposed activities demonstrate a good understanding of the environmental conditions of the full area of proposed operation, for example, through prior experience, or through seeking the advice of relevant experts? Are there any Antarctic Specially Protected Areas (ASPAs), Antarctic Specially Managed Areas (ASMAs) and Historic Sites and Monuments (HSMs) in proximity to their intended activities?

- Have the proposed activities been planned in accordance with *Guidance for those organising and conducting tourism and non-Governmental activities in the Antarctic* (Recommendation XVIII-1(1994))? Are plans in place to ensure that those planning to undertake the activities in Antarctica are fully aware of the *General Guidelines for Visitors to the Antarctic* (Resolution 3(2011)); and *Non-native Species Manual* (Resolution 2(2011)?

- Are the proposed management practices for waste and sewage appropriate for the scale and location of the proposed activities; particularly plans for discarding waste from travelling activities (paying particular attention to the likelihood of temporary camps being dismantled quickly)?

- Do contingency plans include provision for the removal of all equipment in the case of accident or damage to equipment, or in the event of an emergency evacuation?

- Have appropriate measures been identified to avoid introductions of non-native species, both by the members of the expeditions, and by their logistical support operator, if different?

Specific issues, to be considered as relevant:

- Are detailed fuel handling, storage procedures, and spill avoidance measures in place, including any specific procedures where fuel is to be transported long distances, or where vehicles and aircraft are to be refuelled on the ice? (The COMNAP Fuel Manual 2008 may be useful in assessing such measures);

- If vehicle use is proposed, what measures have been taken to demonstrate its appropriateness for the proposed area of operation? Are vehicles proposed to be used in any areas not covered by snow or ice, and if so, what is the potential risk of more than minor or transitory impacts (eg, visible tracks remaining after the activity is completed)?

Contingency Plans (including Search and Rescue and Medical Evacuation)

Overarching issues, likely relevant to all land-based activities:

- Have the proposed activities been planned in accordance with Measure 4(2004) and/or paragraph 1 of Resolution 4(2004), such as to ensure that appropriate contingency plans and appropriate arrangements for health and safety, search and rescue, and medical care and evacuation are in place? Do these contingency plans cover, in particular, weather-related implications, medical emergencies, and equipment failures?

- Can the organisers demonstrate adequate insurance or other arrangements to cover the costs associated with search and rescue and medical care and evacuation, in line with Measure 4(2004) and paragraph 2 of Resolution 4(2004)? Do all insurance policies make specific reference to Antarctica and the types of activities for which the policy/arrangements cover – for both the organisers, and all participants?

- Have the organisers developed a sufficiently detailed risk assessment for the activities proposed, in terms of search and rescue and evacuation (ie, identification of possible scenarios requiring search and rescue and/or evacuation, and clear plans as to how this would be enacted under each scenario)?

- Has radio linkage between each component of the activity (vehicles, groups, medical and/or logistical staff etc), with base camp and with organisers outside Antarctica been prepared and successfully tested?

Specific issues, to be considered as relevant:

- Where activities are planned to take place away from a base camp, are clear agreed protocols in place for regular (eg, at least once per day) reporting to base camp or to a designated contact elsewhere (including whether all necessary communication and location equipment and back-ups will be provided for prior at the beginning of the activities)? Is there a maximum proximity between base camp and the activities to be supported, and is this appropriate? Will search and rescue operations be automatically commenced if no communication is received after an agreed period of time? For travelling activities, will a continuous record of the last known (and regular) location of participants be kept?

Health and Safety of those undertaking the activities

- Do the organisers, or appointed leaders of the activities in Antarctica if different, have previous experience of operating in Antarctica (or other similar environments, combined with a clear understanding of the different conditions and requirements of Antarctica)? What safety equipment will they have available and is this appropriate for the type and scale of the proposed operation?

- Have the organisers identified the potential health and safety risks arising from their activities in Antarctica, and, if appropriate, will all potential participants be medically assessed for their physical aptitude to carry out the planned activities?

- Have standard operating procedures been developed for accidents and emergencies, health and safety and the provision of medical/first aid? What medical equipment will they have available?

- As appropriate: what will the ratio be of medically and specialist polar trained staff/instructors to novice, or less experienced participants – is this appropriate and does it provide for continuous cover throughout the duration of the proposed activity?; or for remote activities, what will the arrangements be for ensuring timely access to medical assistance?

Specific issues, to be considered as relevant:

- Can the organisers of any potential activities to be undertaken in Antarctica without the supervision or support of an experienced operator demonstrate full compliance with paragraphs 3-7 of the Guidelines appended as Annex 1 to Resolution 4(2004)?

- For supervised/supported group activities which will involve participants engaging in endurance or highly physical activities (assessed relative to the abilities of the participants), what specific prior training and preparation will be undertaken, and will this be for all participants (for example, in line with paragraphs 3, 5 and 6 of Annex I of Resolution 4(2004), even where there are also on-site guides present?

- For supervised/supported group activities which will involve participants engaging in endurance or highly physical activities (assessed relative to the abilities of the participants), what arrangements will be in place for regular monitoring of the well-being of participants (eg, for races, this might be at a series of checkpoints)? Are formal procedures in place for the withdrawal or removal of participants on medical grounds?

- For travelling activities, is there a general agreed pre-planned (fixed) route (with contingencies), and if so, has there been reconnaissance and mapping of these routes (with particular emphasis on the location of crevasses and other natural hazards)? Are the organisers aware of recent meteorological data across the proposed routes?

- Where vehicles (including all wheeled, tracked or skied machinery, both powered or unpowered, eg, cars, snow mobiles, quad bikes, 'tractor trains') are to be used, what modifications have been made for Antarctic conditions, for example, will they be fitted with ground radar and other navigational equipment, and are the vehicle operators appropriately trained in the use of such equipment? Is the number of vehicles sufficient to support the proposed activities and what appropriate spare parts will be carried?

- Has the loss of one or more vehicles been taken into account and would such an event endanger lives?

Liaison with other Competent Authorities and Treaty Parties

- In line with Resolution 3(2004), what contact has been made with other national authorities that may have an interest in the activities (eg, sub-contractors, participants etc)?

- Will the proposed activities be taking place in proximity to known scientific research locations, or scientific stations? What contact has been made with relevant National Antarctic Programmes?

Education and Outreach

- How will the activities focus on the enrichment and education of visitors, before and during the period in Antarctica, in line with Resolution 7(2009)?

- Have the organisers fully considered whether, and how, the activities will generate a wider interest in the protection of Antarctica, for example, through education and outreach etc?

Yachting Guidelines

The Representatives,

Recalling Resolution 1 (2003) regarding the provision of advice to yacht and vessel operators about the Protocol on Environmental Protection to the Antarctic Treaty;

Recalling the work of the Antarctic Treaty Meeting of Experts on Management of Ship-borne tourism (Wellington, 2009);

Concerned about the safety of vessels in the Southern Ocean and the possible risk of accidents involving these vessels and the resulting harm to both persons and the environment;

Desiring to bring forward safety issues for yacht operators and private sailors, to promote good practices and to further protect the environment;

Recommend that:

1. consistent with their national law and as they consider appropriate, the Parties utilise the attached *Checklist of yacht specific items for preparing safe Antarctic voyages* when assessing proposed yacht visits to Antarctica;

2. the Antarctic Treaty Secretariat (the Secretariat) place *Yachting Guidelines for Antarctic Cruises,* as discussed by the Antarctic Treaty Consultative Meeting, on its website;

3. the Parties provide details to the Secretariat, to enable it to maintain on its website in conjunction with the *Yachting Guidelines for Antarctic Cruises*:

    a) contact details of national competent authorities; and

    b) details of relevant Maritime Rescue Co-ordination Centres;

and

4. the Parties urge all those intending to undertake a yacht visit to Antarctica to take into account in planning their voyage the *Checklist of yacht specific items for preparing safe Antarctic voyages* and, as appropriate, the *Yachting Guidelines for Antarctic Cruises*.

Checklist of yacht specific items for preparing safe Antarctic voyages

Preamble

Antarctica is one of the most remote and demanding cruising areas in the world's oceans. Weather conditions can be extreme, ice can pose a danger at any time and limited external assistance is available should things go wrong. Any yacht expedition heading south of 60°S needs enhanced planning and preparations and should be crewed by experienced yachtsmen.

The intention of the checklist is to support those planning yacht operations, and to provide guidance as to appropriate standards for Antarctic yacht operation. The safety of a yacht and her crew is the sole and inescapable responsibility of the person in charge who must do his best to ensure that the yacht is fully equipped, thoroughly seaworthy and manned by an experienced crew who have undergone appropriate training and are physically fit to face bad weather and the general conditions of sailing in the Antarctic which can be subject to rapid change.

Yachts heading towards Antarctica must be completely self-sufficient for very extended periods of time, capable of withstanding heavy storms and prepared to meet serious emergencies without the expectation of outside assistance. The materials used in the relevant areas of the vessel structure should provide adequate toughness and ductility to minimise the risk of structure failure due to impact or crushing, brittle failure and other causes. Yachts should be prepared for being "knocked down" and also for encountering extreme weather and sea conditions.

These checklist items for use by stakeholders do not replace, but rather supplement, the requirements of governmental authority, flag states or international regulations. All yachts are to comply with all relevant IMO regulations under SOLAS and MARPOL and with all relevant provisions under the Environmental Protocol and ATCM Resolutions and also appropriate national requirements.

Personal preparation

- Ensure good knowledge and understanding of the appropriate environmental protocols and regulations in the Antarctic Treaty System

- Consideration should be given to visiting Antarctic waters during Austral summer months and preferably areas with low ice concentration to avoid hazards. Only experienced and highly prepared crews should consider voyages outside the Austral summer or to an area outside the more commonly visited areas

- Review appropriate web sites (of national governments, IAATO, IMO, Antarctic Treaty System recommended sites) and other sources of information about the Antarctic, eg, specialised technical publications

273

- Risk assessments for all planned activities should be provided beforehand
- Finding anchoring/mooring sites that offer shelter from wind, waves/tides, and moving ice can be a challenge. Consult appropriate publications and Antarctic sailing experts to identify suitable locations within the area in which you intend to cruise
- Experience, training and knowledge are the basis for pre-expedition decisions:
  - Involve experienced yachtsmen particularly of sailing in high latitudes
  - Ensure absolute self sufficiency for at least two weeks in excess of planned trip duration when operating south of 60 degrees: This includes comprehensive spares, tools and, most importantly, the ability to fit/use them. Carry a reserve of enough food, drinking water and fuel
  - Consideration needs to be given to the fact that Antarctica is a large area remote from search and rescue services and that responders may take days or weeks to find the location
  - Don't rely only on maps and charts-based GPS positioning
  - Detailed study of the nautical charts of the area considered to be sailed
  - Update information on rescue coordination centre responsibilities and contact those early
  - First aid equipment training for crew members verified by necessary certifications
  - All crew and passengers should be comprehensively briefed on vessel operations, safety procedures, environmental considerations and bio-security
  - Specific training for crew members in ship and sailing techniques relevant for high latitude operations (eg, ISAF Sea Survival Course). Particularly courses including "Navigation in icy waters" and "Sailing with severe weather conditions" would be an advantage as well as personal experience
- Reports/ Information:
  - Appropriate procedures based on domestic legislations, including reporting to competent authorities, must be taken prior to the departure towards Antarctica
  - Provide to your authorising government agency the details they require for advance notification of your activity (dates and places of the planned expedition) to include that information in EIES
  - Inform the appropriate MRCC of your intended voyage route, vessel details, equipment carried, and personnel on board; provide, if possible, the vessel's position at 08:00 and 20:00 hours to a MRCC or, alternatively, to a ship located nearby that can relay this information to MRCC
  - Post visit report to permitting authorities afterwards

- Weather and ice observations are encouraged to be reported regularly to the Voluntary Observation Programme

Technical preparation

- Vessel structure and general equipment:

  - All hull types should be strong. For yachts regularly visiting Antarctica, well-built and sturdy metal hulls should be favored. Remember that the hull should be accessible from inside for damage control purposes
  - The vessel should be stable and able to withstand extreme weather conditions and large seas. Consider the vessel's watertight integrity. Small vessels may have great difficulty in these conditions and could expect to be rolled over
  - All items onboard should be prepared for withstanding extraordinary conditions; keep them well protected not to cause damage by flying loosely around
  - Comprehensive tool kit and spare parts inventory
  - Decks should be fitted with safety harness jackstays and attachment points
  - Robust mast & rigging on sailing vessels
  - Heavy weather sails for sailing yachts (storm sails, including a tri-sail and storm jib)
  - Bolt cutters or other appropriate equipment (eg, hydraulic cutters) should be carried on sailboats in order to free a broken rig

- Antarctic specification:

  - Spotlight for ice identification at night
  - Radar
  - Multiple shore landing craft if possible
  - Means to combat icing of the vessel and rig necessary in case of freezing weather conditions
  - Cold weather treatment for fuel
  - Storm boards (storm shutters or blanking plates) with the ability to replace, cover or repair any hatch or opening

- Anchoring and mooring:

  - Multiple sets of anchoring equipment and cables should be carried, suitable for the size of vessel, the type of seabed and the depth of water likely to be encountered. Possibly consider having heavier anchor(s) and chains than it is required as standard for the size of the vessel
  - Shorelines and associated equipment/ good ground tackle are recommended where their use is possible

- Communication equipment (installed on the vessel and portable for carriage onto a lifeboat or liferaft):
    - Long-range communications systems: satellite (Iridium, Inmarsat) and/or HF/SSB radio
    - VHF marine radio to talk to other vessels and aircraft in the event of a rescue, including portable set(s) for use off the vessel
    - Suitable means to receive weather and ice information
    - Preferably two 406 EPIRB (Emergency Position Indicating Radio Beacon)
- Rescue equipment:
    - Comprehensive first aid equipment such as a Category A kit
    - Ocean-going man-overboard marking and retrieval equipment (eg, throwable horseshoe buoys)
    - Ocean-going grade life rafts (SOLAS rafts with a SOLAS A pack), lifejackets (cp. ISO12042 part 2 275N) and survival suits and safety harnesses for at least 100% capacity; Immersion or survival suits should be carried for all onboard which are compatible with the lifejackets
    - Search and rescue transponder (SART) or GPS EPIRB to ensure that in the event of an incident, efforts can be focused upon rescue rather than search
    - Automatic Identification System (AIS) is recommended for collision avoidance as well as detection by search aircraft or ships
    - Personal Locator Beacon (PLB) or related devices, such as a Man Overboard Beacon on larger vessels, may be helpful to ease rescue operations in relation to a single person
    - Fire extinguisher and blanket
    - Flares and other pyrotechnics
    - Collision mat or similar material to be hauled over a damaged part of the hull
    - Portable spotlight
    - Tapered plugs
    - A sturdy boarding ladder or platform is highly recommended
- Other necessary equipment:
    - availability of an appropriate, relevant and up-to-date nautical chart set covering the area planned to be sailed
    - navigation system with redundancy
    - Other critical boat systems (i.e. steering, autopilot) should be robust and where possible with backup system (i.e. with redundancy)

Checklist for visitors' in-field activities

The Representatives,

Recalling Article VII of the Antarctic Treaty, which provides for the designation of observers to carry out inspections, and Article 14 of the Protocol on Environmental Protection to the Antarctic Treaty (the Protocol), which provides that inspections shall be arranged to promote the protection of the Antarctic environment and dependent and associated ecosystems and to ensure compliance with the Protocol;

Taking into account Resolution 5 (1995) *(Antarctic inspection checklists),* Resolution 4 (2008) *(Checklist for inspections of Antarctic Specially Protected Areas and Antarctic Specially Managed Areas),* and Resolution 3 (2010*) (Revised Antarctic inspection Checklist "A"),* which propose a number of checklists to guide the planning and conduct of inspections under Article VII of the Antarctic Treaty;

Considering Resolution 7 (2009) *(General Principles of Antarctic Tourism),* which states that Antarctic Treaty Parties aim to ensure, as far as practicable, that they continue to proactively develop regulations relating to tourism activities that should provide for a consistent framework for the management of tourism;

Reaffirming that inspection checklists are useful as guidelines for those planning and conducting inspections under Article VII of the Antarctic Treaty and in assessing implementation of the provisions of the Protocol;

Noting that inspection checklists are not mandatory and are not to be used as a questionnaire;

Recommend that:

their Governments encourage the use of the attached Checklist for visitors' in-field activities.

Checklist for visitors' in-field activities

The following checklist is aimed to support inspections under Article VII of the Antarctic Treaty and Article 14 of the Madrid Protocol.

The issues included in this checklist are to supplement (but not be a substitute for) information obtained from environmental assessment processes, information exchange, reports by Parties and Experts to the ATCM and CEP, and from documented industry practices and procedures (where applicable). This checklist is neither exhaustive nor prescriptive and is intended for guidance purposes only.

Except where indicated, all the information needed to reply to these questions will be obtained from on site sources (eg, interviews + field observation).

SECTION A. INSPECTION DETAILS

1. Location (name of the site inspected)
2. Date and time of inspection visit
3. Mode of transport to the site (by sea/ by air/land)
4. Name and flag of vessel (if appropriate)
5. Does the vessel comply with agreed restrictions on the number of passengers carried onboard at the site in question (in relation to Measure 15, 2009 and applicable Site guidelines for Visitors)
6. Tour/ Non-Governmental Organisation/ other operator (name, nationality)
7. Any other company involved in the operation (eg, vessel operator, tour operator, sub-charterer, providers of other services)
8. Affiliation to IAATO (yes/no)
9. Name of Expedition leader (or person in charge of disembarking visitors)
10. Duration of visit
11. Persons conducting inspection (name, nationality)

SECTION B. ADVANCE NOTIFICATION AND OTHER LEGISLATION REQUIREMENTS

12. Has the activity undergone authorisation / permit / environmental assessment procedures, and is a copy of the EIA available?
13. Identify if it has been single-year or multiyear, and if it covers the activities of a single-ship or company, or multiple ships and companies
14. Which Party provided the authorisation / permit / or administered the environmental assessment procedures?
15. Was the activity notified in advance to the appropriate Treaty Party?

SECTION C. SITE MANAGEMENT

16. Is the area subject to particular management requirements, like Site Guidelines for Visitors, ASPA/ASMA Management Plan/Codes of Conduct, Facility's internal policies, or similar?

This information should be collected prior to the deployment of the inspection team, from off site sources, such as the ATS, IAATO and National Programmes' websites.

SECTION D. INFORMATION MANAGEMENT

17. Did the expedition party (cruise ship/aircraft/other) contact the facility (station, refuge, hut, field camp) prior to arrival in order to coordinate the visit? (if appropriate)

18. Was the Expedition leader (or person in charge of disembarking visitors) aware of the general provisions of the Antarctic Treaty and its Protocol on Environmental Protection?

19. Did visitors receive, prior to their arrival at the site, information on:

    • the values present in the area, and on ways to avoid their degradation?; and on

    • the contents of relevant guidelines and management instruments on Antarctic tourism? (eg, Site Guidelines for Visitors, General Guidelines for Visitors of the Antarctic, behaviour rules and commitments of Rec. XVIII-I, or ASPA/ASMA-Management Plan)

    Describe ways on which this information was transmitted (board presentation, a briefing prior to landing, a briefing immediately after landing)

SECTION E. VISIT DESCRIPTION

20. Total number of visitors landed during the visit

21. Was there more than one tourist vessel at the landing site at any one time?

22. For vessel landings, what was the maximum number of passengers landed ashore at any one time? (Noting that the limit should be 100, unless a lower number is otherwise specified in applicable ATCM Measures or Site Guidelines)

23. Was the minimum ratio staff: passenger of 1:20 (unless otherwise specified in applicable ATCM Measures or Site Guidelines) maintained during visit?

24. What types of activities were carried out by visitors during their visit to the site? (eg, walks ashore, sea baths, swimming, kayaking, diving, trekking, hiking, climbing, camping, marathons, races, snowboard, skiing, hand gliding, wildlife watching, etc.)

25. Provide details of any on-ground visitor management or environmental protection measures implemented during visit (eg, temporary area markers to guide visitors, additional guides)

26. Describe in situ safety measures implemented during the visit (for example, in the event that the vessel/aircraft is not able to collect the visitors at the expected time)?

27. Were the provisions set out in any applicable ASPA/ASMA Management Plan/ Codes of Conduct, Facilities internal policies, or similar, adhered to in full?

28. Were the provisions set out in any applicable Site Guidelines for Visitors (eg, preferred landing sites, zoning schemes, behaviour ashore, precautionary notes, etc.) adhered to in full?

SECTION F. ON SITE IMPACTS / CONDUCT OF VISIT

29. Was any incident or evidence of direct impacts identified that was caused by visitors on the:

    • site's flora and fauna?

    • the landscape and wilderness values present in the site? (eg, trampling on pristine surfaces, digging bathing pits, building a cairn, graffiti on rocks, etc.)

30. Describe in-situ waste management procedures implemented during visit

31. Where appropriate, and not otherwise covered in site specific guidelines or management plans, describe how visit was managed in order to avoid impacts on historic sites and monuments (including immobile and mobile historic features) present in the site?

32. Describe procedures implemented during visit to avoid causing any disturbance to science and/or logistic operations (only applicable to visits to, *inter alia,* stations, refuges, huts, field camps)

SECTION G. ADDITIONAL INFORMATION ON PRACTICES AND PROCEDURES TO ENSURE SAFETY AND/OR ENVIRONMENTAL PROTECTION

33. Were industry standard practices or operating procedures used (specify if so)?

34. Were guides / expedition personnel accredited according to any specific training standards? (Please, specify)

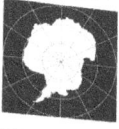

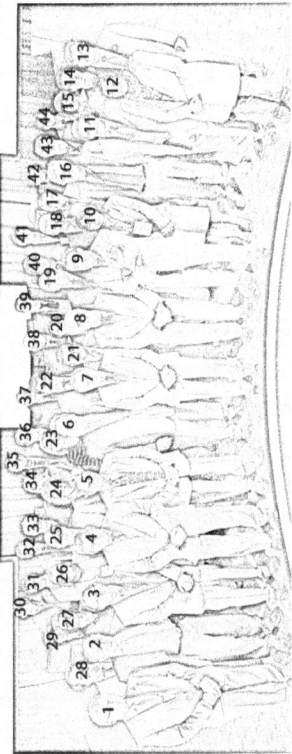

1 Andrew Jackson, Host Country Secretariat
2 Michel Rocard, France
3 Yeadong Kim, Republic of Korea
4 José Olmedo Morán, Ecuador
5 Rasik Ravindra, India
6 Evan T. Bloom, United States
7 Richard Rowe, Chair
8 Ariel Mansi, Argentina
9 Camilo Sanhueza, Chile
10 Masami Fujimoto, Japan
11 Yves Frenot, CEP Chair
12 Sharifah Zarah Syed Ahmad, Malaysia
13 Greg French, Australia
14 Fábio Vaz Pitaluga, Brazil
15 Michelle Rogan-Finnemore, COMNAP
16 Jean-Arthur Régibeau, Belgium
17 Serge Segura, France
18 Krassimir Stefanov, Bulgaria
19 Ismael Alonzo, Uruguay
20 Kim Crosbie, IAATO
21 Feng Gao, China
22 Dmitry Gonchar, Russian Federation

23 Helena Ödmark, Sweden
24 Liisa Valjento, Finland
25 Luis Quesada, Peru
26 Andrii Gurzhii, Ukraine
27 Carolyn Schwalger, New Zealand
28 Henry Valentine, South Africa
29 Olga Bula, Colombia
30 Miroslav Ondras, WMO
31 Stein Paul Rosenberg, Norway
32 Warren Papworth, ACAP
33 James Barnes, ASOC
34 Jane Rumble, United Kingdom
35 Ryszard Sarkowicz, Poland
36 Marcos Gómez Martínez, Spain
37 Oscar Moze, Italy
38 Hugo Gorziglia, IHO
39 René J.M. Lefeber, Netherlands
40 Sönke Lorenz, Germany
41 Manfred Reinke, ATS
42 Mike Sparrow, SCAR
43 Andrew Wright, CCAMLR
44 Kamuran Sadar, Canada

www.ingramcontent.com/pod-product-compliance
Lightning Source LLC
Chambersburg PA
CBHW080719220326
41520CB00056B/7152